CHINESE REGIONAL COOKING

Countryside in Hebei, northern China.
China is still basically an agricultural
country, and 80 per cent of the
population work on the land.

Macdonald

CHINESE REGIONAL COOKING

Deh-Ta Hsiung

A QUARTO BOOK

First published 1979 by Macdonald Educational Limited,
Holywell House, Worship Street, London EC2A 2EN.

This book was designed and produced by Quarto Publishing Limited,
32 Kingly Court, London W1.

Art Director: Robert Morley
Editorial Director: Jim Mallory
Art Editor: Moira Clinch
Editor: Linda Mallory

Phototypeset in Britain by Parker Typesetting Service, Leicester.
Color origination in Italy by Starf Photolitho.
Printed in Hong Kong

ACKNOWLEDGEMENTS
I wish to record my special gratitude to my wife
Thelma and our children Kai-lu, Anna and
Benjamin, for their unfailing encouragement and
forbearance while I was engaged upon this book.
I am also grateful to Ann Sainsbury for her
enthusiastic help and advice. Finally, I am greatly
indebted to Kate Margolis for her patience and
skill in typing my manuscript.

We would like to thank the chefs of the following
restaurants for cooking the dishes photographed
in this book.

Chef Li of Jumbo Floating Restaurant, Hong
Kong
Chef Kuo of Spring Deer Restaurant, Kowloon
Chef Lui of Tree Top Restaurant, International
Hotel, Kowloon

Chef Su and Chef Yang of Kiangsu
and Chekiang
Residents (HK) Association, Hong Kong
Chef Teng of Yung Kee Restaurant, Hong Kong
Chef Tsou of Hoover Sky Restaurant, Hong
Kong
Chef Chen of Lok Ho Fook Restaurant, London
Chef Tsao of Dragon Gate Restaurant, London
Chef Yeh of The Peking Restaurant, London

Shark's fin soup, essential for any grand Chinese banquet

CONTENTS

NOTE *Apart from a few exceptions, I have used the new pin yin system for transliterating Chinese names, with the Wade-Giles system in brackets to help those who are not yet familiar with the newer form.*
D.T.H.

INTRODUCTION

CHINA, or to give it the correct name, the Middle Kingdom, occupies a dominant position in the eastern part of Asia. To understand why the Chinese used to regard themselves as the centre of the world, one has only to look at a map: China has a central location, bordering on virtually all the mainland nations of Eastern Asia.

In all, China borders on 11 nations: Korea, USSR and Outer Mongolia in the east and north; Afghanistan, Pakistan and India in the west; and Nepal, Bhutan, Burma, Laos and Vietnam in the south. Across the sea, it faces Japan to the east, and the Philippines, Malaysia and Indonesia to the south-east.

China's vast land area of 3.7 million square miles (9.6 million square km) is slightly larger than that of the United States, and about the same size as Western Europe. The distance from east to west is over 3,000 miles (5,000 km). 2,000 miles (3,200 km) separate the cities of Shanghai in the east and Urumqi (Urumchi) in the west, about the same distance as between New York and Salt Lake City. From north to south the country measures about 2,500 miles, from sub-arctic Manchuria to tropical Hainan Island.

In topographical outline, China is like a three-step west-east staircase. It begins in the west with the Tibetan plateau, 12,000 ft (4,000 m) above sea level. From the mountains on the eastern edge of this plateau, the land slopes away to highlands in Yunnan and Guizhou (Kweichow) and basins in Sichuan (Szechuan), mostly from 6,000–3,000 ft (2,000–1,000 m). It then descends further eastward to hilly regions and plains below 1,000 ft (300 m) on the middle and lower reaches of the Yangtse River.

In China, some areas are warm all the year round while others have long winters and short summers; however, most of the land lies in the temperate zone with four distinct seasons. A combination of high temperature and

Terraced fields in the hilly country near the Yellow River, north China.
Inset: *Transplanting rice seedlings in the flat lands of the Yangtse River delta, south China*

Sheep and cattle graze along a winding river in Xinjiang. This fertile country provides most of China's dairy produce

plentiful rainfall provides favorable conditions for farming.

China has rich water resources. There are numerous lakes and rivers, and a coastline 8,700 miles (14,000 km) long which touches on three seas of the Pacific Ocean: the Yellow Sea, the East China Sea, and the South China Sea. There is also a fourth sea, the Po Hai, which is the western part of the Yellow Sea. When the Chinese talked about 'within the four seas' in the olden days, they usually referred to the Asian continent which, as far as most people were concerned, was the entire world.

For centuries, the high mountains and deserts of the west and north and the seas to the east and south had protected China from invasion, but they had also isolated her from the rest of the world.

It is difficult to establish the exact date when the Middle Kingdom first made contact with the outside 'barbaric' world, but the Han dynasty (206 B.C.–A.D. 220) was noted, among other things, for expansion, and ex- pansion inevitably opened China to foreign influences. Trade was developed with central Asia, and this contact with the West brought Buddhism to China. In the year 138 B.C. the great Chinese adventurer Chang Chien was sent to 'the western regions' (which covers an area as far west as the Persian Gulf) as China's envoy. He was credited with introducing all sorts of exotic food into China. The list includes grapes, alfalfa, walnuts, sesame, onions, peas, coriander and cucumber. Then,

around 100 B.C., the first traders took the historic Silk Road through central Asia, bringing new spices and vegetables to China. In A.D. 166, the first trade link between the Roman Empire and China was recorded. The barrier that lay between the great civilizations of the East and West was lifted, and not only merchandizè but philosophies were interchanged, with repercussions beyond measure.

The Chinese philosopher Mencius (372–289 B.C.) observed that desire for food and sex is only human nature.

Left: *Kunming Lake in Yunnan, south-west China.* **Above:** *Volcanic rocks rise sharply from the level ground at Guilin, south China*

This may appear to be merely stating the obvious, but there are people who would regard both food and sex purely as part of the chemical process of life. They would hold that no sensual enjoyment should be extracted from either of these two vital activities.

Whatever your view on sex, can you imagine how dull life would be if the entire world treated eating as merely a survival need, everybody eating the same food cooked in the same way, to be measured only in calories, carbohydrates, proteins and vitamins? No, life like that would not be worth living, whatever material comforts this modern world might offer. Many people may try to delude themselves that they 'eat to live', but the Chinese are honest enough to admit that they 'live to eat', and that a good appetite is a blessing.

Sunrise among the mountains,
Huang Shan, in Anhui province,
east China

The classification of Chinese Cuisine

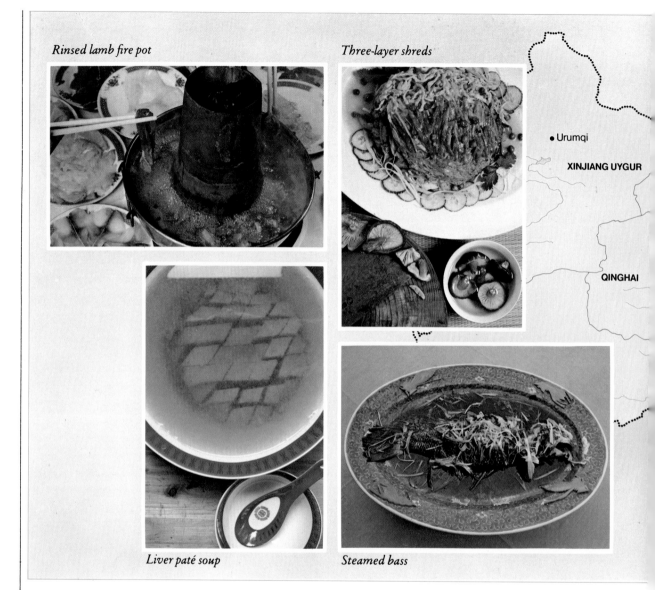

Rinsed lamb fire pot

Three-layer shreds

Liver paté soup

Steamed bass

China – showing the four regional schools of cooking

Looking at a map of China, it is not difficult to understand why there should be such a large variety of different cooking styles throughout the country. The Chinese attach great importance to the use of fresh meat and tender young vegetables, so, because it was difficult to transport food and keep it fresh, each region was forced to make the best use of its own products. Every district has its own specialty , yet all these different forms and styles of cooking can be grouped under four main Schools: Peking, Shanghai, Sichuan (Szechuan) and Guangzhou (Canton).

Peking (Northern School)
Besides the local cooking of Hebei (in which province Peking is situated), Peking cuisine embraces the cooking styles of Shandong (Shantung), Henan (Honan) and Shanxi, as well as the Chinese Moslem cooking of Inner Mongolia and Xinjiang (Sinkiang). Also, being the capital of China for many centuries, it became the culinary center, drawing inspiration from all the different regional styles.
Specialties : Peking duck, Rinsed lamb in fire-pot.

Shanghai (Eastern School)
Also known as the Huaiyang School of the Yangtse River delta, with Shanghai as its culinary center. This region covers the fertile lands of Anhui (Anhwei), Jiangsu (Kiangsu) and Fujian (Fukien). Fujian forms a school of its own, but sometimes is linked with the Southern School.

The two provinces of Hubei

14

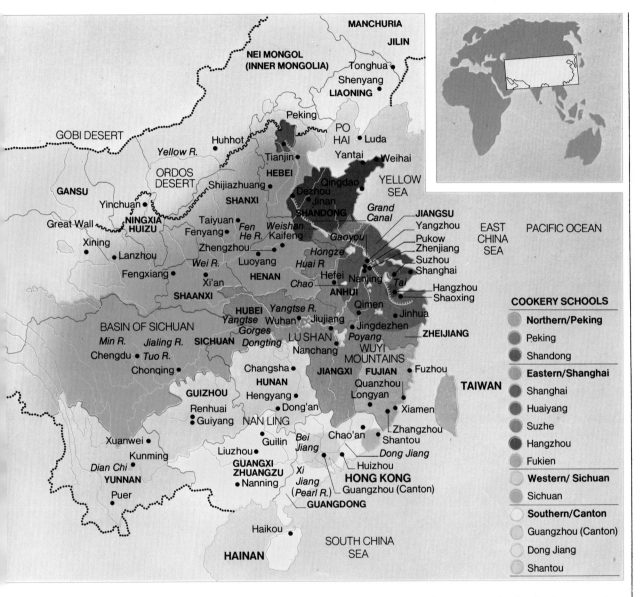

Map labels: MANCHURIA, JILIN, NEI MONGOL (INNER MONGOLIA), Tonghua, Shenyang, LIAONING, Peking, PO HAI, Luda, GOBI DESERT, Huhhot, Yellow R., Tianjin, Yantai, Weihai, ORDOS DESERT, Shijiazhuang, HEBEI, Qingdao, YELLOW SEA, GANSU, SHANXI, Dezhou, Jinan, SHANDONG, JIANGSU, Yinchuan, Taiyuan, Fen He R., Weishan, Kaifeng, Grand Canal, Yangzhou, EAST CHINA SEA, PACIFIC OCEAN, Great Wall, NINGXIA HUIZU, Fenyang, Gaoyou, Pukow, Zhenjiang, Xining, Zhengzhou, Hongze, Suzhou, Shanghai, Lanzhou, Wei R., Luoyang, Huai R., Fengxiang, Xi'an, HENAN, Hefei, Nanjing, Tai, Hangzhou, Chao, ANHUI, Shaoxing, SHAANXI, Qimen, Jinhua, BASIN OF SICHUAN, HUBEI, Yangtse R., Wuhan, Jiujiang, Jingdezhen, ZHEIJIANG, Yangtse Gorges, Min R., Jialing R., SICHUAN, Dongting, LU SHAN, Poyang, Fuzhou, Chengdu, Tuo R., Nanchang, WUYI MOUNTAINS, TAIWAN, Chonqing, Changsha, JIANGXI, FUJIAN, HUNAN, Quanzhou, GUIZHOU, Hengyang, Longyan, Xiamen, Renhuai, Dong'an, Guiyang, NAN LING, Zhangzhou, Xuanwei, Guilin, Bei Jiang, Chao'an, Shantou, Kunming, Liuzhou, Dong Jiang, Dian Chi, GUANGXI ZHUANGZU, Xi Jiang (Pearl R.), Huizhou, YUNNAN, Nanning, HONG KONG, Puer, Guangzhou (Canton), GUANGDONG, Haikou, SOUTH CHINA SEA, HAINAN

COOKERY SCHOOLS

- **Northern/Peking**
- Peking
- Shandong
- **Eastern/Shanghai**
- Shanghai
- Huaiyang
- Suzhe
- Hangzhou
- Fukien
- **Western/ Sichuan**
- Sichuan
- **Southern/Canton**
- Guangzhou (Canton)
- Dong Jiang
- Shantou

(Hupeh) and Jiangxi (Kiangsi) are sometimes grouped under this School because they both belong to China's 'Lands of Fish and Rice'.
Specialties : 'White-cut' pork,'Lions' heads,' 'Squirrel' fish.

Sichuan (Western School)
The red Basin of Sichuan (Szechuan) is one of the richest lands of China. Owing to its geographical position, it was practically inaccessible from the rest of China until recently, therefore it developed a very distinct style of cooking. Its richly flavored and piquant food has influenced its neighboring provinces of Hunan and Guizhou (Kweichow), although the last two have a style of their own.

Sichuan (Szechuan) food has only recently been introduced to the outside world and has a strong following in both Japan and the United States.
Specialties : Tea-smoked duck, Chili chicken cubes, Aubergine in 'fish sauce'.

Canton (Southern School)
The Pearl River delta, with Canton as the capital of Guangdong (Kwang-tung), is undoubtedly the home of the most famous of all Chinese cooking styles. Unfortunately its reputation has been damaged by a great number of so-called 'chop-suey' houses outside China. Authentic Cantonese food has no rival and has a greater variety of dishes than any other School. Because Canton was the first Chinese port opened for trade, foreign influences are particularly strong in its cooking.
Specialties: Cha Shao, Roast suckling pig. Also famous for its *dim sum* (snacks).

15

The fundamentals

Since Chinese civilization is the oldest that has survived to the present day, no-one would dispute the fact that the art of Chinese cooking must also be the oldest.

However, history and tradition are not the only characteristic features of Chinese food. It is closely related to Chinese culture; in fact, it is part of the way of life strongly influenced by the two early philosophies of Taoism and Confucianism.

Both Laotzu (founder of Taoism) and Confucius lived during the later Chou dynasty (770–249 B.C.). It was the Taoist School (*Tao* being the Chinese word for 'way', the mystic path of righteousness which lies at the core of Laotzu's teaching) that developed the hygienic and nutritional science of food, while Confucianism was more concerned with the art of cooking.

Confucius stressed social ritual as a teacher of virtue. It was he who laid

Above: *Confucius and Laotzu.*
Right: *Three cold dishes, clockwise –
Beef and celery salad, Crab balls, and
Braised beef, carefully selected to
give a harmonious balance of color,
flavor and texture*

down the rules to be followed in recipes and the correct custom and etiquette of the table. So for over two thousand years, a Chinese scholar was a true gourmet, since traditional Chinese classical teaching was concerned not only with the mind, but also with the heart and senses – an educated person was not just someone who could read and write but also, at the same time, a poet, painter, calligrapher, chess player, seal carver, musician and so on, besides being a connoisseur who cultivated the art of living, which of course included enjoying food, wine and tea.

THE ELEMENTS OF TASTE

'Everyone eats and drinks', said Confucius, 'but few can appreciate taste.' Since taste is a very personal thing (just as 'beauty is in the eye of the beholder'), one's palate has to be developed both physically and intellectually. Few people in the West, however, are aware that, for centuries, Chinese scholars discussed, analyzed and wrote down their thoughts on food and drink, and that some of them developed an extensive knowledge of the nature of food and the physiology of taste based on Taoist and Confucianist teachings.

No-one would disagree that the essence of the art of cooking lies in the taste of food. The Chinese believe the most important elements that help us to appreciate the taste are: color, aroma, flavor and texture. All these elements have to be well balanced to form a harmonious whole and this is the central principle of culinary art.

Any wine connoisseur will immediately recognize the parallel with wine tasting: first you examine the color, then smell the bouquet, next you taste the flavor and, finally, you judge its body and aftertaste. This may sound very elementary to the expert, but how many uneducated palates can truly appreciate the subtleties of all these elements when they are combined in one single dish?

Color

Each ingredient has its own color, some items change their color when cooked, and others only show off their true color well when supple-

mented with different colored ingredients in contrast.

Aroma

Aroma and flavor are very closely related to each other, and they both form an essential element in the taste experience. The agents a Chinese cook most often uses in order to bring out the true aroma of a certain ingredient are: scallions (spring onions), root ginger, garlic and wine.

Flavor

Each School has its own classification of flavors, but out of scores of subtle taste experiences, the Chinese have isolated five primary flavors: sweet, sour, salty, bitter and piquant. They have also learned how to combine some of these flavors to create an entirely new flavor – sweet and sour, for instance, make an interesting pair, but not sweet and piquant.

Texture

This is another vital element in Chinese cooking. A dish should have one or several textures: tenderness, crispness, crunchiness, smoothness and softness. The selection of different textures in one single dish is as important as the blending of different flavors and the contrast of complementary colors. The art of Chinese cooking lies in the selection, blending and harmonizing of color, aroma, flavor and texture.

Harmony

Very few Chinese dishes consist of only one single ingredient; as it offers no contrast it therefore lacks harmony. This is the basic Taoist philosophy of *yin* and *yang*. So, with few exceptions, all Chinese dishes consist of a main ingredient (be it pork, beef, chicken or fish) with one or several supplementary ingredients (usually vegetables) in order to give the dish the desired harmonious balance of color, aroma, flavor and texture.

For instance, if the main ingredient is pork, which is pale pink in color and tender in texture, one would use either celery (pale green and crunchy) or green peppers (dark green and crisp) as the supplementary ingredient; or one might choose mushrooms (Chinese

Flavors of Chinese cooking: ginger **(top far right);** *chilis, garlic* **(above).** *Contrasts in color: beans, aubergines* **(above right).***The finished dishes preserve a careful balance of texture and flavor: Bean curd à la maison* **(far right;** *recipe p.144), and The four season* **(right;** *recipe p.207)*

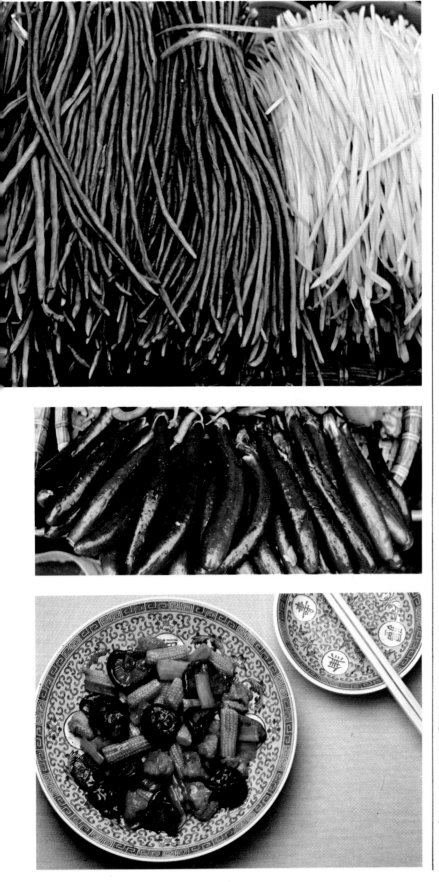

mushrooms are much darker in color with a soft texture) or bamboo shoots (pale yellow and crunchy when fresh), or a combination of both to give the dish an extra dimension.

This principle of harmonious contrast is carried all the way through a meal. No Chinese would serve just one single dish on his table, however humble his circumstances might be. The order in which different dishes are served, either singly or in pairs (often in fours), is strictly governed by the same principles: avoid monotony and do not serve similar types of food one after another or together, but use contrasts to create a perfect harmony. This will be discussed in more detail later. Here we shall concentrate on the various techniques of Chinese cooking.

Techniques & utensils

CUTTING

The main difference between Western and Chinese cooking lies in the fact that most Chinese dishes require a lot of preparation before the actual cooking, which can be very simple and quick, while in Western cooking preparation is usually quick; cooking time often lengthy.

The Chinese attach great importance to cutting. They believe the art of cutting contributes to the harmony of the dish, in that the different ingredients should be cut in a uniform size and a harmonious shape. Flavors are more easily exchanged between the different ingredients when they are cut into small pieces. Small pieces require only a short time to cook, thus preserving the natural flavors and tenderness of the food.

The Chinese cleaver is very versatile. It can be used for all forms of cutting as well as a number of other uses (see illustrations).

The cutting and chopping are carried out on a hardwood block made from a tree trunk. It should be at least 4 in (10cm) thick and 10–12 in (25–30cm) in diameter.

The basic cutting methods are as follows:

Slicing

This is probably the most common form of cutting in Chinese cooking. The ingredients are cut into very thin slices, not much bigger than an oblong stamp, and as thin as cardboard. When slicing meat, always cut across the grain – this makes it more tender when cooked.

Slicing meat across the grain

To preserve vitamins, always wash vegetables before cutting

Shredding

The ingredients are first cut into thin slices, then shredded into thin strips as small as matches but twice as long.

Meat is shredded into thin strips

Shredding bamboo shoots

Chopping

The normal method of cutting a fow is as follows:

1 Remove the two wings

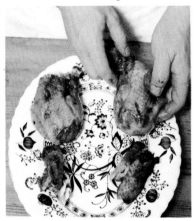

2 Remove both the legs and thighs

3 Separate the breast from the backbone

4 Divide the breast into two sections

5 Cut each breast into 3–4 pieces

6 Cut each wing into 3 pieces and each leg into 5 pieces. Reassemble as neatly as possible.

Dicing

The ingredients are first cut into coarse strips about the size of French fried potatoes, then diced into small cubes.

1 Chicken breast is cut into strips

2 The strips are cut crossways into small cubes

Grinding (mincing)

Finely chop up the ingredients into small bits. Although it is much easier to use a grinder (mincer), the flavor is not quite the same.

1 Slices of pork are finely shredded

2 The shreds are coarsely chopped

3 Grinding (mincing) with a cleaver

Diagonal cutting

Carrots, celery, zucchini (courgettes) and asparagus are normally cut into diamond-shaped pieces.

Carrots are cut diagonally

Sweet peppers are cut into diamond-shaped pieces

Preparing pork spareribs

Spareribs are easy to eat when prepared in this way. There are sparerib recipes on pages 136 and 197.

1 Trim off the large bone

2 Separate the ribs

3 Chop each rib into small pieces

Preparing shrimps (prawns)

The large Pacific or King varieties should be de-veined before cooking.

1 Remove the shell

2 Use a sharp knife to make a shallow incision on the back of the prawn, then remove the black intestinal parts.

Flower cutting

Kidneys, squid, duck gizzard and tripe are usually cut in this way. First score the surface of each piece diagonally in a criss-cross pattern, then cut the ingredients into small rectangular pieces so that when cooked each piece will open up and resemble ears of corn, hence the name 'flower'.

Flower cutting a pig's kidney

Carving and sculpturing

Finally there is a highly sophisticated method of cutting known as 'carving and sculpturing' – quite different from carving a joint in the West. In fact it is a highly skilled craft of cutting certain vegetables into various shapes to resemble flowers or animals.

A fine example of carved and sculptured vegetables

MARINATING

After cutting, the next stage in the preparation of food before actual cooking is marinating, sometimes called 'coating' or 'blending' in Chinese. The basic method is to marinate meat, fish or chicken in salt, egg-white and starch – usually water-chestnut flour, but cornstarch (cornflour) is a good substitute. Sometimes sugar, soy sauce and wine are added. The purpose of this 'coating' is to preserve the vitamins and protein content in meat after it is finely cut up, while retaining its tenderness and delicacy.

Soy sauce is added to the marinade

Mixing the cornstarch with pork

COOKING METHODS

The various cooking methods can be grouped into four basic categories: water cooking, oil cooking, steam cooking and fire cooking. In all these different methods, the degree of heat is the most vital point to remember. It is important to be able to control the degree of heat with perfect ease and that is why, in the Western kitchen, gas is far superior to electricity for Chinese cooking.

The Chinese divide the degree of heat into 'military' (high or fierce) and 'civil' (low or gentle) heat. Closely related to heat is timing; in some cases a fraction of a second can make all the difference to the final result with a particular dish. This is the reason why it is very difficult to give a precise time for cooking most Chinese dishes – so much depends on the size of the cut ingredients and the type of heat you use. A traditional Chinese recipe never gives cooking time or measurement of ingredients, not only because cooking was regarded as a fine art – and art, unlike science, can never be measured or timed – but also because, in olden days, there was no mechanical clock or standard cooking stove in the kitchen. Even today one should learn by experience, use one's intuition, and above all be alert all the time so that one emerges from the kitchen in triumph at the end. Such is the joy of Chinese cooking.

Here is a selection of the more common Chinese cooking methods:

Chao: Stir-frying. By far the most common method of Chinese cooking. Practically all vegetables are cooked in this way. The method is very simple once you have mastered the technique. Here a Chinese frying-pan known as a *wok* is most useful. First you heat up the *wok* or pan, then put in a small amount of oil – say about 3 tablespoons (45ml) for ½ lb (225g) of vegetables, less for cooking meats. Wait until the oil smokes (using high or fierce heat all the time), then throw in the ingredients to be constantly stirred and tossed for a short time, usually no more than two to three minutes, sometimes for only a few seconds. When correctly done, the food should be crispy and wholesome.

Zha: Deep-frying over a high heat. Needs no explanation.

Jian: Shallow-frying over a moderate heat. Similar to the Western way, except that in some cases stock or water is added at the last minute to make a little gravy.

Bao: Rapid-frying. Literally *bao* means to explode; it takes an even shorter time than stir-frying. Very high heat.

Shao: Braising. Literally *shao* means to burn or, in this case, to cook. The ingredients are first fried in a little oil over a moderate heat, then simmered in stock until very little juice is left.

Men: Stewing. Very similar to *shao* (braising), except that it usually takes longer over a lower heat.

Dun: Simmering. No oil is used. Low heat.

Zhu: Boiling over moderate heat.

Chuan: Rapid boiling over a high heat for a very short time.

Zheng: Steaming. Needs no explanation. Traditionally the Chinese use a bamboo steamer which sits in a *wok*.

Lu: Stewing in stock made of soy sauce, five-spice powder and sugar. Low heat.

Hui: Another form of braising. *Hui* literally means 'assembly'. Normally a

Above: *Stir-frying in a* wok
Right: *A Chinese housewife prepares a meal*

number of ingredients, some cooked, some semi-cooked, are blended together for the final stage of cooking in gravy. High to moderate heat.

Kao: Roasting. Hardly needs explanation except that, in China, most kitchens are not equipped with ovens, therefore most roasting is done either as barbecuing or in a restaurant.

Ban: Mixing. The Chinese seldom eat raw food; the so-called salad or cold dishes are pre-cooked, then cooled before mixing in the dressings.

One can go on and list at least another 10 methods of cooking, but they are mostly variations of the methods already described.

Two points to remember when cooking:

1. When frying, always heat up the pan or *wok* first before heating the oil, otherwise the food will stick to the pan.

2. When braising or stewing, use cold water if you want to bring out the natural juice of the ingredients. Hot or boiling water will seal the juice in

1 *Scoopers*
2 *Spatula*
3 *Woks*
4 *Strainers*
5 *Bamboo steamer*
6 *Chopsticks*
7 *Chopping block*
8 *Cleavers*
9 *Sand pot*

KITCHEN UTENSILS

An average Chinese kitchen has far less equipment and tools than one in the West. To start with, as I said earlier, very few Chinese kitchens are equipped with an oven. Most stoves are not suitable for baking or roasting; a great majority of families have to make do with a small brazier, burning either charcoal or firewood. But then, over the years, the Chinese have been refining their utensils to achieve a maximum efficiency and usefulness.

The *wok* and cleaver are two tools in point: with these two basic pieces of equipment, a Chinese cook can work wonders with whatever ingredients he or she is given.

The principal implements found in a Chinese kitchen include *woks* (two or three different sizes and types), cleavers (two or three different weights), a chopping block, bamboo steamers (two types), a strainer, scooper, spatula (fish slice) and sand pots (casseroles).

CHOPSTICKS AND TABLEWARE

The sight of a non-Chinese struggling with a pair of chopsticks in a restaurant must have put many people off trying. Actually they are very simple to use provided one is shown the correct way (see illustrations). Using chopsticks is like learning to ride a bicycle: you must not be too self-conscious about what you are doing, above all try not to concentrate too hard on your fingers, but relax your mind and pretend nobody is looking at you. After a little practice you need not feel ashamed if you drop some slippery item. – even the Chinese sometimes do that!

Is it worth all that effort? After all, the food will taste the same whether one uses chopsticks or spoon and fork. Quite apart from the aesthetic aspect, there is also the question of practicality. All Chinese food is cut up beforehand and prepared in such a way that it is easier to pick up with chopsticks than with any other instrument.

Except at a formal banquet, the Chinese serve all the dishes together on the table, including soup. A place setting usually consists of a medium-sized plate, a pair of chopsticks, a bowl for rice which can also be used for soup, and a porcelain spoon.

Traditionally all Chinese tableware is made of porcelain. Sometimes large serving bowls are made of pottery, though enamel and even plastic tableware is now not uncommon.

In the past, the Emperor used to have his food served on silver; it was believed that the silver would turn black if anybody tried to poison him. This practice was copied by court officials and rich merchants who wanted to show off their wealth and position, and came to be regarded as rather vulgar.

Below: *The place-setting for a formal Chinese banquet.* **Overleaf:** *Giving the finishing touch to sandpots in a kitchenware shop.*

HOW TO USE CHOPSTICKS

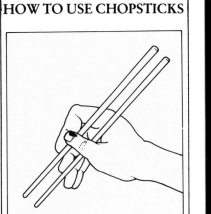

1. *Hold the chopsticks in your thumb and index finger, allowing them to rest on your second and third fingers*

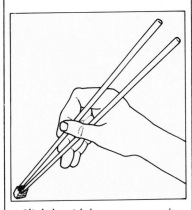

2 *Slightly withdraw your second finger and clamp the two chopsticks around the piece of food*

The serving of Chinese food

When serving a meal, Chinese etiquette is entirely different from the Western tradition. To start with, the guest of honor is placed farthest away from the host and hostess, with the next most important guest sitting on either side of the guest of honor. The least important guest, somebody junior either in rank or age, usually both, sits next to the host and hostess, who always sit side by side with their back to the door. The head of the table facing the doorway is the seat of honor.

Until the beginning of the century, no table linens were used, and it was regarded as bad form to have the wood grains of the table running towards the guest of honor; the table had to be laid so that the wood grains and joints were horizontal to the seat of honor. Another interesting point was that only square tables were used for official and formal occasions, whilst round tables were reserved for home and informal use.

The Chinese do not 'dress for dinner', rather they are often urged to 'loosen' their clothes at table in order to relax and enjoy their food. Do not get the idea that the Chinese indulge themselves starkers in orgies, they merely remove their outer garments and stick rigidly to a set of strict rules and conventions that have governed their table-manners for centuries.

The order in which dishes or courses are served at a formal Chinese meal is again in complete contrast to the Western custom. Soup is always served last or between courses; fruits, both fresh and dried, are always served at the start; while the sweet dishes are not served at the end but in between courses or even at the beginning. The sequence of a formal banquet would run like this:
1. Four sweet dishes (cakes etc.)
2. Four fresh fruits
3. Four dried fruits
4. Four dates and nuts (sweet)
5. Four cold dishes (sometimes eight different dishes)

All these dishes must be on the table before the guests are seated, for it would never do to ask your guest to sit at an empty table. Then:
6. Two or four hot dishes – these are served on slightly larger plates than the cold dishes. They usually consist of stir-fried or deep-fried food to accompany wine.
7. Four big dishes – these are the main course of the meal, served in large bowls or deep dishes. One of them must be either Bird's nest, or Shark's fin, or at least Bêche-de-Mer. After that comes Roast duck Roast suckling pig, chicken, fish, etc., and each of these four 'big' dishes are served with at least two side dishes, sometimes with a sweet dish or soup in between.
8. Two *dim sum* (1 sweet, 1 savory).
9. Four or six bowls – these are served with rice when all wine drinking will cease. These 'bowls' usually consist of one or two soups – nothing fancy, just plain fare to accompany rice.

For an informal feast, you may cut out all the fruits and nuts by starting with say eight cold dishes, followed by four hot dishes; then serve two *dim sum* before the final eight 'big bowls'. Nowadays, to simplify matters further, people entertaining at home or in a restaurant would serve a mixed cold dish as a starter, followed by two or four hot dishes before the main courses, which could be three or four big dishes. Then there would be a sweet course, followed by rice with two or three 'bowls' and soup.

It goes without saying that the Chinese never serve an individual dish to each person, you all share the dishes on the center of the table. When

---

PLANNING A CHINESE MEAL *Dishes marked with an asterisk are illustrated here.*

Here are a few sample menus for you to start with, after that you should have no difficulty in selecting your own according to different taste. The point to bear in mind is the balance between color, aroma, and flavor.

For four to six people
A. Five-fragrant kidney slices (p61)
   Braised bamboo shoots (p65)
   Braised shrimps (prawns) (p 64)
   Twice-roasted pork (p90)*
   Chicken, ham and mushroom soup (p77)

B. Fried duck liver and gizzard (p45)
   Ground (minced) fried pork (p.48)
   Stewed four treasures (p74)*
   Shredded beef with celery (p64)
   'Three Pearls' (chicken, peas and tomato) (p 72)

C. 'White-cut' pork (p106)
   Fu Yung crab meat (p115)
   Braised duck (p.113)
   The 'Two Winters' (bamboo shoots and mushrooms) (p.119)
   Crystal sugar 'silver' ears (p.160)

D. 'Jadeite' prawns (p156)
   Hot and sour kidney (p157)
   Tea-smoked duck (p157)
   Steamed beef with ground rice (p168)
   Red-cooked shad (p116)*

E. Mixed hors d'oeuvres (p214)
   Chicken in bird's nest (p214)
   Salted chicken (p214)
   Beef in oyster sauce (p211)
   Steamed sea bass (p209)

Decadent Shanghai businessmen are entertained by singsong girls

everyone is seated the host will raise his chopsticks and say 'Chin-chin' ('Please-please') – and then you all help yourselves.

HOW TO USE THE RECIPES IN THIS BOOK

I have already mentioned that it is very difficult to give a precise time or measurement of ingredients for Chinese recipes. Similarly, it would be wrong for anybody to expect me to state the exact number of helpings each dish is supposed to serve. Suffice it to say if a dish contains ½ lb (225g) each of meat and vegetables, then it should be enough for two people with average appetites. Of course it would be very dull (for the Chinese anyway) to serve only one dish at a meal, so why not reduce the amount of ingredients but increase the number of dishes? True it requires more work, but the end result is definitely worth the effort. Therefore, when planning a meal, you should allow at least one dish per person. For instance, if you are cooking for six people, prepare at least five dishes plus a soup; if you are cooking for ten, then you should have eight dishes plus a soup and a sweet course and so on.

For eight to ten people

A. Crab balls (p52)
Stewed beef (p72)
Beef and celery salad (p177)
Fried chicken breast (p48)
Egg rolls (p50)
Sunflower duck (p63)
'Cassia' lamb (p76)
Sweet and sour carp (p84)
Chicken and bamboo shoots assembly (p59)*
'Coral' cabbage (p92)

B. 'Three-layer' shreds (p108)
Phoenix tail shrimps (prawns) (p.112)
Oil-soaked duck (p137)
Stewed pork with bamboo shoots (p144)
Bean-curd à la maison (p144)
Sweet-sour crisp fish (p164)
Cantonese fried chicken (p206)
Stuffed green peppers (p211)
Ox tail soup (p176)
Thousand-layer cakes (p47)*

C. Chicken à la Kin Hwa (p.215)
Squid and peppers with shrimp (prawn) balls (p202)*
Scrambled eggs with shrimps (prawns) (p.215)
Red-cooked lamb (p207)
Fried spring rolls (p194)
Steamed bass in salted black beans (p.209)
Braised green cabbage with red ham (p194)
Roasted goose (p205)

PEKING/THE NORTHERN SCHOOL

Ancient myths and legends surround the early history of China, but archaeological evidence shows in 5000 B.C. the inhabitants of north China had begun to farm, settle down and make painted pottery eating and cooking vessels.

We have to wait until about 1500 B.C. when written records appeared before we can piece together a reasonably complete picture of the dietary habits of the ancient Chinese. We learn that the people of the Shang dynasty (from about the eighteenth to the eleventh centuries B.C.) grew millet, wheat, barley and rice, and they fermented their grain to make some form of alcoholic beverage. Later, during the Chou dynasty (eleventh century to 221 B.C.), soy beans were added to the Chinese diet. By this time they already practised the art of blending different flavors by using several ingredients in one dish,

and they cut and prepared their foodstuffs before cooking them – two of the main characteristics of Chinese culinary art.

Some of the most conspicuous traces of early Chinese culture have been found at sites that lie along the valley of the Yellow River, which is why this area is sometimes described as the cradle of Chinese civilization.

In 720 B.C. Peking, a small garrison town, became a capital for the first time – not yet of China but of the feudal state of Yan. Yan was one of the seven 'warring states' that were constantly fighting among themselves until 221 B.C., when the state of Chin conquered and unified all China for the first time. The prince of Chin declared himself 'Chin Shi Huang Di' (Chin, the First Emperor).

The first emperor abolished the feudal system and divided the country into 36 provinces, with civil and military governors directly responsible to the emperor – this system of national administration remained unchanged almost until the present day. He

Below: *Workers from the model Da Zhai commune return from a day in the terraced fields not far from Peking. Their modern aqueduct stands out starkly from the ancient landscape.*
Right: *Sharp-pointed rocks on the banks of the Yellow River. This river valley was the cradle of Chinese civilization.*

extended China's boundaries towards the south coast and, in order to strengthen his defences against the 'barbaric' northern invaders, completed the Great Wall of China, which stretched from the sea north of Peking, westwards across Shanxi to the Yellow River, and finally ended in the Gobi Desert. From end to end it probably measured some 3,000 miles (5,000 km). It took many years to complete and was immensely costly in terms of human life – of the one million laborers who were conscripted to build it, half lost their lives.

Today visitors to Peking can view this ancient monument to the Chinese people about 30 miles north-west of the city. The wall is over 20 ft (7m) thick at the base and up to 28 ft (8.5m) high, and for the most part it is wide enough to allow five horsemen to ride abreast. With battlements dotted all along one side of the wall and watch-towers every 200 yd (183m), it rises and falls with the ridges of the mountains like a gigantic dragon curling through the mountain tops, disappearing into the misty distance. One cannot but marvel at this truly great human construction, and feel both proud and humble at the same time.

Peking has had an extraordinary history. Its name alone has changed at least eight times. It appears in the warring states period (481–221 B.C.) as the city of Chi. As Yenking ('Swallow Capital') it was the capital of the Liao dynasty in the tenth century, and it was called Chungtu ('Middle Capital') by the Chin dynasty in the twelfth century. Ironically, the city's greatest period came in the late thirteenth century when Kublai Khan, whose ancestors, the Mongols, the Great Wall was first built to keep at bay, moved his capital there and gave it the name Tatu ('Great Capital'). When Marco Polo visited it in 1275, he called it Cambaluc from the Mongolian name Khan-balyk, and it was not until 1420 that the city was given the name Peking ('Northern Capital') by the Ming dynasty. It retained the name through the Manchu (Ching) dynasty (1644–

A momument to the Chinese people: the Great Wall of China.

35

1911). When the Kuomintang government moved its capital to Nanking ('Southern Capital') in 1928, Peking was renamed Peiping ('Northern Peace'). In 1949, when the People's Republic was established, the city once again reverted to its political pre-eminence by becoming China's capital under its historic name, though people on the island of Taiwan still stubbornly refer to it as Peiping.

During the 3,000 years of its history, Peking has suffered many catastrophes, including total destruction. It has been rebuilt no less than four times just in the past 800 years. The city pattern dates from the days of Kublai Khan, who adopted the Chinese style of living, and who brought the Mongolian influence into the Northern School of Chinese cuisine.

The Peking we see today was completely rebuilt in the fifteenth century by the Emperor Yung-lo of the Ming dynasty. Some of the original Imperial Palace, known as the Forbidden City, still remains and is now converted into a museum. This central area of the Inner City is the most beautiful part of the capital, set among lakes and parks. Along the south edge of the old Imperial City, one of the capital's main thoroughfares, called Chang An Chieh ('The Boulevard of Long Peace'), leads past the world-famous Tien An Men square ('The Gate of Heavenly Peace').

In his book *Peking Cooking* (Faber), the eminent Chinese gourmet

Kenneth Lo defined Peking cuisine as: 'The crystallization of the many inventions and performances of the generations of Imperial Chefs of the different dynasties which have ruled in Peking for nearly a millennium and the grass-root dishes of the locality which the people of Shangdong (Shantung) and Hebei (Hopei) have been in the habit of preparing, together with all the culinary contributions which have flowed in from the far-flung regions and provinces of China, and which over the years have established their reputation in the Old Capital. Peking cooking is, in short, the top table of Chinese culinary art.' To me, this is the definition of Peking cuisine in a nutshell.

Conventionally, the Chinese always place east first when arranging the four directions in their right order, followed by the south and west, north being the last, as people who are familiar with the game of Mah Jong will know. The reason I have chosen the Northern School as the starting point of this book on Chinese regional cooking is not because Peking food is 'the top table of Chinese culinary art', it is entirely a personal one: Peking happens to be my birthplace, and I cannot possibly leave it to the last when writing about Chinese regional food.

Although I was born in Peking, I only lived there for a few years, and was brought up in the south-east province of Jiangxi (Kiangsi). But I have early memories of life in Peking

in the 'thirties, before the war with
Japan which was to change the entire
course of Chinese history. The two
things I remember most vividly are the
house we lived in and the long,
straight, tree-lined thoroughfares,
longer and much wider than the
Champs Elysées in Paris. Then there
was the climate. I shall never forget the
bitterly cold winters with savage
winds blowing from the plains of
Siberia, nor could I easily forget the
intensely hot and humid summers,
with the air parched and dusty; the
worst feature, however, was the wind
blowing in across the Gobi Desert,
bringing dry, fine sand known as
Peking dust that got everywhere and
into everything.

Yet on looking back, one cannot
help feeling nostalgic for one's early
childhood: life in Peking seemed so
peaceful and tranquil in those days. I
was completely unaware of the unrest
and the civil war that was raging in
China. Just beyond the Great Wall,
the Japanese army had seized
Manchuria and was about to launch a
full-scale war against China that
eventually involved almost the entire
world.

Until recently, almost all of

Far left: *The Imperial Palace,
Peking.* **Left:** *The jade belt bridge
crosses the lake of the Summer Palace
park on the outskirts of Peking.*
Above: *A corner of the Pavilion of
Floating Green in the Imperial
Palace*

Above: *Corner of a Peking market.*
Left: *Aerial view of the single-story houses in Peking's old residential area; looking along a hutung* (**inset, left**); *a four-enclosure courtyard* (**inset, right**).

Peking's residential dwellings were single-story houses. It is believed that an emperor decreed centuries ago that no citizen should be able to look down on him from a tall building, so Peking remained a low city well into the twentieth century.

We lived in one of these single-storey houses amongst a maze of little *hutungs* – narrow alleys or lanes that survived from old Peking. No windows looked onto these *hutungs*, but small doorways led into large courtyards which lay at the center of each building, with rooms on all four sides looking onto the courtyard. They were called *Si He Yuan* ('Four-enclosure Courtyard'). Our courtyard, like others, was paved with stone slates, and there were trees and potted flowers. Our living quarters, known as the North House, faced south and a few stone steps led onto a

verandah. On summer evenings we used to bring out chairs and sit on the verandah for cool air, with bird cages hanging above our heads. From the verandah the entrance led directly into our dining room with two bedrooms on either side. The door was always left open, but there was a bamboo curtain during the summer months to keep the insects out, and the curtains were changed to padded cotton ones in the winter in order to keep out the cold draught. I remember that I always waited in excited anticipation for the change of the curtains as it marked the sharp change of the seasons, even though it only meant we exchanged one extreme type of weather for another.

On the opposite side of the courtyard, facing north, stood the South House. I think it only consisted of two large rooms. In one of them,

scrolls of painting and calligraphy hung on the walls and all the visitors were shown into there, so it must have been the living room. Adjacent to it was my father's study, with shelves full of books. What impressed me most was the fact that they were not ordinary Chinese books which I saw everywhere in other people's houses, but fascinating looking foreign books! For at that time my father, besides being a professor of English at one of the universities in Peking, was also a translator of works by Bernard Shaw, James Barrie, Thomas Hardy, John Galsworthy and Benjamin Franklin.

I have not much recollection of the West House, but the East House opposite I do remember well, for it contained a large kitchen and I spent a lot of time in there with my nanny.

A Chinese kitchen is never small, for more often than not it is also the

living area as well as the dining room. But, in better-off households, it used to be the servants' living quarters.

My nanny, whose name was Zhang, had been with our family for many years. Like my parents, she came from Nanchang in the south, and she had looked after my mother before becoming nanny to me. At that time, my mother was busily studying at the university, so my brother and I were constantly with nanny Zhang during the daytime.

Nanny Zhang, who was a good cook in her own right, told me later that she learned quite a lot from our cook in Peking, and my interest in cooking must have taken root very early.

Shortly before my parents left Peking, they were invited by various friends for farewell feasts, then finally it was their turn to invite everyone

back to say goodbye. I remember that occasion especially well because they ordered the food from a restaurant to be cooked at our home. First the restaurant delivered the food and implements, not by a mule-cart, which was the most popular transport in Peking at that time, but carried on a shoulder pole by a porter. (The porter could avoid the bumps in the road, so the food arrived undisturbed.) All the ingredients were already cut and arranged neatly in several large containers which were stacked taller than the porter. Two men came with the porter and they carried the containers into the kitchen. One of them then dashed about arranging things while the other one put on a white apron and started to cook as the guests began to arrive.

The children were not allowed to be part of such a formal dinner, but we

stayed in the courtyard with our nanny and watched the goings-on with wide-eyed excitement. What impressed me most was when the assistant arranged a huge pile of charcoal at the far end of the courtyard and started a big fire. The chef then skilfully roasted a white duck on a long spit for quite a while without burning any part. When the duck turned a shining golden color he put it onto a plate and showed it around the table for the guests to admire his skill; then he took it back to the kitchen to be carved. The crispy skin and meat were served separately. Meanwhile, the assistant was carrying in the sauce, scallions (spring onions) and 'Lotus-leaf' pancakes which would be eaten with the duck.

The next day, the duck carcass was made into a delicious soup with white cabbage, which we all enjoyed.

Peking duck

One of the most famous dishes in Chinese cuisine must be 'Peking duck'. Its reputation is worldwide, yet it is strictly a regional dish in the same sense that *bouillabaisse* cannot be made away from the shores of the Mediterranean. Just as the Marseillais regard their own recipe as the only authentic one, so do the chefs in Peking. The interesting point is this: neither of these two dishes originated from the cities which claim their monopoly (I do hope no Marseillais will bear a grudge against me for this provocative statement but most culinary experts seem to agree on this).

There are three important factors which make 'Peking duck' unique. Firstly, the duck itself: it is a specially raised species only to be found in and around Peking. Secondly, the way it is cooked as well as the elaborate preparation prior to cooking. And finally, the way it is served and eaten.

A Peking duck has a different appearance from the common duck; it has pure white feathers and is brought by several stages of force-feeding and care to exactly the right degree of plumpness and tenderness before it is prepared for the oven. Its creamy-pink lean flesh has fine streaks of white fat embedded in it, which makes it extra-tender and delicious.

I will spare you here the gory details of how to kill and pluck the bird – I can assure you it is quite a business. Anyway, after the duck is cleaned thoroughly – which again is no easy task – it is inflated by pumping air between the wind-pipe and the skin in order to separate it from the body. Then the skin is doused with boiling water and the duck hung up in an airy spot to dry, which can take anything up to 12 hours. But that is not all: before roasting, the skin of the duck is coated with sugar-water (one part of malt sugar (maltose) or honey to six parts of water) and allowed to dry once more. The purpose of all this is to make the skin look a beautiful golden color, and taste really crispy when cooked.

There are several different ways of cooking a Peking duck. The simplest method is spit-roasting over an open charcoal fire. Another method is to roast it in a specially built coal-fired oven, which is not often found in ordinary Chinese restaurants let alone an average home. The most renowned method, however, is called hung-roasting, and all the best Peking restaurants which specialize in duck dishes use this method.

One of the best-known restaurants for Peking duck in Peking is *Quan Ju*

A Chinese family enjoys a delicious dish of Peking duck

Left: *Ducks in a Chinese market*
Top: *Rows of Peking ducks hanging to dry before cooking*
Above: *The roasted duck is removed from the oven. Barrel-shaped ovens like this one are specially designed for cooking Peking duck*

De, first established in the twelfth year of the reign of Emperor Tong Zhi (1873); their oven is built like a kiln, square outside and curved inside. The ducks are roasted hanging on iron rods with wooden handles, hence the name 'Hung-roasting duck'. The best fuel is Chinese date tree, which gives high heat, burns slowly and does not produce too much smoke. The next best are plum or apricot tree, but they give less heat.

Apparently, the way the firewood is arranged inside the oven is very important. It goes without saying that, once the fire is lit, the heat control is crucial. A book which deals with this subject, first published in Peking in 1958, gives pages and pages of detailed instruction on the oven and heat control (see illustration). There is an interesting section in this book, headed 'How to tell when the duck is done'. The text is worth translating in full:

'An experienced cook can judge if a duck is done or not by timing, color and the degree of heat; another way of judging is to estimate the weight of the duck (when done, the duck should weigh about a third less than when raw).'

Peking duck can be cooked very successfully in an ordinary gas or electric oven. Here is an easy method, adapted for Western kitchens.

3½–4 lb (1.5–1.75kg) duckling
1 tbsp (15ml) malt sugar (maltose) or honey
1¼ cups (½ pt, 300ml) water

For serving:
6 tbsp (90ml) Hoi Sin sauce
10 scallions (spring onions)
½ cucumber
24 'Lotus-leaf' pancakes (for recipe, see page 44)

Do not use a frozen duck, or a duckling smaller than 3½ lb (1.5kg), which will not have much meat on it. If a duck weighs over 5 lb (2.25kg), the meat will be too tough.

Clean the duck well before dousing it with a pot full of boiling water, then

THE QUAN JU DE OVEN

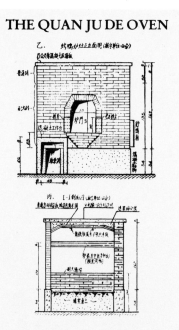

Upper picture: *Front view of the oven. The duck goes in the central door; the fuel goes in below.* **Lower picture:** *The oven in cross-section*

CARVING THE DUCK AND PREPARING IT FOR THE TABLE

The duck is carved at the table, using a peeling action

The skin is removed and served on a separate dish

The crispness of the skin is characteristic of a Peking duck

The meat is carved and put on a separate dish

The tender, juicy meat contrasts with the crisp skin

Finally the duck's beak is cut off, to show that no more meat is left

hang it up to dry thoroughly – either leave it in a drafty place overnight or use a fan heater or hairdryer to speed up the process.

Next mix the malt sugar (maltose) or honey with the water and pour it all over the duck as evenly as possible, then dry it for several hours.

To cook, place the duck on the middle rack of a preheated oven (400° F, 200°C, Gas Mark 6) and roast it for precisely one hour. Do not open the oven during the cooking – the duck should not be basted.

Simple you might say. Yes, but then there is the most important part to come yet: serving and eating it.

What you do is this: while the duck is being cooked, make the 'Lotus-leaf' pancakes; cut the onions into 2–3 in (5–7.5cm) lengths; slice the cucumber into thin strips. All these accompaniments (including the Hoi Sin sauce) are served in separate dishes. The photographs show how the duck is carved and served.

To eat, you spread a teaspoon or so of the Hoi Sin sauce on a pancake, then place a few cucumber strips and onions in the middle, and on top of these you add a piece or two of the crispy skin with some of the meat. Now roll the pancake up tightly, turning up the bottom end to prevent anything falling out, and eat it with your fingers.

The combination of crunchy vegetables, crispy skin and tender meat with the sweetish sauce, all at the same time, is an experience you will never forget.

Returning to my earlier remarks that this dish may not have originated in Peking, it is said that way back when the cities of Luoyang and Kaifeng, just south of the Yellow River in Henan (Honan) province, were ancient capitals, the noblemen and imperial families lived in such luxury that their chefs invented this novel way of cooking and eating a duck, and when the capital moved up north to Peking, so did this famous dish. Whether this is true or not we will have to leave to some future archaeologists, but I do hope that I will not be chastised by the people of my birthplace for daring to put forward this heresy.

SERVING THE PEKING DUCK

First: The Hoi Sin sauce is spread on the Lotus-leaf pancake

Second: Shredded onions and cucumber are added

Third: The pieces of duck skin and meat are placed on top

Fourth: The pancake is folded up, either by hand or using chopsticks

Fifth: The completed package is now ready to be served and eaten

Here the chef is making a party dish – normally you serve yourself

'LOTUS-LEAF' PANCAKES

4 cups (1 lb, 0.5kg) plain flour
1¼ cups (½ pt, 300 ml) boiling water
3 tsp (15ml) vegetable oil

Sift the flour into a mixing-bowl and
very slowly pour in the boiling water,
mixed with 1 tsp (5ml) oil, while
stirring with a pair of chopsticks or a
wooden spoon. Do not be tempted to
add any more water than the amount
given, otherwise the mixture will get
too wet and become messy.

Knead the mixture into a firm
dough, then divide it into three equal
portions. Now roll out each portion
into a long 'sausage', and cut each
sausage into eight equal parts; then,
using the palm of your hand, press
each piece into a flat pancake. Brush
one of the pancakes with a little oil,
and place another one on top to form a
'sandwich', so that you end up with 12
sandwiches. Now use a rolling-pin to
flatten each sandwich into a 6 in
(15cm) circle by rolling gently on each
side on a lightly floured surface.

To cook, place a frying-pan over a
high heat, and when it is hot reduce
the heat to moderate. Put one pancake
sandwich at a time into the ungreased
pan, and turn it over when it starts to
puff up with bubbles. It is done when
little brown spots appear on the
underside. Now remove from the pan
and, very gently, peel apart the two
layers and fold each one in half.

If the pancakes are not to be served
as soon as they are cooked, they can be
stored and warmed up, either in a
steamer, or the oven for 5–10 minutes.

*Duck and cabbage soup: a nourishing
and delicious soup, particularly at the
end of a rich feast. In this picture the
chef has added some transparent
noodles and Chinese mushrooms, and
has garnished the dish with Chinese
parsley (fresh coriander)*

DUCK AND CABBAGE SOUP

Traditionally, when duck has been served, the carcass is made into a soup with cabbage. In a restaurant, this soup will be served at the end of a meal since there will always be more than one duck carcass to make the soup with. But at home you will have to wait until the next day as it takes at least an hour to make.

1 duck carcass (plus giblets if
available)
4 cups (1 lb, 0.5kg) Chinese cabbage
2 slices ginger root
salt and Sichuan pepper

Break up the carcass, place it together with the giblets, if you have not already used them for another dish, and any other bits and pieces in a large pot or pan; cover it with water, add the ginger root, bring it to the boil. Skim off the impurities floating on the surface and let it simmer gently with a lid on for at least 45 minutes.

About 20 minutes before serving, add the washed and sliced cabbage. Season with salt and pepper, then serve.

FRIED DUCK LIVER AND GIZZARD

Whenever I was taken to restaurants in Peking for a roast duck dinner, my favorite food was not the duck itself, but the 'small dishes' which preceded the main course. Not knowing the fine art of eating, like any child of my age, I stuffed myself silly with whatever was served first, thus leaving very little room for the 'big dishes'.

All the duck restaurants served a wide variety of dishes, using different parts of the duck. Nothing was thrown away; things like the duck webs, tongues and intestines, were made into delicious dishes. I was told that at the *Quan Ju De* restaurant there were over a hundred different duck dishes on the menu.

giblets from one duck (the liver and
gizzard)
2 cups (1 lb, 0.5kg) duck fat (or lard)
for deep-frying
salt and Sichuan pepper

Clean and trim off all excess fat on the gizzard. Remove the gall bladder from the liver, making sure that it is not broken, otherwise it will leave a sharp, bitter taste. Now cut the gizzard into six small pieces, and the liver into six triangular pieces. Parboil the liver first – testing it by pressing with your finger to see it is still soft to the touch – remove and drain; parboil the gizzard for roughly the same length of time, then also remove and drain.

Heat up the fat until you can see blue smoke appearing, then fry the gizzard first for three minutes; remove and drain. Wait for the fat to produce more blue smoke, put both the liver and the gizzard into it and fry for another three minutes, then remove and drain. Serve with salt-pepper mixture as a dip (one part ground pepper mixed with two parts salt).

Duck liver and gizzard, crispy outside and tender inside – one of the hundred or more variations of duck

In the style of the palace kitchen

In 1925, a restaurant was opened in Beihai ('North Sea') Park within the Imperial City. Its chefs had formerly served in the Imperial kitchens inside the Forbidden City, and the dishes they prepared became known as 'In the style of the Palace Kitchen'. The interesting point is that on the whole the ingredients used were nothing unusual, but most of the dishes re-quired elaborate and highly skillful preparation in order to achieve their unique and outstanding quality.

The following selection of recipes should not be beyond a competent cook. Even if you do not feel like trying them out, at least they will give you some idea of the type of fare indulged in by the Imperial family of the last dynasty in China (1644–1911).

Below: *A corner of the Imperial Palace, Peking. This beautiful building has recently been reopened to the public after restoration and redecoration*

THOUSAND-LAYER CAKES

Of course there are not a thousand layers in this cake (just as there are not that number in the French *Mille-Feuilles*); there are, in fact, only 81, but that is quite impressive.

6 cups (1½ lb, 0.75kg) flour
2 tsp (10ml) dried yeast
1½ cups (12 fl oz, 350ml) warm water
¾ cup (6 oz, 150g) sugar
½ cup (4 oz, 100g) lard
3 tbsp (40g) walnuts, crushed

Sift the flour into a mixing bowl and add the sugar; dissolve the yeast in warm water and slowly pour it in, then knead it well for 5 minutes. Cover the dough with a damp cloth and let it stand for 3 hours or until it doubles in volume.

Now divide the dough into three equal portions, then roll out each portion into a thin rectangle measuring about 1 ft (30cm)×8 in (20cm). Spread some lard and sprinkle a few chopped walnut pieces on the surface of one portion, and place another one on top to make a 'sandwich'. Then spread some lard and walnut pieces on top of the sandwich, and place the third portion on top to form a double-decker sandwich.

Now roll this sandwich flat until it measures roughly 2½ ft (75cm)×1 ft (30cm). Spread some lard and walnuts over two-thirds of the surface of the dough, then fold one-third over to

Thousand-layer cakes, served on a silver dish for a special occasion

cover the middle section and spread lard and walnuts on top of that, then fold the other one-third over.

Turn the dough around so that the folded edge faces you. Repeat the rolling, spreading and folding twice more so that you end up with the dough measuring roughly 1 ft (30cm)× 8 in (20cm) again but with 81 layers.

Let it stand for about 30 minutes, then place it on a wet cloth in a steamer and steam over boiling water for 50–60 minutes.

Remove and let it cool a little, then cut the cake into squares or diamonds before serving.

FRIED CHICKEN BREAST

This dish was first created by the Palace chefs and has since been imitated by many others. 'Fu Yung chicken slices' (p.57) is a variation on this recipe.

½ lb (225g) chicken breast boned
3 egg whites
1 cup (4 oz, 100g) green peas
2 cups (1 lb, 0.5kg) lard for
*   deep-frying*
salt, cornstarch (cornflour), rice wine
*   (or sherry), chicken stock,*
*   monosodium glutamate and sesame*
*   seed oil*

Separate the meat from the white tendon and membrane of the chicken breast. First pound the meat by using the blunt edge of the cleaver for about 30 minutes, adding a little water now and again. Then chop the meat with the sharp edge of the blade for a further 30 minutes or until the meat has a creamy texture (if you think this is tough going, wait till you see the recipe for 'Shark's fin'!). Add a little more water (about 1 tbsp, 15ml), the whites of 3 eggs and mix well – but very gently so as not to disturb the consistency of the egg whites, otherwise the meat will come apart when deep-fried. Finally, add a pinch of salt and about 2 tsp (10ml) of cornstarch (cornflour).

Heat up a *wok* or deep-fryer over a high heat before putting in the lard; this is important, otherwise the meat will stick to the bottom during frying. When the lard has been heated for about 2 minutes, reduce the heat to low. Now squeeze the creamy chicken meat through the holes of a perforated spoon so that they become little balls the size of peas. Deep-fry them for about 1 minute, then quickly scoop them out with the perforated spoon and drain.

Mix in a bowl ½ cup (4 fl oz, 100ml) of chicken stock, 1 tbsp (15ml) rice wine or sherry, 1 tbsp (15ml) cornstarch (cornflour), and ½ tsp (2ml) each of salt and monosodium glutamate; stir until they are well blended. (You will notice that the Palace chefs often used monosodium glutamate although it is rather frowned on by some chefs as being

Ground (minced) fried pork (left) and fried chicken breast (right). Both these dishes are served with sesame seed bread (above) which opens up, rather like Greek pitta bread. The meat can be placed inside the bread, and then eaten like a sandwich.

somewhat unsubtle; it proves there are no hard and fast rules.)

Pour out the excess lard from the *wok* and over a high heat make the chicken stock mixture into a white sauce; add the peas followed by the chicken balls. Cook together for a short while (about 30 seconds), add ½ tsp (2ml) sesame seed oil and serve.

This dish not only looks pretty (pure white with bright green peas), it should taste so tender that it almost melts in your mouth – well worth the effort if you have the staying power, or chefs scurrying around to do it for you!

GROUND (MINCED) FRIED PORK

This fried dish is rather unusual in that it is fried without any oil. In fact, the fat it produces during cooking should be drained, a process known as 'dry-frying'.

1 lb (0.5kg) pork fillet
½ cup (4oz, 100g) Sichuan preserved
*   vegetable*
1 tbsp (15ml) crushed yellow bean
*   sauce*
2 tsp (10ml) brown sugar
½ tsp (2ml) salt
½ tbsp (10ml) soy sauce
1 slice ginger root
1 scallion (spring onion)
1 tbsp (15ml) rice wine (or sherry)
1 tsp (5ml) sesame seed oil

Trim off all sinew and gristle from the meat, but keep the fat; now chop the pork coarsely with a cleaver into rice

CHICKEN 'CASSEROLE'

*1 young chicken weighing about
    2½–3 lb (1.25–1.5kg)*
1 tbsp (15ml) five-spice powder
2 tbsp (30ml) sugar
2½ cups (1 pt, 600ml) soy sauce
1 slice ginger root
1 scallion (spring onion)
*5 cups (2 pt, 1.2l) vegetable oil for
    deep-frying*

Use a fresh chicken, wash and dry it
thoroughly.

Put the five-spice powder into a
large pot or casserole, add sugar, soy
sauce and about 5 cups (2 pt, 1.2l)
water, bring it to the boil, then reduce
the heat and simmer until it turns dark
brown. This is the master sauce,
which can be used over and over again;
the flavor improves each time it is
used, though after using it four or five
times, you will have to add more five-
spice powder.

Now parboil the chicken for 2 to 3
minutes, then place it in another pot of
clean boiling water; add the ginger
root and onion; cook for about 40
minutes over a gentle heat; remove
and let it cool for a short while. Cook
the chicken in the 'master sauce' for
about 15 minutes, turning it over once
or twice so that the entire chicken has
become dark red. Remove the meat
from the sauce and drain.

Heat up the oil over a high heat
until smoking, then fry the chicken for
about 15 minutes until the skin
becomes dark brown but not quite
burnt; remove. Chop up the chicken
with a sharp cleaver (see p.21) and
arrange it neatly on a plate and serve.

Below: *Chicken 'casserole' – delicious
and tender and good to look at*

grain-sized pieces. Chop the Sichuan
preserved vegetable into small pieces.

Finely chop the ginger root
(peeled) and onion.

Heat up a *wok* or frying-pan over a
high heat and stir-fry the pork for 1 or
2 minutes; as soon as it starts to stick
on the bottom, reduce the heat to low
and scrape the pan well. After about 1
minute, increase the heat to high again
until it starts to stick, then reduce
heat. Repeat this rather fiddly high-
low heat procedure three or four
times, when the pork will turn pale in
color. Then drain off the fat which the
meat will have produced.

Over high heat add the bean sauce,
sugar, salt and soy sauce, mixing well;
by now the meat should have turned
light brown. Now add the chopped
Sichuan preserved vegetable, ginger
root, onion and wine or sherry, blend
well, and finally add the sesame seed
oil and serve.

FRIED GREEN PEAS WITH PORK

½ lb (225g) pork fillet
2 cups (½ lb, 225g) fresh or frozen
* peas*
1 slice ginger root, peeled
1 scallion (spring onion)
2 tbsp (30ml) lard
1 tbsp (15ml) crushed yellow bean
* sauce*
1 tbsp (15ml) rice wine (or sherry)
1 tbsp (15ml) soy sauce
½ tsp (2ml) monosodium glutamate
2 tsp (10ml) cornstarch (cornflour)
1 tbsp (15ml) stock
1 tsp (5ml) sesame seed oil

Dice the pork into small cubes about the same size as peas, and finely chop the ginger root and onion. Blanch the peas for about 1 minute and drain.

Heat up a *wok* or frying-pan over high heat, then melt the lard and stir-fry the pork for a while. When it starts to sizzle in its own juice, reduce the heat; when the noise becomes subdued, increase the heat again. Continue cooking for 6–7 minutes, then add ginger root, onions and crushed bean sauce, cooking for 2–3 minutes more; now add the peas, sherry, soy sauce and monosodium glutamate.

Fried green peas with pork, an ideal start to a meal

When it starts to get dry, add cornstarch (cornflour) mixed with the stock and blend well. Add the sesame seed oil when the juice thickens, stir a few more times, then serve.

This was one of the 'everyday' dishes in the Imperial Palace, and is most appetizing.

EGG ROLLS

4 oz (100g) pork
1 slice ginger root, peeled
1 scallion (spring onion)
½ tsp (2ml) salt
2 tsp (10ml) rice wine (or sherry)
1 cup (4 oz, 100g) bean sprouts
4–5 Chinese dried mushrooms, soaked
1 tbsp (15ml) cornstarch (cornflour)
2 eggs
1 tbsp (15ml) plain flour
2½ cups (1 pt, 600ml) oil for
* deep-frying*
salt and Sichuan pepper for dip

Finely grind (mince) the pork; mix it with finely chopped ginger root and onion; add salt, wine or sherry and about ½ tbsp (10ml) cornstarch (cornflour). Blend well.

Beat up the eggs with the rest of the cornstarch (cornflour), then warm up a *wok* or frying-pan over a moderate heat; grease the pan with a little oil and pour in half the beaten eggs. Tip the pan from side to side until a thin,

round pancake of egg forms (about 6 in (15cm) in diameter). Gently lift the pancake up with a spatula and lay it flat on a plate. Make another pancake with the remaining eggs in the same way.

Mix the plain flour with a little water to form a thin paste and spread some of it on the surface of the egg pancake. Chop the Chinese dried mushrooms into small pieces. Place about half of the pork mixture, bean sprouts and Chinese dried mushrooms on the pancake. Fold up the pancake as though doing up a package, sealing the edges with a little more flour paste, then press them down firmly.

Warm up the oil over a moderate heat; deep-fry the rolls for about 2–3 minutes, then increase the heat to high and continue cooking for about 10 minutes or until golden. Remove and drain.

Serve by dipping in salt and Sichuan pepper mix.

PORK VARIETY MEATS (OFFAL) IN CASSEROLE

This dish originated in a restaurant known as 'The Sand-Pot (Casserole) Cottage', first opened in the sixth year of the reign of Emperor Chien Lung (1741) in what was then the night-watchman's lodge belonging to a member of the Imperial Household.

At that time over two hundred years ago, so the story goes, the Imperial Court and palaces made ritual sacrifices at dawn and dusk, as well as on other occasions, in which a pig of the highest quality was used. The slaughtered pigs were given to the nightwatchmen (they would be called security guards in modern terms) as a reward. Being enterprising fellows, the nightwatchmen collaborated with the ex-workers from the Imperial kitchen, cooked the whole pig together with its variety meats (offal) in an enormous casserole and started a flourishing business.

The following recipe has been modified somewhat for the Western kitchen; the original ingredients in-

Egg rolls with some of the ingredients used to make them – eggs, bean sprouts and Chinese dried mushrooms

cluded things like lungs (lights), and melts which I do not think would appeal to the average Western taste!

pig's heart, liver, tripe (stomach),
* kidneys and tongue*
2 cups (½ lb, 225g) Chinese cabbage
* (or spinach)*
⅔ cup (4 oz, 100g) bamboo shoots
3–4 Chinese dried mushrooms
1 slice ginger root
1 scallion (spring onion)
1 tbsp (15ml) rice wine (or sherry)
salt to taste

The tripe should be cleaned thoroughly, parboiled for about 10 minutes, and then marinated in a little salt and vinegar for 2 minutes. After that, rinse well in clean, cold water.

First place the tripe on the bottom of a big pot or casserole, followed by the tongue and heart, and finally the kidneys and liver. Add enough cold water to cover, then bring it to a rapid boil. Skim off the impurities floating on the surface, then reduce the heat and let it simmer with a lid on.

After simmering for half-an-hour, remove the liver and kidneys; next remove the tongue and heart, after about an hour's cooking. The tripe will have to be cooked for two hours or more, so take it out when it is well done. Reserve the stock in which the meat has been cooked.

Cut the tripe and heart into small chunks, the tongue, kidneys and liver into slices.

Wash the cabbage or spinach in cold water and cut it into small pieces. Soak the dried mushrooms in warm water for about 20 minutes, then remove the hard stalks and cut them into small pieces together with the bamboo shoots.

Place the cabbage or spinach on the bottom of a pot or casserole, then put the tripe, heart, tongue, kidneys and liver over it, followed by the bamboo shoots and Chinese dried mushrooms; finally, add the ginger root and onions, salt and rice wine or sherry. Add enough of the stock in which the meats have been cooked to cover the entire contents, cover with a tightly fitting lid and bring to a rapid boil,

To serve, bring the casserole or pot to the table.

CRAB BALLS

½ lb (225g) crab meat
¼ cup (2 oz, 50g) pork fat
½ cup (2 oz, 50g) water chestnuts,
* peeled*
2 eggs
2 tbsp (30ml) rice wine (or sherry)
1 tsp (5ml) monosodium glutamate
1 tsp (5ml) salt
2 tbsp (30ml) cornstarch (cornflour)
1 slice peeled ginger root, finely
* chopped*
1 scallion (spring onion), finely
* chopped*
½ cup (4 fl oz, 100ml) chicken
* stock*
2 cups (1 lb, 0.5kg) lard for
* deep-frying*
1 oz (25g) cooked ham

Finely chop the crab meat, pork fat and water chestnuts and add 2 eggs, 1 tbsp (15ml) wine or sherry, ½ tsp (2ml) monosodium glutamate, ½ tsp (2ml) salt, and 1 tbsp (15ml) cornstarch (cornflour) together with the

Crab balls served cold, garnished with flower-cut cucumber and Chinese parsley (fresh coriander)

finely chopped ginger root and onion. Blend well, then make into small balls about the size of walnuts.

Heat up the lard over high heat for about 3–4 minutes, then reduce the heat to moderate and deep-fry the crab balls for about 5 minutes until pale golden. Scoop them out with a perforated spoon and serve them hot or cold. Alternatively place them in a bowl with a little chicken stock – not quite enough to cover them – then place the bowl in a steamer and steam for 15 minutes.

Now mix the remaining sherry, monosodium glutamate, salt and cornstarch (cornflour) with the chicken stock and make a white sauce over a moderate heat, then pour it over the crab balls. Garnish with finely chopped ham and serve.

This dish is delicious as well as being very pretty to look at.

FRIED BEAN-CURD

2–3 cakes of bean-curd
1 slice peeled ginger root
1 scallion (spring onion)
2 tbsp (30ml) oil
1 tsp (5ml) salt
1 tbsp (15ml) rice wine (or sherry)
½ tsp (2ml) monosodium glutamate
2 tsp (10ml) cornstarch (cornflour)
2 tbsp (30ml) chicken stock
1 tsp (5ml) sesame seed oil

Coarsely cut the bean-curd and finely chop the ginger root and onion.

Heat up a *wok* or frying-pan over high heat before putting in the oil. Fry the ginger root and onion, followed almost immediately by the bean-curd; stir-fry for about 2–3 minutes, breaking up the bean-curd into even smaller bits. Then add salt, sherry and monosodium glutamate together with cornstarch (cornflour) mixed in chicken stock. Blend well.

Finally add sesame seed oil and serve.

This dish was one of the Empress Dowager's favorites in her old age. As it is so delicate and easy to digest, it is good for invalids. I remember my nanny used to cook it for me whenever I was ill and it became one of my favorites as well.

A bean-curd factory run by a unit of the People's Liberation Army on the outskirts of Peking

FISH SLICES IN SWEET AND SOUR SAUCE

½ lb (225g) fish fillet (flounder, plaice or sole)
2 tbsp (30ml) cornstarch (cornflour)
2½ cups (1 pt, 600ml) oil for deep-frying

For the sauce:
1 tbsp (15ml) sugar
1 tbsp (15ml) soy sauce
1 tbsp (15ml) vinegar
1 tbsp (15ml) rice wine (or sherry)
1 tbsp (15ml) cornstarch (cornflour)
½ tsp (2ml) monosodium glutamate
1 tbsp (15ml) lard
1 slice ginger root, finely chopped
1 scallion (spring onion), finely chopped

Cut the fish into small, thin slices about the size of a book of matches and coat them with cornstarch (cornflour).

Heat up the oil in a *wok* or deep-fryer over a high heat until smoking. Then reduce the heat and use a pair of

Fish slices in sweet and sour sauce. Most people associate this sauce with Cantonese cooking, but in fact it originated in the north

chopsticks to put the fish slices into the oil and deep-fry them for about 2 minutes or until golden. Remove and drain.

Heat up the lard in a hot *wok* or pan; meanwhile, mix the sugar, soy sauce, vinegar, wine or sherry, cornstarch (cornflour) and monosodium glutamate in a bowl. Toss the finely chopped ginger root and onion into the hot lard, then pour in the sauce mixture and stir until thickened; now add the fish slices, blend well so that each piece is coated with the sauce, then serve.

This recipe was created by the famous chef Wang from the Palace kitchen. It forms part of a series of four dishes all using the same method; the other three use pork kidney, pork fillet and peeled shrimps (prawns) as their main ingredient.

SHARK'S FIN SOUP

This recipe is included here purely for academic interest. Should any reader be adventurous enough to attempt it, I had better warn you that to start with, one or two of the ingredients are unobtainable in the West, and there are no substitutes that I know of. If that does not deter you from going ahead, I must tell you that it takes days to clean the shark's fin in the preliminary stage before you can even proceed to the preparation proper, which is in itself lengthy and fiddly.

1½ lb (0.75kg) shark's fin, which has been soaked for at least 3 days with several changes of water
4 oz (100g) 'yolk' (roe) of the female or hen crab extracted from 2 lb (1kg) cooked crab meat
6 tbsp (90ml) rice wine (or sherry)
2½ tsp (12ml) salt
1½ tsp (7ml) monosodium glutamate
2–3 slices ginger root
2–3 scallions (spring onions)
2½–3 pt (about 1.5l) stock (made from simmering a whole chicken and a whole duck in 5–6 pt (about 3l) water until the liquid is reduced by half, discarding both the chicken and duck and straining the stock for use)
½ cup (4 oz, 100g) lard
2 tbsp (30ml) cornstarch (cornflour)

After the shark's fin has been soaked, it is cleaned again before simmering for 4–5 hours or until the sandy skin and decayed bone hidden in the meat at the top of the fin can be removed, but do not boil it hard. Rinse in cold water and scrub off the sandy skin and decayed bone. After simmering gently for a further 8 hours or so the fin will gradually reveal itself as a transparent color and curl into the shape of a crescent.

Now place the absolutely clean fin in a bowl, add 2 tbsp (30ml) rice wine or sherry, 1 tsp (5ml) salt, ½ tsp (2ml) monosodium glutamate, ginger root, and onion. Use about a third of the stock to cover the fin. Then place the bowl in a steamer and steam over a high heat for about 1–1½ hours or until the fin is really soft.

Place about half of the remaining stock in a *wok* or pan, add ¼ tsp (1ml)

monosodium glutamate, ¼ tsp (1ml) salt, and 1 tablespoon rice wine or sherry together with the fin, but discard the stock in which it has been steamed. Simmer gently for about 15 minutes or until the fin is quite tender, then remove and discard the stock in which it has been cooking, and start all over again with fresh stock, wine, salt and monosodium glutamate. After a further simmering, remove the fin (yes, again discard the stock!) and place it neatly on a plate.

Finally (this is quite serious in case you may think I am pulling your leg) the fin is ready for its last stage of cooking.

Warm about half of the lard in a *wok* or pan, put in the crab 'yolk', add the remaining 2 tbsp (30ml) rice wine or sherry, 1 tsp (5ml) salt, ½ tsp (2ml) monosodium glutamate together with the last 3 or 4 tbsp (45–60 ml) of stock and cook gently for 10 minutes. The crab 'yolk' will then have broken up and the flavor of both the lard and rice wine will have merged into it. Now thicken it with cornstarch (cornflour) until smooth; take it off the heat and add the remaining lard, stirring and pouring it all over the fin. It is now at last ready to be served.

You may well wonder why all these complicated preparations and this waste of good stock are necessary. The answer is that the stock in which the fin has been cooked will have acquired a rather unpleasant odor due to the curing process used to preserve the fin, and each time you cook it in fresh stock the fin absorbs some of the concentrated flavors from the rich stock; so all the lengthy cleaning and wasteful cooking are in fact necessary. Economy has no place in the realm of delicacies.

Shark's fin soup – the essential part of any grand banquet

Regional dishes found in Peking

Amongst more than a thousand restaurants in Peking, not surprisingly a great number specialize in regional food from all over China.

Like most shops in Peking, all the famous restaurants look just like a private residence from outside apart from a sign over the entrance. Once inside, you feel as though you have stepped into someone's private dining room. There are a number of separate rooms, each with a round table in the middle and armchairs on both sides. While you are waiting for the meal to start, you sit in the armchairs at the sides drinking tea and cracking melon-seeds (and jokes!). You only sit down at the table when the first course is served – more details of Chinese table manners and etiquette will be found on pages 30–31.

The following nine recipes are selected from well-known Shandong restaurants in Peking. Of all the schools of Chinese cuisine, the style of Shandong cooking must have the strongest influence on Peking food. In fact some people would go so far as to say that the Peking School *is* Shandong food. For instance, the famous Peking duck restaurant *Quan Ju De* ('Complete Amalgam of Virtues') is of Shandong origin.

TOP-RANK BIRD'S NEST

Compared with the other Chinese delicacy 'Shark's fin', 'Bird's nest' is very simple to prepare though it does require a certain amount of patience. I think what might have put people off it is the name 'nest'. I shall never forget the expression of a Scottish friend of my father's when offered a real bird's nest from the garden in a soup bowl at the table. Being a well-mannered fellow he was about to tackle it manfully when my young sister, who played this rather cruel joke, burst out laughing. You should have seen how relieved the poor fellow was when he was told the truth!

The so-called 'bird's nest' is in fact predigested protein from a seaweed used by swallows for building their nests on the cliffs of islands along

The bird's nest after cleaning, ready to be added to the chicken broth in the bowl above it

China's coast (ornithologists might like to know that the swallow is a petrel of the *Procellariidae* family).

'Bird's nests', and the Chinese alkali powder used in their preparation, are not usually available in the West. If you do try this dish, be sure to use the correct alkali powder, and do not use more than the quantities given here.

2 oz (50g) 'bird's nest'
4⅜ cups (1¾ pt, 1l) good chicken
  stock
1½ oz (40g) Chinese alkali powder
1 tsp (5ml) salt
½ tsp (2ml) monosodium glutamate
1 tbsp (15ml) rice wine (or sherry)

Soak the 'nest' in lukewarm water for about 15 minutes and pick out all the feathers and other bits and pieces with tweezers – this is where patience is required; then rinse very gently in lukewarm water two or three times.

Dissolve the alkali in 2½ cups (1 pt, 600ml) of boiling water, then add the cleaned 'bird's nest' and stir gently with chopsticks or a fork. Leave it to stand for 5 minutes, then drain and soak in 4⅜ cups (1¾ pt, 1l) fresh boiling water for a further 5 minutes. Drain again. Finally rinse the 'nest' in 4⅜ cups (1¾ pt, 1l) fresh warm water for 4 minutes more and drain well; by now it is clean and ready for the last stage of cooking.

Bring the chicken stock, salt, monosodium glutamate and rice wine or sherry to the boil, skim if necessary, then add the well-drained 'bird's nest' and serve immediately.

FU YUNG CHICKEN SLICES
This is a variation of 'Fried chicken breast' on p.48, and makes an interesting comparison.

4 oz (100g) chicken breast meat (boned
  and skinned)
4 oz (100g) white fish fillet (sole,
  haddock, etc.)
½ cup (2 oz, 50g) water chestnuts,
  peeled
3 egg whites
1 slice ginger root, peeled and finely
  chopped
1 scallion (spring onion), finely
  chopped

1 tsp (5ml) salt
2 tbsp (30ml) cornstarch (cornflour)
5 tbsp (75ml) chicken stock
3¾ cups (1½ pt, 900ml) oil for
  deep-frying

Finely chop the chicken meat and fish into pulp. If you can get fresh water chestnuts, peel and boil them in water for a while, then finely chop them; canned water chestnuts have already been boiled, so just drain and finely chop them.

Place the chicken, fish and water chestnuts in a mixing bowl, add finely chopped ginger root and onion, ½ tsp (2ml) salt and 1 tbsp (15ml) cornstarch (cornflour), blend them well, then slowly add the egg whites; do not stir too vigorously but mix gently.

Heat up oil in a deep-fryer; before the oil gets too hot, use a spoon to slide the chicken-fish mixture into the oil from the side of the pan – a spoonful at a time. On meeting the hot oil, the mixture will slip out of the spoon and form a slice. Repeat until all the mixture is used up. Turn the slices over and cook for about 10 seconds only, then scoop them out with a perforated spoon.

Heat up the chicken stock in a pan together with the remaining salt. When it starts to boil, put in 1 tbsp (15ml) cornstarch (cornflour) mixed with a little water; stir until it thickens; add the chicken slices; blend well, then serve.

Fu Yung chicken slices, garnished with green peas and lettuce heart

Kwei-fei chicken cooked in a Chinese sand-pot. Like a casserole, a sand-pot can be used over direct heat or in the oven.

KWEI-FEI CHICKEN (DRUNKEN CHICKEN)

Yang Kwei-fei was an empress of the Tang dynasty (A.D. 618–907), noted for her beauty as well as her fondness for alcohol. Whether this dish actually had anything to do with her is open to question.

1 chicken weighing about 3 lb (1.5kg)
⅝ cup (¼ pt, 150ml) Chinese red wine, or port
7½ cups (3 pt, 1.8l) chicken stock
6 tbsp (90ml) soy sauce
3 tbsp (45ml) rice wine (or sherry)
2–3 scallions (spring onions), cut to 2 in (5cm) lengths
1 tsp (5ml) salt
oil for deep-frying

Clean and dry the chicken. Mix 2 tbsp (30ml) each of soy sauce and rice wine and pour it all over the chicken both inside and out.

Heat up the oil in a deep-fryer, fry the chicken with onions until golden, then immerse the chicken (keeping the onions for later) in a large pot of boiling water for 3 minutes. Now transfer to another large pot or casserole, add the remaining soy sauce, rice wine or sherry, salt, Chinese red wine or port and the chicken stock, as well as the onions, and simmer gently for at least 2 hours, turning it over several times during cooking. Serve in a large bowl or in the casserole itself. You will find it very similar in flavor to the French *Coq au vin*.

CHICKEN AND BAMBOO SHOOTS ASSEMBLY

6 oz (175g) chicken breast meat
⅔ cup (4 oz, 100g) bamboo shoots
1 egg white
1½ cups (12 fl oz, 350ml) chicken stock
2 tbsp (30ml) cornstarch (cornflour)
1 tbsp (15ml) rice wine (or sherry)
1 slice ginger root, peeled
2 tbsp (30ml) lard
1½ tsp (7ml) salt
oil for deep-frying

Cut the chicken into fine shreds about the size of matches and mix them with the egg white and ½ tbsp (7ml) cornstarch (cornflour). Cut the bamboo shoots into shreds roughly the same size as the chicken. Finely chop the ginger root.

Heat up the oil in a deep-fryer, fry the chicken shreds in oil over a moderate heat for about 10 seconds only. Separate the shreds, scoop them out and drain.

Heat up the lard in a *wok* or frying pan, stir-fry the bamboo shoots, add ginger root, salt, wine or sherry and chicken stock. Bring it to the boil, then add the remaining cornstarch (cornflour) mixed with a little cold water; stir until the ingredients are well blended. When the gravy starts to thicken, add the chicken shreds, blend well and serve.

This is a semi-soup dish, ideal for serving with rice.

Chicken and bamboo shoots assembly, usually served with rice at the end of a banquet, for those who still have some room left

CHICKEN AND SHRIMP (PRAWN) BALL SOUP

This soup *par excellence* was invented at the beginning of the century. If the mange-tout peas are out of season, then by all means use any other greens such as watercress or lettuce leaves, for it is the color rather than the flavor that is important here.

½ lb (225g) uncooked shrimps
    (prawns)
¼ cup (2 oz, 50g) pork fat
2 oz (50g) chicken breast meat
2 oz (50g) cooked ham
half a cucumber
2 egg whites
1½ tbsp (25ml) cornstarch (cornflour)
1 slice ginger root, peeled and finely
    shredded
2 tbsp (30ml) rice wine (or sherry)
2 tsp (10ml) salt
3¾ cups (1½ pt, 900ml) stock

Shell the shrimps (prawns) and finely grind (mince) to a pulp. Grind (mince) the pork fat and chicken breast meat. Finely chop the ham. Slice the cucumber thinly.

Mix ½ tbsp (10ml) cornstarch (cornflour) with 4 tbsp (60ml) water, add the ground (minced) chicken breast and 1 egg white, blend well. This is called chicken paste (purée).

Mix together the shrimps (prawns), pork fat, the remaining cornstarch (cornflour), egg white, finely chopped ginger root, 1 tbsp (15ml) rice wine or sherry and 1 tsp (5ml) salt; blend well.

Bring the stock to the boil, then reduce the heat and put in the shrimp (prawn) and pork fat mixture made into small balls about the size of walnuts. Increase the heat to bring it back to the boil. Now add the remaining salt and rice wine or sherry, then reduce heat again and simmer gently for about 10 minutes.

Stir the chicken paste (purée) and add it to the soup, stirring all the time so it does not form into lumps.

Add the ham and cucumber; turn up the heat to bring to a rapid boil; serve in a large bowl.

Chicken and shrimp (prawn) balls soup, here shown garnished with Chinese parsley (fresh coriander)

FIVE-FRAGRANT KIDNEY SLICES

½ lb (225g) pigs' kidneys
1 tsp (5ml) red coloring
1½ cups (12 fl oz, 350ml) chicken stock
1 tbsp (15ml) soy sauce
1 tbsp (15ml) rice wine (or sherry)
1 slice ginger root
1 tsp (5ml) salt
1 tsp (5ml) five-spice powder
1 scallion (spring onion)

Place the kidneys in cold water in a pan; bring to the boil; skim off any impurities floating on the surface; reduce heat and simmer for 30 minutes. Remove and drain.

Place the kidneys in fresh cold water (just enough to cover), add the red coloring (if Chinese red-powder is unobtainable, then use a little cochineal). Bring to the boil, then remove and rinse in cold water and drain.

Put the chicken stock in a pot or pan; add the soy sauce, wine or sherry, ginger root, onion, salt, five-spice powder and the kidneys. Boil for 5 minutes, then place the kidneys with the stock in a large bowl to cool. This will take 5–6 hours.

Take the kidneys out and cut them into as thin slices as you possibly can – it is possible to cut 80–90 slices from each kidney if your cleaver is really sharp!

Place the unevenly cut slices in the middle of a plate to make a pile, then neatly arrange the rest of the slices all the way around it in two or three layers like the petals of an opened flower, then through a sieve pour a little of the juice in which the kidneys have been cooking over the 'flower', but be careful not to disturb the beautiful 'petals'. Serve cold as an hors d'oeuvre. The name 'five-fragrant' is, of course, referring to the five-spice powder used.

Five-fragrant kidney slices, skillfully cut in the form of a flower

61

WON'T STICK THREE WAYS

This is a well-known sweet from Peking, so called because it won't stick to the spoon or to the chopsticks, or to your teeth.

5 egg yolks
2 tbsp (30ml) cornstarch (cornflour)
5 tbsp (75ml) water
½ cup (4 oz, 100g) sugar
3 tbsp (45ml) lard

Beat the egg yolks, add sugar, cornstarch (cornflour) and water, blend well.

Heat the lard in a frying-pan over a high heat, tilt the pan so that the entire surface is covered by lard, then pour the excess lard (about half) into a jug for later use. Reduce the heat to moderate, pour the egg mixture into the pan, stir and scramble for about 2 minutes and add the remaining lard from the jug little by little, stirring and scrambling all the time until the eggs become bright golden, then serve.

Personally I find this much too sweet for my liking, so you can reduce the amount of sugar or increase the number of eggs if preferred.

CHICKEN CUBES IN BEAN SAUCE

½ lb (225g) chicken breast meat
1 egg white
2 tsp (10ml) cornstarch (cornflour)
2½ cups (1 pt, 600ml) oil
*   for deep-frying*
2 tbsp (30ml) lard
2 tbsp (30ml) crushed yellow bean sauce
1 tsp (5ml) sugar
1 tbsp (15ml) rice wine (or sherry)
1 slice ginger root, peeled and finely
*   chopped*

Soak the chicken meat in cold water for 1 hour, separate the meat from the white tendon and membrane, then dice it into ⅓ in (7mm) cubes. Mix them with the egg white and cornstarch (cornflour) together with a little water – say 2 tsp (10ml).

Heat up the oil in a deep-fryer, lower the chicken cubes in and separate them with chopsticks or a fork. As soon as they start to turn golden scoop them out with a perforated spoon and drain.

Won't stick three ways, a favorite dish for sweet-toothed Chinese, served on a bed of fried seaweed

Meanwhile heat the lard in a *wok* or frying-pan, add the crushed bean sauce, stir until the sizzling noise dies down, then add the sugar followed by wine (or sherry) and finely chopped ginger root. After about 10–15 seconds, it should have a smooth consistency. Now add the chicken cubes and stir well for 5 seconds so that each cube is coated with this bright reddish sauce. Serve.

This is a very popular dish, usually served during the early stages of a banquet.

BRAISED FOUR TREASURES

The 'four treasures' are duck webs, wings, tongues and kidneys.

6 duck webs
4 duck wings
10 duck tongues
5–6 duck kidneys
1 cup (½ lb, 225g) lard for
*   deep-frying*
1 scallion (spring onion), finely
*   chopped*
1 slice ginger root, peeled and finely
*   chopped*
1¼ cups (½ pt, 300ml) chicken stock
2 tbsp (30ml) rice wine (or sherry)
½ tsp (2ml) monosodium glutamate
1 tbsp (15ml) crushed bean sauce
2 tsp (10ml) soy sauce

Clean the duck webs in warm water and remove the outer coat of skin, then parboil for 20 minutes. Cool them in cold water and cut into small pieces about ½ in (1cm) in length.

Parboil the wings for 20 minutes. Cool them in cold water and cut into small pieces about ½ in (1cm) in length.

Clean the tongues in warm water and remove the outer layer of skin; parboil for 10 minutes, then cool in cold water.

Parboil the kidneys for 15 minutes and remove the outer layer of fat. Split each in half, cut each half in two, then marinate in a little soy sauce. Heat up the lard in a *wok* or pan until smoking; fry the kidney pieces for 5 minutes or until golden, then remove and drain.

Leaving about 2 tbsp (30ml) lard in the pan, first fry the finely chopped onion and ginger root; add the chicken stock with wine, monosodium glutamate, crushed bean sauce and the remaining soy sauce, stir and add the 'four treasures'. Bring to the boil, then reduce the heat and simmer for about 15 minutes. When the stock is reduced by half, increase the heat to high to thicken the gravy, and serve.

PREPARING THE DUCK

The duck is split down the middle with a heavy cleaver

The duck is placed on a plate, then in a bamboo steamer

The bamboo steamer allows steam to escape through the lid

SUNFLOWER DUCK

In China, the Cantonese have always been regarded as the people who really know how to enjoy themselves as far as good food is concerned. One of the Cantonese restaurants in Peking is called 'Food of Tan's Family' and was first opened by a Mr. Tan from Canton, whose father was a court official during the Manchu dynasty. Both father and son were gourmets and food from their family kitchen was much appreciated at the time, so other officials used to entertain at Tan's place and thus its reputation became widespread. Eventually Tan junior went into business and established this restaurant; here is one of their specialties:

1 duckling weighing about 4 lb (1.75kg)
1 oz (25g) Chinese dried mushrooms
4 oz (100g) cooked ham
1¼ cups (½ pt, 300ml) good chicken and duck stock
2 tbsp (30ml) soy sauce
1 tbsp (15ml) sugar
1 tsp (5ml) salt
1 tbsp (15ml) cornstarch (cornflour)

Clean the duck inside and out, then split it down the middle lengthwise with a cleaver. Place the two halves on a plate, skin side down, and steam

Sunflower duck tastes particularly delicious when accompanied by wine

vigorously for 2–3 hours. Remove and leave it to cool for a while with the skin side up.

Soak the mushrooms in warm water for 10 minutes, discard the stalks and cut the large ones into two to three pieces. Cut the ham into thin slices about the size of a matchbox.

Cut off the neck and wings of the duck, then very carefully remove the meat from the carcass and bones. Cut the meat into thin slices and neatly arrange them on a plate in the shape of the duck with the skin side up, alternately overlapping each piece of meat with a piece of mushroom and a slice of ham. Then very carefully turn the meat out into a large, deep dish or bowl, pour in about a third of the chicken/duck stock, and steam vigorously for about 20 minutes, then turn it out back onto the plate and rearrange if necessary.

Warm up the rest of the stock, add soy sauce, salt, sugar and cornstarch (cornflour) mixed with a little cold water. Stir to make it into a smooth, thickish gravy; pour it all over the duck and serve.

This is a very colorful and aromatic dish, but I fail to see why it is called *sunflower*.

Above: *Braised shrimps (prawns) cooked in their shells with a rich sauce*

½ lb (225g) Pacific shrimps (prawns), unshelled
1 slice ginger root, peeled and finely chopped
1 clove garlic, finely chopped
2 scallions (spring onions), finely chopped
4 tbsp (60ml) lard

For the sauce:
2 tbsp (30ml) rice wine (or sherry)
1 tbsp (15ml) vinegar
1 tbsp (15ml) sugar
1 tbsp (15ml) salt
1½ tbsp (25ml) tomato paste (purée)
1 tsp (5ml) finely chopped Sichuan preserved vegetables
4 tbsp (60ml) chicken stock

Wash and dry the unshelled shrimps (prawns), split them in half lengthwise and discard the black intestinal parts.

Finely chop the ginger root, garlic and spring onions. Have the sauce mixture ready.

Heat up 3 tbsp (45ml) lard in a *wok*, put in the ginger root and garlic first, followed by the shrimps (prawns); stir a few times then add the onions. Continue cooking for 2–3 minutes, stirring all the time. Now add the sauce mixture and reduce heat to simmer until all the sauce has evaporated. Add the remaining 1 tbsp (15ml) of lard and make sure each piece of shrimp (prawn) is coated. Serve hot.

Shredded beef with celery – a piquant dish typical of the Sichuan School, but highly popular in Peking

SHREDDED BEEF WITH CELERY

This dish originated in Sichuan and, like so many other dishes from that province, it has now become a national favorite.

½ lb (225g) beef steak
½ cup (2 oz, 50g) celery
½ cup (2 oz, 50g) leek or scallion (spring onion)
2 slices ginger root
1 tbsp (15ml) chili paste (purée)
2 tbsp (30ml) soy sauce
½ tsp (2ml) salt
1 tsp (5ml) sugar
1 tbsp (15ml) rice wine (or sherry)
1 tsp (5ml) vinegar
3 tbsp (45ml) oil

Shred the beef into thin strips about the size of matches. Shred the celery and leeks the same size (Chinese leeks are a cross between the Western leek and scallion (spring onion) with thin skin and green foliage). Peel the ginger root and cut it into thin shreds as well.

Heat up the *wok* or pan and put in the oil. When it starts to smoke, stir-fry the beef for a short while, add the chili paste (purée), blend well, then add the celery, leek and ginger root, followed by the soy sauce, salt, sugar and wine. Stir for 1–2 minutes, then add vinegar and serve.

BRAISED SHRIMPS (PRAWNS)

This and the next recipe are examples of Eastern School cooking from Jiangsu, adopted by a large Peking restaurant. It is interesting to compare them with the method used by the Western School

BRAISED BAMBOO SHOOTS

I am afraid you cannot use canned bamboo shoots for this dish; if fresh ones are unobtainable then there is no substitute.

1½ lb (0.75 kg) fresh bamboo
*   shoots*
1 oz (25g) green seaweed, or
*   1 cup (4 oz, 100g) green cabbage*
1 slice ginger root, peeled and finely
*   chopped*
2 cups (1 lb, 0.5kg) lard for
*   deep-frying*
2 tbsp (30ml) oyster sauce
1½ tbsp (25ml) sugar
1 tsp (5ml) monosodium
*   glutamate*
1 tbsp (15ml) rice wine (or sherry)
4 tbsp (60ml) chicken stock
1 tbsp (15ml) sesame seed oil

Peel off the skin of the bamboo shoots and discard the tough parts of the root. Cut them into small slices about ¼ in (5mm) thick, then into strips about 1½ in (3.5cm) long.

Finely chop the seaweed or cabbage and ginger root.

Warm up the lard, deep-fry the bamboo shoots for 1–2 minutes, then reduce heat and continue cooking for 2–3 minutes. When their color turns golden, scoop them out and drain.

Keep about 2 tablespoons lard in the *wok* or pan, increase the heat and put in the seaweed or cabbage and ginger root, followed by the bamboo shoots; add the oyster sauce, sugar, monosodium glutamate and rice wine or sherry, blend well. Add the chicken stock, bring it to the boil, then reduce heat and let it simmer until almost all the juice is evaporated. Now increase the heat again, add the sesame seed oil, stir a few times and serve.

Braised bamboo shoots, served on a bed of seaweed and garnished with chopped dried shrimps

The Moslem School

Mongolian nomads with their flock. They live in tents called yurts, padded with thick felt which is excellent protection against the cold in these high mountainous regions. As you can see, they are preparing a meal out of doors over an open fire, and beneath the red flag on the left two women are preparing dumplings

The Chinese Moslems known as the *Hui*, though Chinese speaking, are distinguished from ethnic Chinese by their affiliation with the Sunni branch of Islam. One theory is that they are descendents of Moslems who settled in China in the thirteenth century and adopted the Chinese language and culture. There are nearly four million *Hui* widely distributed throughout almost every province of China, but their traditional area of settlement is the north-west, with heavy concentrations in Henan, Shanxi, Shaanxi, Hebei and Shandong. They form the Chinese Moslem School of cooking together with two other national minorities: the Uygur group in Xinjiang (3.7 million), virtually all Moslems, and the Mongols (1.5 million). The Mongols are traditionally nomadic and therefore do not eat pork. Beef and mutton, milk and butter are the most important foods in their daily diet.

In addition, we can group with these three about 2.5 million ethnic Manchus, whose ancestors conquered China in the seventeenth century and founded the Qing (Ching) dynasty (1644–1911). The Manchus adopted the Chinese language and culture and are virtually indistinguishable from ethnic Chinese, except that they consider mutton to be their main diet (but, unlike the Moslems, not on religious grounds). Though still mainly settled in Manchuria, there is a large concentration of Manchus in Hebei and Peking, and very few, if any, can claim to have preserved any cultural traits of the original Manchu people. But, as far as their dietary habits are concerned, they have been grouped together with the Hui, Uygurs and Mongols under the Moslem School.

Here are some recipes from the fairly extensive repertoire of the Moslem School.

TUNG-PO MUTTON

Su Tung-po (1036–1101), poet, painter, calligrapher as well as epicure, is credited with a number of dishes. Although a native of Sichuan, he actually lived in almost all parts of China. There is another of Su Tung-po's recipes later in this book (Tung-po pork, page 135). Whether or not he invented this particular recipe is open to question.

½ lb (225g) stewing mutton
1 cup (4 oz, 100g) potato
1 cup (4 oz, 100g) carrot
2 tbsp (30ml) soy sauce
1 tbsp (15ml) sugar
2 scallions (spring onions)
1 slice ginger root, peeled
1 clove garlic, crushed
1 tsp (5ml) five-spice powder
½ tsp (2ml) Sichuan pepper
oil for deep-frying

Cut the mutton into 1 in (2.5cm) cubes, then score one side of each square half way down. Peel the potato and carrot and cut them the same size and shape as the mutton.

Heat up quite a lot of oil in a *wok* or deep-fryer. When it is smoking, deep-fry the mutton for 5–6 seconds or until it turns golden; scoop out and drain, then fry the potato and carrot also until golden.

Place the mutton in a pot or casserole, cover the meat with cold water, add soy sauce, sugar, onions, ginger root, garlic, pepper, five-spice powder and rice wine or sherry, and bring it to the boil. Then reduce the heat and simmer for 2–3 hours; add potato and carrot, cook together for about 5 minutes and serve.

This colorful and aromatic dish has a rich sauce which goes particularly well with rice.

Tung-po mutton, typical of the Moslem School, and a popular everyday family dish

67

The picture on page 69 shows fire-pot as served in southern China, where, in addition to lamb, other meats such as beef steak, chicken breast, fish, prawns (shrimps) and oysters are served
Below: *Entrance to a covered market in Peking*

RINSED LAMB IN FIRE-POT
Of the scores of markets in Peking, the biggest and also the most famous must be Dong An ('Eastern Peace') Market. Like all the others in this city, it is a covered one, but the word 'market' is used here in its widest sense; it is more like a small town, where there are shops of every description selling practically everything under the sun.

There are bookshops (particularly second-hand bookshops), antique shops, jewelry shops, silk shops, toy shops, tea-houses, theaters, movies and, of course, restaurants. Without a doubt, the most famous restaurant of the market, if not of Peking, is *Dong Lai Shun*, which can be very loosely translated as 'Eastern Luck'. It was opened as a food stall at the beginning of the century by an enterprising

Moslem, and within a few years it expanded into a large restaurant. Then in 1912 it acquired some highly skilled 'meat carvers' from a more established restaurant whose specialty was a dish called 'Rinsed lamb in fire-pot'. In their new home, the carvers improved and developed this unique dish, both in their selection of ingredients and in the technique of carving. From then on, the restaurant went from strength to strength.

The fire-pot came originally from Mongolia and is very similar to a fondue with a funnel at the center in which charcoal is burned. The moat is filled up with water and you cook your own piece of thinly sliced lamb in the boiling water, then dip it in the specially prepared sauce before eating it. Even people who normally dislike

Held firmly by chopsticks, a piece of lamb is rinsed in the boiling water of the fire-pot's moat

the strong taste of lamb can enjoy it.

If you cannot obtain a Chinese fire-pot, sometimes known as a chafing pot, then use a fondue or an electrically heated pan on the table. The following recipe should be ample for four to six people.

3–3½ lb (1.5kg) boned shoulder, loin or leg of lamb
4 cups (1 lb, 0.5kg) Chinese cabbage
4 cups (1 lb, 0.5kg) spinach

2 cakes of bean-curd (fresh or frozen)
1½ cups (4 oz, 100g) transparent noodles
4–5 pt (about 2l) water or stock

Sauce:
finely chopped scallions (spring onions), garlic and ginger root; soy sauce; sherry; Hoi Sin sauce; vinegar; sugar; chili sauce and sesame seed oil.

Cut the lamb into fairly large but very, very thin slices – you will find that it is much easier to do this if the meat is half frozen.

Wash and cut the cabbage and spinach into biggish pieces; cut each cake of the bean-curd into 10 to 12 slices; soak the transparent noodles in warm water for a few minutes, then drain.

Now arrange the cabbage, spinach, bean-curd, transparent noodles and

At the end of the meal, when all the meat is finished, the remaining vegetables are cooked in the fire-pot for a few minutes, then ladled into individual bowls and served as soup

the meat in separate serving dishes and place them on the table with the fire-pot in the middle. Here a round table would be ideal, a square one is almost as good, but a long table – well, you will have to arrange your seats in such a way that nobody is too far from the fire-pot.

While waiting for the water or stock to boil in the moat of the fire-pot, each person prepares his or her sauce by mixing a little of the various ingredients in individual sauce dishes according to his or her own taste.

When the water or stock is boiling vigorously, each person picks up a piece of lamb with chopsticks and dips it in the water to cook it, occasionally dunking it as if rinsing,–hence the name of the dish.

Depending on the thickness and cut of the meat, it should not take more than 20–30 seconds to cook, otherwise it will be too tough. Now you dip the cooked meat in the sauce mixture and eat it. Delicious!

After a while, you can start adding the vegetables to the moat and eating them with the meat. As the cooking progresses, the pot is re-charged with charcoal; the remaining water or stock is put in the moat, and the contents get tastier and tastier.

When all the meat is eaten, put the rest of the vegetables into the moat, to make a delicious soup.

Above: *'Three pearls' soup in the making*
Right: *The finished dish. Here we have chicken meat as the main ingredient; its pale color provides a pleasing contrast to the brightness of the green peas, while the third ingredient, the tomato or ham, helps to create an esthetically-pleasing effect, and adds an extra dimension to the flavor*

'THREE PEARLS' SOUP

The 'three pearls' are chicken, peas and tomato: three contrasting colors, textures and flavors.

4 oz (100g) chicken breast meat
1 egg white
2 tbsp (30ml) milk
1½ tbsp (25ml) cornstarch (cornflour)
½ cup (2 oz, 50g) green peas
2 red tomatoes
2½ cups (1 pt, 600ml) stock
1 tbsp (15ml) rice wine (or sherry)
1 tsp (5ml) salt
½ tsp (2ml) monosodium glutamate
1 tsp (5ml) chicken fat

Remove all white tendon and membrane from the chicken meat, finely grind (mince) it into a pulp, mix it with ½ tbsp (10ml) cornstarch (cornflour) and milk, add the egg white and blend it all together well.

Skin the tomatoes by dipping in boiling water and cut them into small cubes the same size as the peas.

Bring the stock to a rolling boil, add the peas and tomato, bring it back to the boil then remove it from the flame. Now use a single chopstick to pick up a little bit of chicken mixture at a time and flip it into the stock until all the chicken is used up and you end up with lots of tiny chicken balls the size of peas. Then place the pan back on a high heat and bring the stock to a boil. Mix the rest of the cornstarch (cornflour) in a little water and add to the soup together with salt, rice wine or sherry and monosodium glutamate. When it starts to boil again, all the 'three pearls' will float on top; add the chicken fat and serve.

Should you use ham instead of tomato, you will still have the three colors of white, green and pink.

MIXED 'THREE WHITES'

4 oz (100g) cooked chicken breast meat
2 oz (50g) white asparagus (canned)
1½ cups (6 oz, 175g) white cabbage
*   heart*
½ cup (4 fl oz, 100ml) milk
1 tbsp (15ml) cornstarch (cornflour)
2 tsp (10ml) rice wine (or sherry)
1 tsp (5ml) salt
½ tsp (2ml) monosodium glutamate
1 slice ginger root, peeled
2 scallions (spring onions), cut into
*   short lengths*
½ cup (4 fl oz, 100ml) stock
3 tbsp (45ml) chicken fat

Thinly slice the chicken meat and arrange it in a neat row on a long plate. Drain the asparagus and arrange side by side next to the chicken meat.

Cut the cabbage heart into about eight pieces, blanch in boiling water until soft, then arrange the pieces neatly on top of the chicken breast and asparagus spears.

Heat up about 1 tbsp (15ml) chicken fat, toss in the onion and ginger root followed by rice wine or sherry and stock; bring it to the boil, then discard the ginger root and onion. Now very carefully slide the 'three whites' (i.e. chicken, asparagus and cabbage) into the pan without disturbing the neat arrangement. Add salt and monosodium glutamate; wait for it to boil again before adding milk, and pour the cornstarch (cornflour) mixed with 1 tbsp (15ml) cold water evenly all over the surface. Now pour the remaining chicken fat along the edge of the pan. Toss the 'three whites' on to the serving dish so that the cabbage is now at the bottom with the chicken and asparagus on the top – but still in their neatly arranged rows. You need luck and a steady hand!

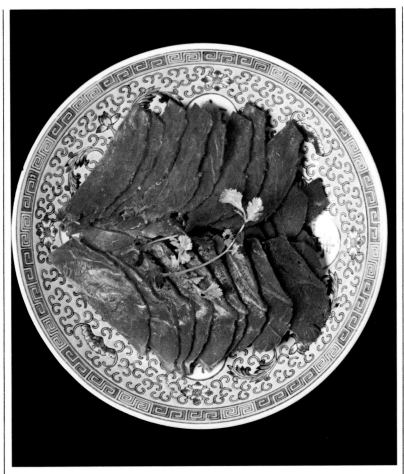

Mixed 'Three whites' – subtle in color, but with strong contrasts in flavor and texture

STEWED BEEF

2 lb (1kg) shin of beef
2 tbsp (30ml) sugar
6 tbsp (90ml) soy sauce
2 tbsp (30ml) rice wine (or sherry)
1 tsp (5ml) five-spice powder
3–4 scallions (spring onions)
2–3 slices ginger root
2 tbsp (30ml) oil

Stewed beef – this is an ideal starter, thinly sliced and served cold on an attractive dish

This dish makes excellent use of a cheap cut of meat. It is cooked slowly so that the meat becomes really tender.

Cut the beef into 1 in (2.5cm) cubes. Cut the onions into 1 in (2.5cm) lengths.

Heat up the oil and brown the beef before blanching it in a pot of boiling water for a few seconds. Pour the water away and cover with fresh cold water, add onions, ginger root, five-spice powder, sugar, soy sauce and rice wine or sherry, and place a tightly fitting lid over the pan. Bring it to the boil over a high heat, then reduce the heat and simmer gently for 3–4 hours, after which there should be very little juice left. Serve hot or cold.

STEWED FOUR TREASURES

If you have never heard of fish lip, then you do not know what you are missing! It is the lip of a special type of fairly large fish and is preserved like shark's fin but much easier to prepare.

It is bought in a dried state with bones attached and therefore has to be soaked in cold water for two or three days until the lip part becomes soft. After that, simmer it until all the bones can be easily removed. When this is done, clean the lip thoroughly. It is now ready for final preparation.

4 oz (100g) soaked fish lip
4 oz (100g) abalone (canned)
1 cup (4 oz, 100g) broccoli
⅔ cup (4 oz, 100g) bamboo shoots
2 slices ginger root
2 cloves garlic
2–3 scallions (spring onions)
3 tbsp (45ml) chicken fat
2 tbsp (30ml) rice wine (or sherry)
½ cup (4 fl oz, 100ml) chicken stock
1½ tbsp (25ml) soy sauce
2 tsp (10ml) sugar
1 tbsp (15ml) cornstarch (cornflour)

After the fish lip has been soaked and cleaned, cut it into pieces about the size of a matchbox, wash it once more, then steam over a high flame for about 30 minutes or until soft. Drain the abalone and cut it into pieces roughly the same sizes as the fish lip.

Wash the broccoli, cut it into small chunks diagonally and parboil for a few minutes only. Drain.

Cut the bamboo shoots also into thin slices the size of a matchbox. Now arrange these 'four treasures' in four overlapping rows on a plate.

Slice the ginger root and garlic and cut the onions into short lengths.

Warm up about 1½ tbsp (25ml) chicken fat and, before it gets too hot, toss in the garlic, ginger root and onions. Fry until golden, add rice wine or sherry and stock, bring it to the boil, then scoop out the garlic, ginger root and onions and discard. Now take a deep breath: with one smooth movement deftly transfer the 'four treasures' into the bubbling stock without disarranging them. Add soy sauce and sugar, bring it to the boil again, then pour the cornstarch (cornflour) mixed with a little water to

cover the entire surface and add the rest of the chicken fat round the edge. Will you now have the nerve to toss the entire contents out and catch them on a plate without disturbing them? I have seen it done, and it requires skill as well as nerve. Try it and see: whatever the result, it will make tossing a pancake seem like child's play!

LAMB IN SWEET AND SOUR SAUCE

It is believed that this dish originated from the Palace kitchen, though whether during the Mongol (Yuan) or Manchu dynasty, no-one seems to know.

½ lb (225g) fillet lamb
2 slices ginger root, peeled
1 tbsp (15ml) crushed yellow bean
   sauce
2 tbsp (30ml) cornstarch (cornflour)
1½ tbsp (25ml) soy sauce
1 tbsp (15ml) rice wine (or sherry)
1 tbsp (15ml) vinegar
2 tbsp (30ml) sugar
oil for deep-frying
½ tbsp (10ml) chicken fat or sesame
   seed oil

Thinly slice the fillet lamb and finely chop the ginger root.

Mix the lamb with ½ tbsp (10ml) cornstarch (cornflour), a little water and the crushed bean sauce.

Mix the remaining cornstarch (cornflour) with soy sauce, rice wine or sherry, vinegar, sugar and the finely chopped ginger root.

Heat up the oil in a *wok* or pan, fry the lamb slices for about 15 seconds and stir to separate them. When they turn pale, scoop them out and return the lamb slices to the *wok* over a high heat. Add the sauce mixture, stir and blend well for about 1 minute; add chicken fat or sesame seed oil, stir a few more times, then serve.

Stewed four treasures. The neatly-arranged four treasures have been disturbed somewhat as you can see, but I can assure you that they tasted absolutely delicious

CASSIA LAMB

The cassia is a tiny, yellow, four-petaled flower that blooms in late September; the dish is named from the similar color of the eggs.

4 oz (100g) fillet lamb
3 eggs
½ tsp (2ml) monosodium glutamate
2 tsp (10ml) rice wine (or sherry)
1 tsp (5ml) salt
1 slice ginger root, peeled
2 tbsp (30ml) chicken fat

Cut the lamb into thin shreds. Finely chop the ginger root. Beat up the eggs and mix them with the lamb shreds and ginger root.

Heat up the chicken fat in a *wok* or pan, put in the egg mixture, stir and scramble for about 10 seconds and add salt, monosodium glutamate and rice wine or sherry. Stir and scramble for another 10 seconds. Serve.

Top: *Scrambling the 'cassia' with chopsticks in a* wok. **Right:** *Cassia Lamb, simple but delicious*

GROUND (MINCED) DUCK WITH CROUTONS

4 oz (100g) cooked duck meat
½ cup (2 oz, 50g) green peas
3 slices white bread
2½ cups (1 pt, 600ml) stock
1 tsp (5ml) salt
½ tsp (2ml) monosodium glutamate
2 tsp (10ml) rice wine (or sherry)
1 tbsp (15ml) cornstarch (cornflour)
    mixed with 1 tbsp (15ml) water
1 tsp (5ml) chicken fat
oil for frying the bread

Finely grind (mince) the duck meat.
Add it to the stock together with the
peas, rice wine or sherry, salt and
monosodium glutamate. Bring it to
the boil over a high flame, then slowly
pour in the cornstarch (cornflour) and
water mixture. When it boils again,
stir in the chicken fat, and remove.

Fry the bread cut into small cubes
until they become golden and crispy;
drain and place them on a soup plate,
pour the ground (minced) duck all
over them so they make a sizzling
noise and serve at once before the fried
bread croûtons become soggy.

RAPIDLY – FRIED BEEF STEAK

½ lb (225g) best beef steak
1½ tbsp (25ml) soy sauce
1 tbsp (15ml) cornstarch (cornflour)
2 cloves garlic, finely chopped
2 scallions (spring onions), white parts
    only, cut into ½ in (1cm) lengths
1 tsp (5ml) vinegar
2 tsp (10ml) rice wine (or sherry)
oil for deep-frying

Cut the beef into thin slices and
marinate with 1 tbsp (15ml) soy sauce
and cornstarch (cornflour).

Heat up the oil until smoking,
deep-fry the beef slices for about 30
seconds only, stir with chopsticks to
separate them, then quickly scoop
them out with a perforated spoon.

Now heat up about 1 tbsp (15ml)
oil in a *wok* and toss in the onions and
garlic. When they start to turn golden,
put in the beef slices, add vinegar, rice
wine (or sherry) and the remaining soy
sauce, stir-fry for about 30 seconds,
then it is done.

A simple dish, but the quality of
the beef steak, the degree of heat and
the timing all must be right.

RED-COOKED FISH 'MILK'

½ lb (225g) white fish fillet (sole,
    flounder, plaice or halibut)
½ cup (2 oz, 50g) water chestnuts
½ cup (2 oz, 50g) carrot
½ cup (2 oz, 50g) cucumber
4–5 Chinese dried mushrooms,
    soaked
2 egg whites
6 tbsp (90ml) chicken and duck stock
2 scallions (spring onions)
2 slices ginger root
1 tbsp (15ml) cornstarch (cornflour)
1½ tbsp (25ml) soy sauce
1 tbsp (15ml) sugar
2 tbsp (30ml) rice wine (or sherry)
1 tsp (5ml) salt
3 tbsp (45ml) chicken and duck fat

Discard the skin and any soft bone
from the fish, finely chop into a pulp
with a little salt and water, beat up the
egg whites in a bowl, put in the fish
with a little fat and continue beating
until smooth.

Half fill a large bowl with warm
water, spoon in the fish mixture,
shaking gently until it becomes solid.
Then place the bowl in a steamer and
steam over a low heat for 5 minutes;
remove – you have made fish 'milk'.

Skin the carrot and water chestnuts, wash the cucumber but keep the
skin on, then cut them into small, thin
slices. Squeeze the mushrooms dry,
discard the hard stalks, and cut the
mushrooms into small slices. Cut the
ginger root and onions into shreds.

Warm up the remaining fat, fry the
onions and ginger root until golden,
add rice wine or sherry and soy sauce
followed by the stock, bring it to the
boil, then scoop out the ginger root
and onions and discard. Now add the
carrot, water chestnuts and mushrooms. Cook for a short while, then
very gently drain the fish 'milk'
through a sieve, add it to the pan
together with the sugar and salt,
reduce heat and simmer until there is
hardly any juice left. Then increase
heat to high, add the cornstarch (cornflour) mixed in a little water, shaking
the pan constantly. Add the cucumber
slices, blend very gently and serve.

*Rapidly-fried beef steak: the degree of
heat is very important*

Shandong dishes

Emerging from the Tibetan Plateau, the Yellow River flows in a great loop through the Ordos Desert in Inner Mongolia and, on meeting the Wei River at the junction of Shaanxi, Shanxi and Henan, continues eastwards across the North China Plain into the Gulf of Po Hai in Shandong. This course has remained unaltered since 1947, but in the past the river has many times changed its course to the sea, often causing catastrophic floods.

The predominantly calcareous alluvium of the North China Plain and the hot, wet summers have made the region one of the most important agricultural areas of China. Its main crops are wheat, barley, Kao Liang (sorghum), millet and corn as well as soybeans, peanuts, tobacco and cotton.

Fisheries are widely developed along the North China coast, particularly the rocky Shandong peninsula.

Fruits are also a Shandong specialty, and grape wines from Yantai (Chefoo) and Qingdao (Tsingtao) are exported worldwide, as are Qingdao beers.

CLEAR AND THICK STOCK

What makes Shandong cuisine outstanding is the use of stock made from chicken, duck and pork, without resorting to the ubiquitous monosodium glutamate which can sometimes give the dishes a uniform and therefore dull taste.

The basic ingredients for both stocks are:

1 duck weighing about 4 lb (1.75kg)
3 chickens weighing about 2 lb (1kg) each
1 picnic shoulder (hand of pork) weighing about 3 lb (1.5kg)
3 lb (1.5kg) pork bones
2–3 scallions (spring onions)
2 slices ginger root, peeled
2 tbsp (30ml) salt
2 tbsp (30ml) soy sauce

Clear stock
Remove the breast meat from all three chickens and the meat from the legs of two chickens; put the meat aside.

Break the leg bones of the third chicken and the duck.

Cut through to the meat of the picnic shoulder (pork hand) as far as the bone, then break the bone with the back of the cleaver.

Put 10–12 pt (about 5l) cold water in a large pot. Place the pork bones in the water, then put in the chickens (but not the breast and leg meat you removed earlier), followed by the duck and finally the picnic shoulder (pork hand). Bring the pot to a rapid boil, skim off the scum, simmer for about 1 hour, then ladle out about 4–5 pt (about 2l) of the stock into a bowl, add the chicken leg meat finely chopped, together with the ginger root and onions, and leave it to cool.

Now add about 5–6 pt (about 2.5l) fresh boiling water to the pot, simmer for 1½ hours, then scoop out the picnic shoulder (pork hand), chickens, duck and pork bones. Skim once more, turn off the heat and let it cool for about 20 minutes, then put it back on a high heat again; add salt, stir and add the stock containing the chicken leg meat; continue stirring. When all the leg meat starts floating on the surface, reduce heat and scoop it out with a perforated spoon, then ladle out about 4–5 pt (about 2l) stock into a bowl. Let it cool a while before putting in the finely chopped chicken breast meat, blend well and pour it back to the stock pot. Increase heat, add soy sauce, stir until all the meat is floating on the surface, scoop it out then pour the stock through a fine sieve, and you will have the famous clear stock.

Thick stock
Use the picnic shoulder (pork hand), pork bones, chickens and the duck carcass and bones with the meat removed left over from the previous recipe.

Place first the pork bones on the bottom of a large pot, then the chickens all the way around the bones with the picnic shoulder (pork hand) in the middle, and finally place the duck carcass and bones on top. Fill the pot up with 10–12 pt (about 5l) water, bring it to a rapid boil then reduce heat to moderate and simmer for 2½ hours or until the stock is reduced by half, remove all the bones and meat; then strain the stock through a fine sieve.

CHICKEN, HAM AND MUSHROOM SOUP

4 oz (100g) chicken breast meat
¼ cup (2 oz, 50g) pork fat
¼ cup (1 oz, 25g) water chestnuts,
*   peeled*
⅙ cup (1 oz, 25g) bamboo shoots
4–5 Chinese dried mushrooms
2 oz (50g) cooked ham
1 egg white
1½ tsp (7ml) salt
2 tsp (10ml) cornstarch (cornflour)
2 scallions (spring onions)
3 tbsp (45ml) oil
3¾ cups (1½ pt, 900ml) thick stock
2 tbsp (30ml) rice wine (or sherry)
1¼ cups (½ pt, 300ml) clear stock
1 slice ginger root, peeled and finely
*   chopped*

Soak the chicken breast in cold water for 20 minutes, then remove the white tendon from the meat and finely chop it into a pulp.

Next peel the water chestnuts and parboil for a few minutes, then chop them finely. Finely chop the pork fat as well.

Soak the dried mushrooms in warm water for 20 minutes, squeeze dry and discard the hard stalks, then cut them into small pieces. Cut the bamboo shoots into thin slices of the same size. Cut the ham into thin slices roughly the same size as the bamboo shoots.

Beat the egg white until frothy, mix in the chicken meat, ½ tsp (2ml) salt, cornstarch (cornflour), pork fat and water chestnuts; blend well.

Heat 2 tbsp (30ml) oil in a *wok*, toss in 1 onion cut into short lengths, after a few seconds discard the onion and reduce the heat to as low as possible. Now wet your hands and make the chicken mixture into small round balls no bigger than cherries; fry them in the oil, turning them round, and press them flat with a spatula. Put the chicken into a bowl, add bamboo shoots, mushrooms and ham, together with ⅝ cup (¼ pt, 150ml) thick stock, ½ tbsp (10ml) rice wine or sherry and ½ tsp (2ml) salt. Steam over a high heat for 5 minutes, remove and discard the stock, place the entire contents in a large serving bowl.

Heat up the remaining oil, fry the other onion (cut into short lengths) for a few seconds and discard, add the remaining thick stock plus the clear stock, salt, finely chopped ginger root and the remaining rice wine or sherry; bring it to the boil then pour it over the chicken.

Serve as a soup for banquets and special occasions.

Chicken, ham and mushroom soup: this dish is so rich that you need only serve a small portion for each person

SHREDDED KIDNEYS IN WINE SAUCE

1 lb (0.5kg) pigs' kidneys
5–6 Chinese dried mushrooms
⅓ cup (2 oz, 50g) bamboo shoots
½ cup (2 oz, 50g) green cabbage heart
*   or broccoli*
1½ tbsp (25ml) rice wine (or sherry)
1 tsp (5ml) salt
1 tbsp (15ml) soy sauce
½ tsp (2ml) monosodium glutamate
1 slice ginger root, peeled
1 scallion (spring onion)
Sichuan peppercorns

Peel off the thin white skin covering the kidneys, split them in half lengthways and discard the white parts in the middle. Shred each half into thin slices and soak them in cold water for an hour or so.

Soak the mushrooms in warm water for 20 minutes, squeeze dry and discard the hard stalks, then cut them into thin shreds. Cut the bamboo shoots and greens into thin shreds, blanch them in boiling water for a few minutes (if using canned bamboo shoots this will be unnecessary as they have already been cooked), then drain and mix them with 1 tsp (5ml) salt.

Parboil the kidneys in about 4⅜ cups (1¾ pt, 1l) boiling water for a few minutes, scoop them out, rinse in cold water and drain. Place them in a bowl, add the bamboo shoots, mushrooms, greens, soy sauce, rice wine or sherry and monosodium glutamate; mix well and marinate for 20 minutes or so. Arrange the contents on a serving plate and garnish with finely chopped onion, ginger. root and freshly ground pepper.

This is an ideal starter for a formal meal or dinner party.

Shredded kidneys in wine sauce – an hors d'oeuvre dish of contrasting colors, flavors and textures

STEAMED CHICKEN

1 young chicken weighing about 2 lb
*   (1kg)*
4–5 Chinese dried mushrooms
⅔ cup (4 oz, 100g) bamboo shoots
2 oz (50g) cooked ham
1 cup (4 oz, 100g) broccoli stalks
2 tbsp (30ml) soy sauce
2 scallions (spring onions)
2 slices ginger root, peeled
1⅞ cups (¾ pt, 450ml) clear stock
3 tbsp (45ml) rice wine (or sherry)
1 tsp (5ml) salt

Clean the chicken thoroughly; place it in a large pot, cover with cold water and boil for 25 minutes. Remove and cool it in cold water, then carefully remove the meat from the bones and carcass (but keep the skin on). Cut the meat into thin slices the size of a matchbox.

Soak the mushrooms in warm water for about 20 minutes, squeeze dry and discard the hard stalks, then cut them into slices as well. Cut the bamboo shoots and ham into pieces the same size as the chicken. Split the broccoli stalks in half lengthwise, cut them into 2 dozen sticks, parboil for a few minutes and drain.

Place the bamboo shoots, mushrooms and ham slices in alternating rows in the bottom of a large bowl and arrange the chicken pieces on top with the skin side down. Place the broccoli stalks all around the chicken with the crushed carcass in the middle, add onions cut into short lengths, ginger root, 1½ tbsp (25ml) rice wine or sherry, ½ tsp (2ml) salt, 1¼ cups (½ pt, 300ml) stock and steam vigorously for 1½ hours. Remove and discard the onions and ginger root, then turn the bowl out into a large serving dish.

Heat up the remaining stock with the stock in which the chicken has been steamed and add soy sauce, the remaining salt and rice wine or sherry. When it starts to boil, skim off any scum; pour the stock over the chicken and serve.

Right: *Steamed chicken – not so simple to make, but well worth the extra effort if you want to serve a special dish for your friends. It is both delicious and attractive*

BRAISED FISH

In China, only carp from the lower reaches of the Yellow River would be used in this dish; it has golden yellow scales and a delicate flesh. The best season for eating them is the summer months (May to September).

1 Yellow River carp weighing about
  1½ lb (0.75–1kg)
2 tbsp (30ml) soy sauce
½ tbsp (10ml) sugar
2½ cups (1 pt, 600ml) clear stock
1½ tbsp (25ml) rice wine (or sherry)
1 tbsp (15ml) crushed yellow bean
  sauce
2 scallions (spring onions), finely
  chopped
1 slice ginger root, peeled and finely
  chopped
oil for deep-frying

Should you find the Yellow River a little too far for you to catch your carp, then by all means use any freshwater fish, only do not expect the same result. No other fish has quite the same taste and I think it is an experience everyone has the right to at least once in their lifetime.

Scale and gut the fish and clean it thoroughly. Score both sides of the fish diagonally down to the bone at intervals of about ¼ in (6mm). There are two reasons for doing this; since the fish is to be cooked whole, it prevents the skin from bursting; and it allows the heat to penetrate quickly and at the same time helps to diffuse the flavor of the seasoning and sauce.

Heat up about 4⅜ cups (1¾ pt, 1l) oil in a *wok* or deep-fryer, fry the fish until golden, take it out and drain.

Leave about 1 tbsp (15ml) oil in the *wok*, put in the finely chopped onions, ginger root and sugar; stir to dissolve the sugar, then add the bean sauce, followed by the rice wine or sherry, soy sauce, stock and the fish. Bring to the boil, then reduce the heat and cook until the juice is reduced by half; turn the fish over and continue cooking until the juice is almost completely evaporated.

Be careful not to break up the fish when lifting it out of the *wok*; it does not look right unless the fish is served whole with both head and tail intact.

Right: *Frying a whole fish in a* wok. *Always heat the* wok *first before putting in oil, and let oil get really hot before you put the fish in. Then reduce the heat to moderate during the cooking, otherwise the fish will be burnt outside and undercooked inside*

Left: *Braised fish. The diamond-patterned scoring helps to diffuse the heat, and also makes the finished dish look attractive*

SWEET AND SOUR CARP

This is *the* specialty of Jinan (Tsinan), the provincial capital of Shandong. The locally produced vinegar made from Kao Liang (sorghum) and millet, matured in the hot sun, has the same color as the muddy waters of the Yellow River. It tastes much stronger than ordinary vinegar.

1 Yellow River carp weighing about
    1½ lb (0.75kg)
a little salt
a little plain flour
oil for deep-frying
5–6 Wooden Ears, soaked
4–5 water chestnuts, peeled
⅓ cup (2 oz, 50g) bamboo shoots
2–3 scallions (spring onions)
2 slices ginger root, peeled
1 clove garlic, finely chopped

For the sauce:
3 tbsp (45ml) wine vinegar
3 tbsp (45ml) sugar
2 tbsp (30ml) soy sauce
2 tbsp (30ml) rice wine (or sherry)
2 tsp (10ml) cornstarch (cornflour)
⅝ cup (¼ pt, 150 ml) clear stock

Scale and gut the carp and clean thoroughly. Score the fish on both sides diagonally in a crisscross pattern down to the bone. Lift the fish up by the ends so the cuts open up, spread a little salt into them followed by a little flour, then coat the whole fish from head to tail with flour.

Cut the Wooden Ears into thin slices together with the bamboo shoots and water chestnuts. Shred the onions and ginger root into the size of matches, and finely chop the garlic.

Heat up the oil in a *wok* until it smokes. Holding the fish by the tail, gently lower it into the hot oil, bending the body so that the cuts open up; use a spatula beneath the body to prevent it from sticking to the *wok*. After 2 minutes turn the fish on its side with its stomach facing up, still holding the tail to make sure the body is kept curved. Cook for 2 more minutes, then turn the fish over so that its stomach is now facing down; after 2

Above: *A Chinese fish stall*
Right: *Sweet and sour carp, a specialty of Shandong*

minutes cook the fish on its flat side again, tilting the *wok* so that the head is in the oil. When the fish has been cooked for 8 minutes in all, take it out (carefully!) and place it on a long dish.

Pour off the excess oil and leave about 2 tbsp (30ml) oil in the *wok*. Fry the onions, ginger root and garlic; add the vinegar followed by the rest of the ingredients, together with the sauce mixture; stir and bring to the boil; pour it all over the fish and serve.

FISH-STOCK SOUP

After the fish is eaten, you can make a delicious soup from the leftovers. In a *wok* place the head and tail of the fish together with any leftovers from the sauce and dressings; crush the head, add 1⅞ cups (¾ pt, 450ml) clear stock and bring it to the boil. Put a little finely chopped onion, Chinese parsley, freshly ground pepper and 1 tbsp (15ml) vinegar in a large bowl; pour the strained fish soup into it and serve hot.

STIR-FRIED KIDNEY FLOWERS

½ lb (225g) pigs' kidneys
5–6 Wooden Ears
⅓ cup (2 oz, 50g) bamboo shoots
½ cup (2 oz, 50g) water chestnuts
1 cup (4 oz, 100g) greens in season
1 tbsp (15ml) cornstarch (cornflour)
3 tbsp (45ml) clear stock
1 tbsp (15ml) soy sauce
1 tbsp (15ml) vinegar
1 tsp (5ml) salt
2 scallions (spring onions)
1 slice ginger root, peeled
1 clove garlic
oil for deep-frying

Peel off the thin white skin covering the kidneys, split them in half lengthways and discard the white parts.

Score the surface of the kidneys diagonally in a criss-cross pattern and then cut them into small oblong pieces. When cooked they will open up and resemble ears of corn – hence the name 'flowers'. Mix the kidney pieces with a little salt and ½ tbsp (10ml) cornstarch (cornflour).

Soak the Wooden Ears in water for

Top: *Stir-fried kidney flowers. There is a similar dish in the Sichuan School, Hot and sour kidney , page 157*

about 20 minutes and slice them together with the water chestnuts and bamboo shoots. Cut and blanch the greens and finely chop the onions, ginger root and garlic. Mix the remaining cornstarch (cornflour) with the soy sauce and stock.

Heat up the oil in a *wok* until it smokes; deep-fry the kidney 'flowers', separate them with chopsticks or a fork, then quickly scoop them out with a perforated spoon. Now pour out the excess oil leaving about 2 tbsp (30ml) in the *wok*; toss in the onions, ginger root and garlic, add the vinegar followed by the bamboo shoots, water chestnuts, Wooden Ears and greens and finally the kidneys. Pour in the sauce mixture, blend well and serve.

This dish should have a harmonious balance of aroma, flavor, texture and color and is ideal as an accompaniment to wine. It is one of my favorite dishes.

SWEET AND SOUR SHRIMPS (PRAWNS)

1 lb (0.5kg) unshelled, uncooked
*   Pacific shrimps (prawns)*
1 egg white
2 tbsp (30ml) sugar
2 slices ginger root, peeled
1½ tbsp (25ml) cornstarch (cornflour)
1½ tbsp (25ml) vinegar
1 scallion (spring onion)
2 tbsp (30ml) chicken stock
oil for deep-frying

Shell the shrimps (prawns), make a shallow incision down the back of each prawn and remove the black intestinal parts. Wash and clean, then cut each shrimp (prawn) in half lengthwise. Make a criss-cross pattern on each half and marinate them with the egg white and ½ tbsp (10ml) corn-starch (cornflour).

Finely chop the onion and ginger root. Heat up about 4⅜ cups (1¾ pt, 1l) oil in a *wok* and, before the oil gets too hot, put in the shrimps (prawns) piece by piece; fry until golden, take them out and drain.

Leave about 1 tbsp (15ml) oil on the *wok*; stir-fry the finely chopped onion and ginger root until their color changes, then put in the shrimps (prawns); stir and add sugar and con-tinue stirring until all the sugar has dissolved. Add the remaining corn-starch (cornflour) mixed with the chicken stock, blend well, then serve.

You will find this dish quite dif-ferent from the ones you have tasted in ordinary Chinese restaurants; the secret is in the method of cooking.

Top left: *Sweet and sour shrimps (prawns).*
Lower left: *Raw Pacific shrimps (prawns) in their shells ready for the market. These are abundant off the north China coast, particularly around the rocky Shandong peninsula.* **Right:** *Both freshwater and saltwater shrimps are offered for sale in this fish market*

'DRAGON AND PHOENIX' LEGS

6 oz (150g) lean pork
4 oz (100g) chicken breast meat
6 oz (150g) shelled shrimps (prawns),
    uncooked
¼ cup (2 oz, 50g) onions
1 tbsp (15ml) rice wine (or sherry)
2 tsp (10ml) salt
5 tbsp (75ml) cornstarch (cornflour)
freshly ground Sichuan pepper
2 eggs
A large sheet of cellophane paper
1 tbsp (15ml) sesame seed oil
oil for deep-frying

Coarsely chop the lean pork, chicken, shrimps (prawns) and onions; mix with salt, rice wine or sherry and pepper and divide into 10 portions.

Beat the eggs and mix with 2 tbsp (30ml) cornstarch (cornflour).

Cut the cellophane paper into 10 pieces roughly 2×4 in (5×10cm). On the middle of each piece place a portion of the filling, rub some egg and cornstarch (cornflour) mixture all around it, then wrap the sheet round the filling to make the shape of a chicken leg, making 10 'legs' in all. Put them on a plate and steam for about 10 minutes, then take them out and place on a cold plate.

Mix the remaining 3 tbsp (45ml) cornstarch (cornflour) with 3 tbsp (45ml) water to make a batter; heat the oil in a *wok* or deep-fryer, deep-fry each of the 'legs' in the batter until golden and serve hot.

This dish of 'Dragon and phoenix' legs is served with deep-fried seaweed as garnish. 'Dragon' refers to the shrimps (prawns), and 'phoenix', of course, is the chicken. Traditionally you are supposed to place a piece of chicken bone on the edge of the 'legs' to be used as a handle when eating

TWICE-ROASTED PORK

The first part of the roasting is ideally done on an open fire or barbecue. The second part is supposed to be done in an oven, but there is no reason why it should not be barbecued as well.

3–4 lb (1.5–2kg) loin of pork (in one piece)
4 egg whites
1 cup (4 oz, 100g) plain flour
3–4 scallions (spring onions)
¼ cup (2 oz, 50g) Hoi Sin sauce
½ cup (4 oz, 100g) Chinese pickles

Pierce the pork with a spit, singe the skin over a high flame then plunge it into a large pot of hot water for 5 minutes. Take the pork out and scrape off any burnt skin. Place it in a large pot, cover with cold water and cook for about 1 hour. Remove.

Make a paste with the egg whites and flour, rub it all over the meat (not the skin), roast in a moderate oven (400°F, 200°C, Gas Mark 6) skin side up for 20 minutes, then turn it over and roast for a further 15–20 minutes.

To serve, carve the crackling, the fat, the meat and spareribs separately and arrange each in a row.

Cut the onions into shreds, to be eaten with the pork together with the Hoi Sin sauce and the Chinese pickles. Wrap the pork and its accompaniments in 'Lotus-leaf' pancakes, or place them inside Greek *pitta* bread which is very similar to a type of bread eaten in northern China.

PAN-FRIED PORK

1 lb (0.5kg) boned picnic shoulder (hand of pork)
1 egg
4 tbsp (60ml) cornstarch (cornflour)
1½ tbsp (25ml) soy sauce
1 tsp (5ml) salt
1½ tbsp (25ml) rice wine (or sherry)
3 scallions (spring onions)
1 slice ginger root
2 tbsp (30ml) Hoi Sin sauce
Sichuan peppercorns
5 cups (2 pt, 1.2l) oil for deep-frying

Place the pork in a pot of water and boil over a fairly high heat until soft. Remove and rinse in cold water, then cut it into thin slices across the whole joint, keeping the shape of the joint. Place the pork skin side down in a large bowl, add 1 tbsp (15ml) soy sauce, ginger root, 1 onion cut into short lengths, 1 tbsp (15ml) rice wine or sherry; steam for 1 hour; remove and drain off juice.

Mix the cornstarch (cornflour), egg and salt with the remaining rice wine or sherry and soy sauce, make it into a paste, put half of it on a plate, then place the pork skin side down on it (try to keep the original shape) and spread the remaining paste on top.

Warm up the oil in a deep-fryer, reduce heat and place the plate on the edge of the pan. Gently but firmly push the pork as a whole into the oil; after a while, increase the heat to high, then reduce the heat again when the pork starts to turn golden. Carefully turn it over, continue cooking until the sizzling noises are subdued, then lift it out and drain. Cut it into small pieces, arrange them on a place and garnish with Sichuan pepper.

Cut the remaining 2 onions into shreds, place them on one side of the plate and put the Hoi Sin sauce on the other side as a dip. Serve with 'Lotus-leaf' pancakes (p.44).

Left: *An early nineteenth-century print of a Chinese meat vendor.*
Right: *Twice-roasted pork. In this picture the skin and meat are shown served together. The jugs contain different types of Shaoxing wine, the famous rice wine from Zhejiang in south-east China (see page 135).*

STEAMED FISH

One of the simplest, and probably the best, ways of cooking fish is to steam it. If you have difficulty in getting the dried shrimps called for in this recipe, fresh peeled shrimps (prawns) can be substituted; similarly, use fresh mushrooms instead of the dried ones if so desired.

1 fish weighing about 1 lb (0.5kg)
3–4 Chinese dried mushrooms
½ oz (15g) dried shrimps, or 2 oz (50g)
  fresh peeled shrimps (prawns)
2 slices ginger root, peeled
2–3 scallions (spring onions)
2 tbsp (30ml) rice wine (or sherry)
1 tsp (5ml) salt
1 tbsp (15ml) soy sauce
1 cup (8 fl oz, 250ml) chicken stock

Scale and gut the fish, then clean thoroughly inside and out in cold water.

Soak the dried mushrooms in warm water for 20 minutes, squeeze dry and

Steamed fish. A Peking cook would usually use a carp, but almost any Western variety tastes good when cooked this way

discard the hard stalks; if they are large, cut them into small pieces no bigger than the shrimps or prawns. Peel the ginger root and cut the onions into short lengths.

Plunge the fish into boiling water for a few seconds, remove and place it on a large plate and arrange the mushrooms, onions, ginger root and shrimps on top of the fish. Add salt, rice wine or sherry, soy sauce and chicken stock; place the plate in a steamer and steam vigorously for 20 minutes.

'CORAL' CABBAGE

Chinese white cabbage, also known as Chinese leaves or celery cabbage, is now widely available in the West.

Discard the outer tough leaves and use the tender heart only.

4 cups (1 lb, 0.5kg) Chinese white
  cabbage
4–5 Chinese dried mushrooms
½ cup (3 oz, 75g) bamboo shoots
4–5 dried red chilis
2 tbsp (30ml) sugar
1 tbsp (15ml) soy sauce
½ tbsp (10ml) rice wine (or sherry)
1½ tbsp (25ml) vinegar
1 tsp (5ml) salt
1 scallion (spring onion)
1 slice ginger root, peeled
2 tbsp (30ml) sesame seed oil

Parboil the cabbage; remove and drain, marinate with ½ tsp (2ml) salt for 5 minutes, then squeeze dry and cut into matchbox-sized pieces; arrange on a serving dish.

Soak the mushrooms in warm water for 20 minutes, then squeeze dry and discard the stalks. Cut the mushrooms, bamboo shoots, red chilis, onions and ginger root into thin shreds the size of matches.

Heat up the sesame seed oil in a

wok, stir-fry all the vegetables (except the cabbage) for 2 minutes. Add the sugar, soy sauce, rice wine or sherry, vinegar and salt with about 2 tbsp (30ml) water or stock; stir-fry for 1–2 minutes more and pour over the cabbage.

This is a multi-colored dish and is especially delicious when served cold.

OIL-BRAISED CHICKEN

1 young chicken (poussin) *weighing about 1¼ lb (0.5kg)*
2 tbsp (30ml) soy sauce
2 tbsp (30ml) rice wine (or sherry)
2 scallions (spring onions), finely chopped
1 slice ginger root, peeled and finely chopped
½ tsp (2ml) five-spice powder
oil for deep-frying

For the dip:
chili sauce
Sichuan peppercorns, crushed

Chop the chicken down the middle into two halves. Marinate with soy sauce, the wine or sherry, five-spice powder, finely chopped onions and ginger root. After 20–30 minutes, take the chicken halves out and pat them dry with paper towels.

Heat up the oil in a deep-fryer and,

Oil-braised chicken garnished with deep-fried shrimp crackers

before the oil gets too hot, deep-fry the halves for about 5 minutes or until they start to turn golden, then take them out. Wait for the oil to get really hot, then fry the halves again until brown, take them out and chop them into small pieces, arrange on a plate.

Heat up the marinade, let it bubble for a while then pour it all over the chicken. Serve with chili sauce and Sichuan pepper as a dip.

The skin of the chicken should be crispy, and the meat very tender and highly aromatic.

DICED LAMB WITH SCALLIONS (SPRING ONIONS)

½ lb (225g) fillet lamb
1⅓ cups (½ lb, 225g) scallions (spring onions)
1½ tbsp (25ml) cornstarch (cornflour)
1 tsp (5ml) salt
2 tsp (10ml) soy sauce
1 egg white
½ tbsp (10ml) rice wine (or sherry)
oil for deep-frying
1 tsp (5ml) sesame seed oil

Dice the lamb into ½ in (1cm) cubes, marinate with ½ tsp (2ml) salt, egg white and ¾ tbsp (12ml) cornstarch (cornflour). Cut the onions into ½ in (1cm) lengths.

Heat about 2½ cups (1 pt, 600ml) oil in a *wok*. Before the oil gets too hot, add the lamb cubes, separate them with chopsticks or a fork, then scoop them out and drain.

Diced lamb with scallions (spring onions) – a popular dish of Moslem origin

Pour off the excess oil and leave about 2 tbsp (30ml) in the *wok*. Put in the onions followed by the lamb cubes, salt, soy sauce, rice wine or sherry and the remaining cornstarch (cornflour); stir for 1–2 minutes; add the sesame seed oil, stir a few more times, then serve.

PLUM-BLOSSOM AND SNOW COMPETING FOR SPRING

2 apples
2 bananas
2 eggs
½ cup (4 oz, 100g) sugar
3 tbsp (45ml) milk
3 tbsp (45ml) cornstarch (cornflour)
2 tbsp (30ml) water

Skin and remove the cores of the apples, then cut the apples and bananas into thin slices. Arrange them in alternate layers on an oven-proof dish. Separate the yolks from the whites and mix the yolks with the sugar, milk, water and cornstarch (cornflour). Heat this mixture over a gentle heat until smooth, then pour it over the apple and banana.

Beat the egg whites, pour on top of the yolk mixture and bake in a hot oven (425°F, 220°C, Gas Mark 7) for about 5 minutes. Serve hot or cold.

A Natural Divide

It is a curious fact that a river often seems to divide people into two different groups separated not only physically, which is understandable, but in almost every aspect of their daily lives.

In a narrow sense, the south bank of the Thames in London represents quite a different way of life from the rest of that great city; just as one talks of the 'left bank' of Paris as though it is an entirely different world. In a wider sense, the Yangtse River tends to divide China into 'northerners' and 'southerners' – people who live north or south of the river.

Traditionally a meal in China is never served in an individual container with a clear division of meat and vegetables, but rather as a communal affair – each person helping him- or herself from several dishes in the middle of the table; each person with an individual bowl of rice. The dish or dishes they share, be it fish, meat, vegetable or a combination of any number of them, are called *cai*, and the cooked rice they eat with the *cai* is called *fan*. Northerners, however, do not eat much rice; instead, they eat wheat in the form of bread, noodles, dumplings and pancakes; other grain such as corn, millet and Kao Liang; and soybean. All these when cooked are also

Above: *Cooking dumplings, a typical northern dish.* **Right:** *Rice-plating in south China; wheat-harvesting in north China* (**inset**).

Above: *Beer from Qingdao. The label shows the old spelling, for the export market.* **Right:** *A selection of Chinese wines and spirits.*

called *fan*, which has mistakenly been equated with rice in English.

There also seems to be a big difference between the southerners and northerners in their beverages. Although tea is universal in China, tea drinking in the north is less sophisticated than in the south, partly because there is a far wider variety of teas grown south of the Yangtse River. Then there is the question of alcoholic drinks. The northerners drink mostly a strong spirit made from Kao Liang (sorghum), known as 'white wine' because it is colorless, while the southerners seem to prefer, not surprisingly, the milder 'yellow wine', a rice wine made from glutinous rice. Confusion is caused by the word *Jin*, which can mean wine, but is also used for other alcoholic drinks.

In north China, the undisputed pearl of Kao Liang spirit is *Fen Jui* from a village called Apricot Blossom , north-east of Fenyung in the province of Shanxi. It owes its

FEN JUI AND ZHU YE XING

Right: *Storehouse in the Fen Jui distillery in the Apricot Blossom village, Shanxi. The distilled liquor is sealed into these huge pots and stored for a number of years. It is marketed in porcelain jars (shown near left) decorated with apricot blossom and with a quotation from China's most popular poet Li Bai (701–762): "'May I beg to enquire where I can find a good wine?" The shepherd boy pointed to the Apricot Blossom village in the distance.'*
Far left: *Zhu Ye Xing (bamboo leaf green), a liqueur made from Fen Jui blended with aromatic herbs.*

unique quality in part to the waters of the Fen He, a tributary of the Yellow River. *Fen Jui* has a long history: it was first made over 1,400 years ago.

Fen Jui is used as the basis for a liqueur called *Zhu Ye Xing* ('Bamboo-leaf Green') and is blended with a dozen aromatic herbs including bamboo leaves. It is quite refreshing and is very popular as an after-dinner digestif in Japan, and south-east Asia.

Mention must be made here of another Kao Liang spirit called *Xifeng* ('West Phoenix') from Fengxiang, north of the Wei River in the province of Shaanxi.

According to historical records, rice wine and beer were both first made in China more than 4,000 years ago but, strangely, beer drinking has only been popular during the last two decades or so. Besides Qingdao (Tsingtao), other well-known centres for beer are Yantai (Chefoo), Peking and Manchuria.

Although the vine, *Vitis vinifera*, was first introduced into China more than 2,000 years ago from Iran, the art of wine-making was not acquired until the seventh century. But again, for some unknown reason, the Chinese never really 'took' to grape wine; it has always remained a connoisseur's drink.

In 1898 part of the Shandong peninsula was ceded to Germany as a colony. Besides the brewery for beer at Qingdao (Tsingtao), the Germans also established a winery to make a hock-type wine in Yantai using the high-quality grapes produced locally. Today Yantai and Qingdao are two of China's leading wine-producing centers, making white wine even sweeter than the German hock, as well as sparkling wine and a type of vermouth. Elsewhere, grape wines are made in Peking and Manchuria.

China's largest and most modern winery is situated in Tonghua, just north of the Korean border. Both red and white wines are made here; the red resembles a tawny port and the white is very similar to a medium sherry. Wines from Peking are drier – both red and white – but even so none of them has any distinctive character to make them of serious interest to the Western wine connoisseur.

FROM NORTH TO SOUTH

The new Nanjing bridge links the north and south banks of the Yangtse river.

To go back in time about 40 years, when we left Peking for the south, we first went to Tianjin (Tientsin) by rail to change to the Tianjin-Pukow line for Nanjing (Nanking). Pukow was the terminus on the north bank of the Yangtse River opposite Nanjing – the bridge linking the north and south was not to be built for another 30 years.

It was the first time that I had traveled for such a long distance, and the prospect of sleeping the night on a train greatly excited me and my brother. I remember the attendant frequently brought boiling water to fill our flasks for us so that we could make our own tea.

For the first part of our journey, the train ran along very close to the Grand Canal which links Peking with Hangzhou (Hangchow) in the south, a distance of over a thousand miles. Also known as the Imperial Canal, it was built section by section starting in 486 B.C. and eventually completed in 1292 during the Yuan (Mogol) dynasty. When we stopped at Dezhou, the border town

between Hebei and Shandong, there were vendors selling baskets of cooked chickens. We bought four for one Chinese dollar (I checked with my mother on this and she assures me that my memory is correct. The chickens came from local villages and they tasted delectable. It seemed that we could only get fried rice aboard the train, so most passengers either brought their own food or had to rely on the stops, which were both frequent and long.

For the children it was more like a gastronomic tour sampling the specialties of the region. For instance, we had enormous juicy pears in Jinan – I cannot remember tasting anything quite like them before or since. Then at one country stop – there were no platforms so it could not have been a proper station – a group of women and young girls were selling hot tea-eggs from steaming pots held high above their heads (see recipe on p141). Looking back, it is the food I remember better than anything, even though we must have passed through some of the most scenic parts of China.

When we finally reached Pukow on the north bank of the great Yangtse River, it was almost like arriving at a sea port, for the river was so wide that you could hardly see the opposite bank. Here we say good-bye to the north and move on, first to Shanghai where lots more delicacies are waiting for us.

SHANGHAI/THE EASTERN SCHOOL

Shanghai

The Yangtse, China's longest river, leaving its mountain source in the Tibetan Plateau, flows first through the basin of Sichuan, then winds through the Yangtse Gorges and rushes on through the basin of Hubei and Anhui. Here a net of lakes and tributary rivers slows down its progress until it reaches its journey's end, roaring into the East China Sea just north of Shanghai.

The Yangtse has traveled for more than 3,000 miles (4,800 km) by the time it reaches its Lower Plain, which includes the provinces of Anhui, Jiangsu (with the independent City of Shanghai) and Zhejiang. This is one of China's leading agricultural regions, for the plain contains some of the most fertile land in China. Both wheat and rice are grown here as well as other crops including barley, corn, sweet potatoes, peanuts and soy beans. Fisheries abound in the multitude of lakes and rivers, and deep sea fishing has long been established in the coastal provinces of Jiangsu and Zhejiang. Usually referred to as the 'Lands of Fish and Rice', this region boasts a number of distinctive styles.

Shanghai, which lies on the Yangtse estuary, is the biggest city in China and has the world's third largest population after Tokyo and New York. It used to be very cosmopolitan; even today it remains China's greatest port and an important trading and industrial centre. The characteristics of Shanghai cooking can be summarized as exquisite in appearance, rich in flavor, and sweet in taste.

Above: *The famous Bund, or commercial center, which surrounds the harbour at Shanghai.* **Near right:** *A Moslem food store in Nanjing Road. Specialities from all over China can be found in this cosmopolitan city.* **Right:** *A cake-shop does a roaring trade.* **Opposite:** *Part of old Shanghai still remains today. This traditional tea-house overlooks a quiet lake.*

Just outside Shanghai the countryside remains tranquil and unchanged. This peaceful scene reflects the traditional life in an agricultural area of the Yangtse River delta.

Shanghai dishes

In Shanghai we stayed with my mother's aunt and uncle. What impressed me most was the fact that their house was three stories high; there were stairs for my brother and me to climb, and banisters to slide down. After our single-story house in Peking, this was a great novelty.

My mother's aunt was a good cook, and our uncle enjoyed good food and wine. Although they employed a Shanghai cook, he would eat dishes prepared only by our aunt for he complained that the cook used too much sugar for his liking – 'Sweet food and wine do not go together', our aunt explained.

Here are four recipes my mother learned from her aunt.

BRAISED FISH

1 bream (carp, perch or trout)
*   weighing about 1 lb (0.5kg)*
3–4 Chinese dried mushrooms
⅙ cup (1 oz, 25g) bamboo shoots
⅛ cup (1 oz, 25g) pork fat
2 tbsp (30ml) soy sauce
4 tbsp (60ml) lard
1 slice of ginger root, peeled
1 scallion (spring onion)
2 tbsp (30ml) rice wine (or sherry)
1 tbsp (15ml) sugar
1 tbsp (15ml) vinegar
4 tbsp (60ml) chicken stock

Use freshwater bream, otherwise substitute carp, perch or trout. Scale and gut the fish, then clean thoroughly inside and out in cold water. Trim off the fins and slash both sides of the fish diagonally as deep as the bone at intervals of about ½ in (1cm). There are two reasons for doing this: it prevents the skin from bursting during the cooking; and it allows the heat to penetrate more quickly, to diffuse the flavor of the seasoning and sauce.

Soak the dried mushrooms in warm water for about 20 minutes; squeeze dry and discard the hard stalks, then cut them into 2 or 3 pieces if they are large ones. Cut the bamboo shoots into match-size strips and dice the pork fat into small cubes the size of peas. Cut the onion into 2–3 short lengths.

Heat up about 3 tablespoons (45ml) lard over high heat. While

waiting for it to get really hot, rub the outside of the fish with soy sauce, then fry it in the lard until golden on both sides. Remove and keep warm.

Heat up the remaining lard; fry the ginger root, onion, mushrooms, bamboo shoots and pork fat; stir a few times then put the fish back and add soy sauce, wine, sugar, vinegar and chicken stock. Bring to the boil then reduce heat and simmer for 5–6 minutes; turn the fish over and cook for another 5–6 minutes. By then there should be little juice left; discard the ginger root and onion and serve.

PRESERVED EGGS AND GROUND PORK

Preserved eggs are sometimes called ancient or thousand-year-old eggs. In fact they are duck's eggs preserved in a mixture of alkali, lime ashes, mud and other materials. After a few months the chemicals penetrate the eggshell,

turning both the white and yolk a dark brownish-green color. Normally they are served uncooked; children and Westerners do not always find them to their taste to start with, but I became a convert after eating them at our aunt's house.

2 Chinese preserved eggs
½ lb (250g) pork
1 tbsp (15ml) oil
1½ tbsp (25ml) soy sauce
1 tsp (5ml) sesame seed oil

Remove the mud covering the egg shells, then clean them in water thoroughly before cracking them. Coarsely chop the eggs and the pork, keeping the two ingredients separate.

Heat the oil and fry the pork. When its color changes, put in the chopped eggs, add the soy sauce and mix well. Stir for 3–4 minutes; add sesame seed oil and serve.

Preserved eggs with their outer coating of rice husks. To remove the coating, soak in water until the mud softens and comes off easily

PORK AND BAMBOO SHOOT SOUP

Preserved pork is first salted, then dried in the open air and stored in oil. If unobtainable in the West, unsmoked bacon makes a possible substitute.

½ lb (225g) unsmoked bacon in one piece
1 lb (0.5kg) leg of pork in one piece
2⅔ cups (1 lb, 0.5kg) bamboo shoots
3–3½ pt (about 1.75l) water

Place the two pieces of meat in a large pot; add the water, bring to a rolling boil, skim off the scum and reduce the heat to moderate. Replace the lid and simmer for about 2–3 hours, then add the bamboo shoots cut into chunks and continue cooking for 20–30 minutes.

When serving, you should be able to pull small pieces of the meat off with your chopsticks or with a serving spoon. The preserved pork or bacon should not taste too salty and the fresh pork should have acquired some of the flavor of the preserved pork. The bamboo shoots should taste fantastic having absorbed the flavors of both. (Fresh bamboo shoots absorb flavor even better, but unfortunately they are not usually available in the West.)

'HAPPY FAMILY' (ASSORTED MEATS AND SEAFOOD STEW)

This is a superior version of 'chop suey'. Despite its unusual ingredients (Bêche-de-Mer, etc.), it is not generally served at banquets, but rather as a home dish for special occasions such as birthdays or New Year family dinners. Our aunt cooked this for us at the farewell dinner before we left for the south. The variation of subsidiary ingredients is a matter of personal and seasonal choice. It is important to bear in mind the balance between flavor, color and texture.

4 oz (100g) Bêche-de-Mer (soaked)
2 oz (50g) fish maw (soaked)
2 oz (50g) cooked tripe
1 pig's kidney
4 oz (100g) shrimps (prawns), peeled
⅓ cup (2 oz, 50g) cooked chicken meat
1 egg
8 fish balls, can be bought pre-prepared
6 meat balls, can be bought pre-prepared
⅓ cup (2 oz, 50g) bamboo shoots
1 cup (4 oz, 100g) cauliflower
1 cup (4 oz, 100g) broccoli
2 slices ginger root, peeled
2 scallions (spring onions)
1½ tbsp (25g) dried shrimps
3 tbsp (45ml) lard
1 tbsp (15ml) sugar
2 tbsp (30ml) rice wine (or sherry)
3 tbsp (45ml) soy sauce
2 tbsp (30ml) cornstarch (cornflour)
1¼ cups (½ pt, 300ml) chicken stock
vinegar and salt

Bêche-de-Mer, also known as sea-cucumber or sea-slug, is regarded by the Chinese as a delicacy. It must be soaked overnight to become gelatinous. Cut it diagonally into thin slices.

Fish maw is bought already fried. It has a puffy, spongy, yet crispy texture. It too should be soaked in water overnight before being cut into small pieces about the same size as the Bêche-de-Mer. Cut the tripe into similar sized pieces.

Split the kidney in half lengthwise and discard the fat and white parts in the middle. Score the surface of the kidney diagonally in a cross-cross pattern and then cut into medium size pieces; marinate in a little salt and vinegar; blanch in boiling water for a few seconds until the kidney pieces curl up; remove and drain.

Marinate the peeled shrimps (prawns) in a little salt and cornstarch (cornflour). Cut the cooked chicken meat into thin slices. Wash the cauliflower and broccoli and cut them into small pieces; blanch in boiling water for a while, remove and drain. Slice the bamboo shoots; finely chop the ginger root and onions.

Beat up the egg with a little salt and 2–3 teaspoons (10–15ml) water. Rub some lard on the bottom of a bowl, pour the beaten egg into it and steam for 2–3 minutes, then open the lid of the steamer for a few seconds to let out some hot air; replace the lid and steam for 5–6 minutes more. When the steamed egg is cooled, remove from the bowl and cut it into thin slices.

Parboil all the ingredients together for a few seconds; remove and drain. Heat up the lard in a large pot; fry the finely chopped ginger root and onions; add dried shrimps and rice wine (or sherry) followed by the rest of the ingredients. Now add soy sauce, sugar and chicken stock; bring it to the boil then reduce heat and simmer for a few minutes.

Finally mix the remaining cornstarch (cornflour) with a little water and add to the pot to thicken the gravy. Serve in a large bowl with rice.

Overleaf: *'Happy Family', a beautiful dish of contrasts, in color, texture and flavor*

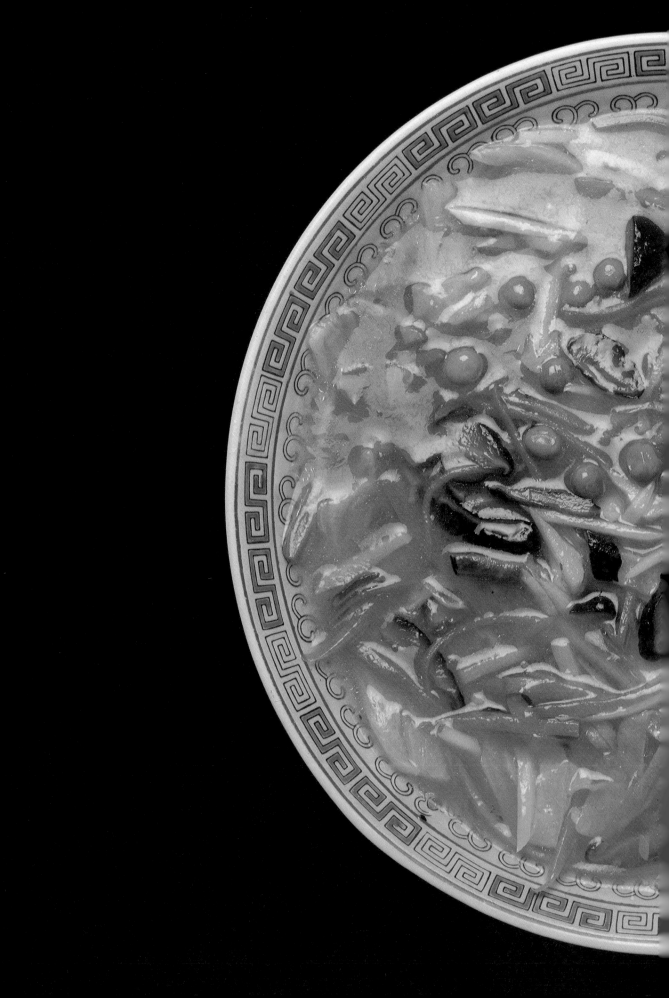

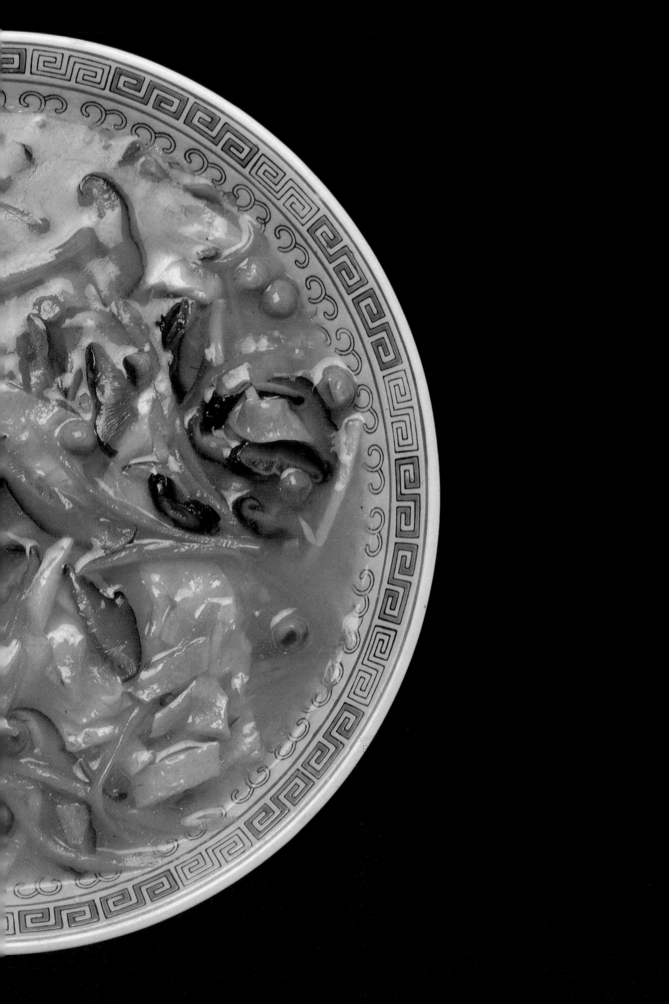

While in Shanghai, we were taken out to several of the local restaurants to sample their specialties. The difference in the flavors and styles of this Shanghai food compared to the Peking food we were used to was apparent even to my unsophisticated palate as a child.

'WHITE-CUT' PORK

2 lb (1kg) leg of pork (skinned and boned)

Dip:
4 tbsp (60ml) soy sauce
1 tbsp (15ml) Kao Liang spirit (or brandy)
2 scallions (spring onions) finely chopped
2 slices ginger root, peeled and finely chopped
1 tsp (5ml) sesame seed oil
1 tsp (5ml) chili sauce (optional)
3–3½ pt (about 1.75l) water

'White-cut' pork: simplicity itself to make, but absolutely delicious

Place the pork (in one piece, tied together with string if necessary) in a large pot; add cold water, bring it to a rapid boil; skim off the scum. Cover and simmer gently for about 1 hour. Remove from the pot and leave it to cool under cover with the fat side up for 6–8 hours.

Just before serving, cut off any excess fat, leaving only a very thin layer (about ¹⁄₁₀ in (2mm)) of fat on top, then cut the meat into small thin slices across the grain. Put any uneven bits and pieces in the center of a plate; arrange the well-cut slices in two neat rows, one on each side of the pile, then neatly arrange a third row on top of the pile so that it resembles an arched bridge.

You can either pour the sauce mixture all over the pork and serve, or use the sauce as a dip.

SWEET AND SOUR SPARERIBS

1 lb (0.5kg) pork spareribs
2 tbsp (30ml) soy sauce
1 tbsp (15ml) rice wine (or sherry)
½ tsp (2ml) monosodium glutamate
2 tbsp (30ml) cornstarch (cornflour)
2 tbsp (30ml) sugar
1½ tbsp (25ml) vinegar
lard for deep-frying
salt and Sichuan pepper for dipping

Chop the spareribs into small bits using a cleaver. Mix ½ tablespoon (10ml) soy sauce with the rice wine or sherry and monosodium glutamate. When they are all well blended together, add 1 tablespoon (15ml) cornstarch (cornflour). Coat each bit of the sparerib with this mixture.

In a bowl mix the remaining soy sauce with sugar and vinegar. Warm up the lard in a *wok* or deep-fryer, put in about half of the spareribs, fry for 30 seconds, scoop them out. Wait for a while to let the lard heat up again, then fry the rest of the spareribs for 30 seconds, scoop out. Now wait for the lard to get hot before returning all the spareribs to the *wok* to fry for another 50 seconds or so; scoop them out when they turn golden and place them on a serving dish.

Pour off the excess lard, leaving about 1 tablespoon (15ml) in the pan; add the sauce mixture. When it starts to bubble, add the remaining corn-

Sweet and sour spareribs, another easy dish, using a cheap cut of meat

starch (cornflour) mixed in a little cold water; stir to make a smooth sauce, then pour it over the spareribs.

Serve with salt and pepper mixed as a dip.

CHICKEN 'SAUCE'

1½ lb (0.75kg) young chicken
2 scallions (spring onions); cut into 1 in (2.5cm) lengths
1½ tbsp (25ml) rice wine (or sherry)
2 tbsp (30ml) soy sauce
1¼ cups (½ pt, 300ml) stock
2 tbsp (30ml) lard
1 tbsp (15ml) cornstarch (cornflour)
1 tbsp (15ml) sugar

Cut off the wings and parson's nose of the chicken, then chop it into about 20 pieces with the bone still attached.

Heat up the lard over a high heat; stir-fry the chicken pieces for about 30 seconds; add wine or sherry, soy sauce and sugar; stir until the chicken turns brown then add the stock. Bring it to the boil, reduce heat to simmer for 10 minutes or until the stock is reduced by a third; now increase the heat, add the cornstarch (cornflour) mixed in a little water, blend well. When the juice is further reduced by half add the onions and serve.

Each chicken piece should be wrapped in a dark, thickish sauce, hence the name of this dish. This was one of our uncle's favorites to accompany his wine drinking.

Chicken 'sauce', here served with two varieties of Kao Liang spirit. It goes equally well with red or white wine

'THREE-LAYER SHREDS'

⅓ cup (2 oz, 50g) cooked ham
⅓ cup (2 oz, 50g) cooked chicken meat
⅔ cup (4 oz, 100g) cooked pork
   (perhaps left over from White-cut pork)
⅓ cup (2 oz, 50g) bamboo shoots
1 large Chinese dried mushroom
2 tsp (10ml) salt
½ tsp (2ml) monosodium glutamate
1 tbsp (15ml) lard
2½ cups (1 pt, 600ml) stock

Cut the ham, chicken, pork and bamboo shoots into match-size shreds, but keep them separate. Discard the stalk of the mushroom after soaking it in warm water for 20 minutes. Place the mushroom smooth side down in the middle of a large bowl, and arrange the ham shreds around it in three neat rows, forming a triangle. Now arrange the chicken shreds on one of the outer edges and the bamboo shoots on the second edge with the pork on the third. Spread 1 teaspoon (5ml) salt all over it, add about 4 tablespoons (60ml) stock and steam vigorously for 30 minutes. Remove and turn the bowl out into a deep serving dish without disarranging the contents. The success of this dish depends on the cutting and arranging, which must be done with skill and care.

Bring the remaining stock to the boil, add salt, monosodium glutamate and lard; let it bubble for a second or two then pour it all over the 'Three-layer shreds' and serve.

'Three-layer shreds', here seen garnished with cucumber slices, green peas and Chinese parsley (fresh coriander) to provide a contrast in color

Dishes from the Yangtse delta

Like Peking, Shanghai has a number of restaurants specializing in dishes from other regions, notably the two local schools known as Huaiyang and Suzhe. The Huaiyang School, the school of the Yangtse River delta area, besides being famous for its noodles and dumplings, boasts a host of other popular dishes. The famous 'Lion's head' (pork meatballs with cabbage) originated in Yangzhou, and Zhen-jiang's vinegar is supposed to be the best in China. Suzhe (the provinces of Jiangsu and Zhejiang) covers a larger area than Huaiyang. Apart from Shanghai, which has a style of its own, it also includes culinary centers such as Nanjing and Hangzhou (Hangchow). The Hangzhou School will be dealt with later. First we have a few examples from the Yangtse delta.

Below: *This fish farm in the Yangtse River delta produces giant carp*

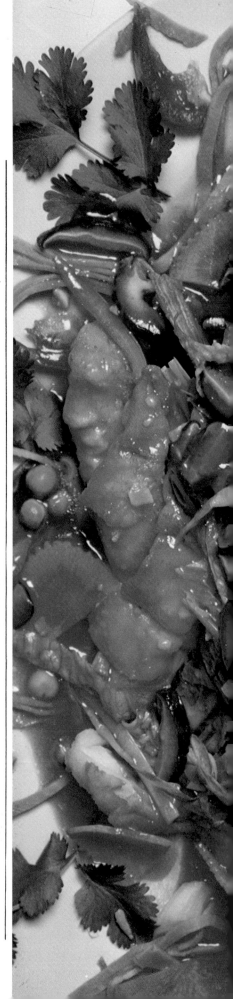

SQUIRREL FISH

This is another recipe from Nanjing. The fish should be a bream from the Yangtse River; there is no reason, however, why you should not use an ordinary bream or even a bass or carp.

1 bream, bass or carp weighing about
*   1½ lb (0.75kg)*
3–4 Chinese dried mushrooms
⅓ cup (2 oz, 50g) bamboo shoots
2 scallions (spring onions)
1 slice ginger root, peeled
2 tbsp (30ml) wine vinegar
2 tbsp (30ml) sugar
6 tbsp (90ml) chicken stock
3 tbsp (45ml) cornstarch (cornflour)
oil for deep-frying

Soak the mushrooms and cut them into thin shreds; do the same with the bamboo shoots. Finely chop the onions and ginger root.

Scale and gut the fish; split it in half, leaving the head whole; remove the backbone, then with the skin side down, score the flesh diagonally in a criss-cross pattern about 24 times almost through to the skin. Coat the whole fish with cornstarch (cornflour) and deep-fry in hot oil for about 10 minutes; by then the body of the fish will curl up, resembling a squirrel.

Above: *The first stage in cutting the fish. It has been split in half and the backbone removed*
Left : *Squirrel fish ready for serving*

Take it out to cool for a while then return it to re-fry for 1–2 minutes or until golden. Place it on a long dish and arrange it in such a way that the tail is sticking out.

When frying the fish for the second time, heat the chicken stock, sugar, wine vinegar, onions, ginger root, mushrooms and bamboo shoots all together; bring to the boil; add about 1 tablespoon (15ml) cornstarch (cornflour) mixed with a little cold water to thicken the gravy. Finally add about ½ tablespoon (10ml) hot oil and pour it all over the fish; serve hot.

PHOENIX TAIL SHRIMPS (PRAWNS)

This recipe originated from a Moslem restaurant in Nanjing. Oil can be used instead of the duck fat it calls for.

½ lb (225g) unshelled shrimps
 (prawns)
½ cup (2 oz, 50g) green peas
2 scallions (spring onions), white parts
 only
1 egg white
1½ tbsp (25ml) cornstarch (cornflour)
½ tbsp (10ml) rice wine (or sherry)
1 tsp (5ml) salt
½ tsp (2ml) monosodium glutamate
6 tbsp (90ml) chicken stock
duck fat or oil for deep-frying

Parboil the peas for 3 minutes, drain and rinse in cold water in order to keep the bright green color. Finely chop the onion whites. Pull off the heads and shell the shrimps (prawns), but leave the tail pieces firmly attached. Marinate them with ½ teaspoon (2ml) salt, egg white and ½ tablespoon (10ml) cornstarch (cornflour).

Heat the duck fat (or oil); deep-fry the shrimps (prawns) for about 1 minute; stir to separate them; remove and drain.

Pour off the excess fat; add the stock, salt, rice wine or sherry, cornstarch (cornflour), monosodium glutamate and onions. Bring it to the boil; stir to make a thickish smooth gravy; add the shrimps (prawns) and peas; blend well and serve.

Two contrasting dishes: **at the top of the picture,** *crystal-sugar pork;* **below,** *Phoenix tail shrimps*

CRYSTAL-SUGAR PORK

1 leg or picnic shoulder (hand) of pork
 weighing about 2½–3 lb
 (1.25–1.5kg)
5 tbsp (75ml) soy sauce
¼ cup (2 oz, 50g) crystal sugar
4 tbsp (60ml) rice wine (or sherry)
2 scallions (spring onions)
2 slices ginger root
2–2½ pt (about 1l) water

Clean the skin or rind of pork well, making sure it is smooth and free of hairs; score an X mark down the middle as far as the bone; this will prevent the skin sticking to the pan.

Place the pork in a large pot with the skin side down, cover it with cold water, bring it to a rapid boil, skim off the scum; add all the other ingredients, place the lid on tightly, reduce heat and simmer for 30 minutes. Then turn the pork over, replace the lid and continue cooking for about 2 hours. The juice should by now be reduced to less than ⅝ cup (¼ pt, 150ml). Turn the heat up for 5 minutes to thicken the gravy, then take the pork out and place it on a bowl or deep dish. Pour the gravy over it and serve. Like many casseroles this is even more delicious cooked in advance and then reheated and served the following day.

Braised duck, crisp and tender, can be served cold as a starter, or hot as a main dish

BRAISED DUCK

1 duckling weighing about
   4½ lb (2kg)
5½ tbsp (40ml) red fermented
   rice
5½ tbsp (40ml) sugar
1½ tbsp (25ml) cornstarch (cornflour)
2 tbsp (30ml) rice wine (or sherry)
¼ cup (2 fl oz, 50ml) soy sauce
5½ tbsp (40ml) crystal sugar,
   crushed
2 slices ginger root
2 scallions (spring onions)
1 tsp (5ml) salt
2 tsp (10ml) Chinese cinnamon bark
1 tsp (5ml) fennel seeds

Clean the duck thoroughly; place it in a large pot with its back facing upwards; add enough water to cover it, then add red fermented rice, soy sauce, salt, rice wine or sherry, crystal sugar, cinnamon bark, fennel seeds, onions and ginger root. Bring it to a rapid boil and keep the heat fairly high for 1 hour; turn the duck over and simmer gently for ½ hour; take it out to cool.

Leave about half the juice in the pan (keep the other half for future use), add sugar and when it is dissolved, strain through a sieve to get rid of the spices; mix the cornstarch (cornflour) with a little cold water to thicken the gravy, then leave to cool. Chop the duck into small pieces, pour the gravy over it and serve.

'BRIGHT MOON AND RED PINE' CHICKEN

This dish originated from the boat restaurants of Suzhou (Soochow), one of China's water cities.

1 chicken leg, boned but with skin
   attached
3 oz (75g) pork
1 egg
½ cup (3 oz, 75g) snow peas
   (mange-tout)
1 tbsp (½ oz, 15g) cooked ham
3 tbsp (45ml) lard
1½ tbsp (25ml) soy sauce
1 tsp (5ml) salt
1 tbsp (15ml) rice wine (or sherry)
1 tbsp (15ml) sugar
1 tbsp (15ml) cornstarch (cornflour)
1 slice ginger root, peeled and finely
   chopped

Break the egg into a bowl; cut the ends off a few snow peas (mange-tout) and place them half way round the egg to resemble the leaves of a flower. Finely shred the ham and arrange the shreds in the middle to make it look like a chrysanthemum. Warm up 1 tablespoon (15ml) lard in a *wok* or frying-pan and with one swift movement empty the bowl into the *wok* to be fried on one side until the egg just sets; lift the 'chrysanthemum' out.

Finely chop the pork and mix it with ½ tablespoon (10ml) rice wine or sherry, ½ teaspoon (2ml) salt, 1 teaspoon (5ml) sugar and 1 teaspoon (5ml) cornstarch (cornflour).

Spread the chicken leg out flat with the skin side down, score the meat with a criss-cross pattern (not too deep), then press the ground (minced) pork hard on top. Make sure it is stuck firmly to the chicken, and add a little more cornstarch (cornflour) to bind them together.

Heat another tablespoon (15ml) lard; fry the chicken-pork piece on both sides until golden; add rice wine or sherry, 1 teaspoon (5ml) sugar, soy sauce, finely chopped ginger root and a little water. Bring it to the boil, then reduce heat and simmer for about 40 minutes. Remove and cut it into three strips with the pork side up; place them on a serving dish.

Now steam the egg 'chrysanthemum' for 2 minutes. In the meantime, stir-fry the rest of the snow peas (mange-tout) with the remaining lard, salt and sugar. Arrange the peas around the chicken-pork pieces, and place the egg higher up in the middle. The egg is the 'bright moon' and the chicken-pork is the 'red pine'.

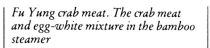

Fu Yung crab meat. The crab meat and egg-white mixture in the bamboo steamer

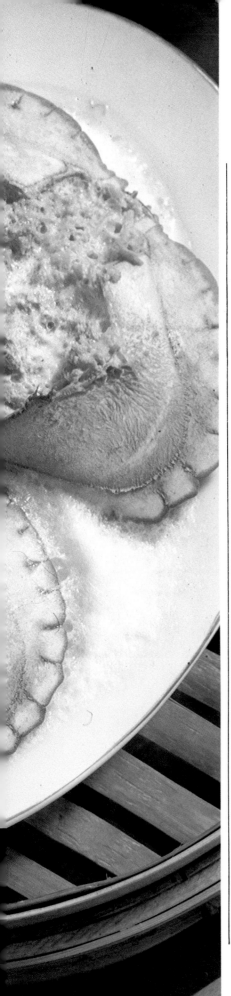

FU YUNG CRAB MEAT

This is another recipe from Suzhou. Ideally you should use freshwater crabs as their meat is much more delicate, but they are almost impossible to obtain in the West.

10 oz (275g) crab meat
3 tbsp (45ml) lard
2 tbsp (30 ml) rice wine (or sherry)
1 tbsp (15ml) soy sauce
1 tbsp (15ml) wine vinegar
1 tbsp (15ml) sugar
6 egg whites
1 tsp (5ml) cornstarch (cornflour)
2 cloves garlic, finely chopped
1 slice ginger root, peeled and finely
　　chopped
2 scallions (spring onions), finely
　　chopped
2 large crab shells (or 4 small ones)
3 tbsp (45ml) stock

Warm up about 2 tablespoons (30ml) lard; fry about half of the finely chopped ginger root and onions followed by the crab meat. Add rice wine or sherry, continue stirring until all the liquid has evaporated, then put the crab meat into the empty shells.

Beat the egg whites with salt and a little water until foamy; pour on top of the crab meat and steam the stuffed shells vigorously for 6 minutes. By then the egg whites will have become solid. Remove and place them on a long serving dish.

Heat the last tablespoon (15ml) lard, add the finely chopped garlic together with the remaining onion and ginger root, followed by soy sauce, vinegar, sugar and stock. When it starts to bubble, add the cornstarch (cornflour) mixed with a little cold water. When it is smooth and thickened pour it over the crab meat and serve.

The sauce is poured over the crabs and they are ready to serve

Red-cooked shad. This shad is served on a cast-iron plate, and brought to the table still sizzling hot

RED-COOKED SHAD

The shad is a migratory fish which swims up the Yangtse from the Yellow Sea every spring to spawn somewhere near Zhenjiang. It is said that a shad found beyond Zhenjiang has less delicate meat.

1 shad (bass can be substituted)
    weighing about 1½ lb (0.75kg)
3 tbsp (45ml) lard
3 tbsp (45ml) soy sauce
1 tbsp (15ml) sugar
2 tbsp (30ml) rice wine (or sherry)
⅓ cup (2 oz, 50ml) bamboo shoots, cut
    into small slices
2–3 Chinese dried mushrooms, soaked
1 tsp (5ml) salt
2 scallions (spring onions)
2 slices ginger root, peeled
1 tbsp (15ml) cornstarch (cornflour)
1¼ cups (½ pt, 300ml) water

Clean the shad or bass, wash and dry it thoroughly. The fish can be prepared whole or cut into slices of uniform thickness.

Warm up the lard, coat the skin of fish with soy sauce and fry for 5 minutes. Turn it over, add the remaining soy sauce, sugar, rice wine or sherry, bamboo shoots, mushrooms, salt, onions, ginger root and water; bring it to the boil and bubble over a high heat for 5 minutes. Reduce heat and simmer for 15 minutes; by then the juice should be reduced somewhat. Remove the fish onto a plate, add the cornstarch (cornflour) to thicken the gravy, then pour it over the fish and serve.

CHICKEN AND NOODLES IN SOUP

⅓ cup (2 oz, 50g) cooked chicken meat
1½ cups (4 oz, 100g) egg noodles
½ cup (2 oz, 50g) cabbage or lettuce
    heart
1½ tbsp (25ml) lard
1 tbsp (15ml) soy sauce
½ tsp (2ml) salt
¼ tsp (1ml) monosodium glutamate
1¼ cups (½ pt, 300ml) stock

Dice the chicken into small cubes;

wash and cut the cabbage or lettuce heart into small bits.

Heat 1½ tablespoons (25ml) lard until smoking; stir-fry the cabbage heart for about 30 seconds; add the stock; bring it to the boil. Put in the noodles, cook for about 1 minute or until the noodles are soft; add monosodium glutamate, soy sauce, salt and chicken; stir with chopsticks, reduce heat and simmer for 2 minutes.

SHREDDED FISH AND CELERY

½ lb (225g) fish fillet or steak
2 cups (½ lb, 225g) celery heart
2 egg whites
1 tsp (5ml) salt
½ tbsp (10ml) rice wine (or sherry)
1 tsp (5ml) monosodium glutamate
2 tsp (10ml) sesame seed oil
1½ tbsp (25ml) soy sauce
½ tbsp (10ml) cornstarch
   (cornflour)
⅝ cup (¼ pt, 150ml) stock
lard for deep-frying

Garnish
⅙ cup (1 oz, 25g) cooked ham, cut into
   small shreds

Discard all skin and bones from the fish; cut it into match-size shreds; marinate it with rice wine or sherry, salt, egg whites and cornstarch (cornflour).

Parboil the celery heart for 1–2 minutes; cool it in cold water then cut it into small shreds. Place it on a serving plate; add ½ teaspoon (2ml) monosodium glutamate and 1 teaspoon sesame seed oil, mix well.

Deep-fry the fish shreds in lard over a medium heat for about 4 minutes; separate them with chopsticks or a fork. When all the shreds are floating on the surface of the lard, scoop them out and drain. Gently press them with a spatula, then put them to soak in the stock for a while to cool. Take them out and place on top of the celery. Garnish with ham shreds.

Make a dressing by mixing a tablespoon (15ml) stock with the soy sauce and the remaining monosodium glutamate and sesame seed oil. Pour it all over the dish and serve.

WATERMELON CHICKEN

This is a very complicated method of serving a very simply cooked dish. It requires skill that far exceeds even that of a really good cook. You will have to be an artist of the first order if you are not going to make a mess of the whole thing.

1 young chicken weighing about 2½ lb
(1.25kg)
1 watermelon weighing about 3½ lb
(1.5kg)
⅓ cup (2 oz, 50g) ham
⅓ cup (2 oz, 50g) bamboo shoots
2 tbsp (30ml) rice wine (or sherry)
1 tbsp (15ml) salt
2 slices of ginger root, peeled
3–4 Chinese dried mushrooms
2½–3 pt (about 1.5l) water

Clean the chicken well; place it in a pot and add the water. Bring to the boil; take the chicken out and plunge it into cold water, then place it in a large bowl.

Add salt and rice wine or sherry to the water in which the chicken has been boiled; skim off any scum. Pour the liquid over the chicken in the bowl. Soak the dried mushrooms for 20 minutes, remove the hard stalks. Add the soaked mushrooms, the ham, bamboo shoots and ginger root to the bowl; place in a steamer and steam for 2 hours.

Slice off a piece across the top of the watermelon; scoop out the 'flesh' from the lower part using a plastic or porcelain spoon, then carve some pretty pictures on the skin. Blanch the melon in boiling water, cool in cold water, then take it out and place it in a bowl.

Now place the steamed chicken inside the watermelon, breast side up. Cut the ham and bamboo shoots into small slices; place these and the mushrooms on top of the chicken; fill the melon with the chicken soup. Cut up the scooped-out melon; and add this to the soup. Place the 'lid' on top, using tooth picks to secure it, then steam it for 10 minutes. Carefully carry the whole melon to the table; remove the tooth picks, take off the 'lid' and serve.

If you can manage it, this is a real *pièce de resistance*.

FRIED PRAWN-BALLS

1 lb (0.5kg) uncooked shrimps
(prawns)
¼ cup (2 oz, 50g) water chestnuts,
peeled
2½ tbsp (1½ oz, 40ml) glutinous rice
powder
1 egg
1 tsp (5ml) salt
1 tbsp (15ml) rice wine (or sherry)
½ tsp (2ml) monosodium glutamate
oil for deep-frying

Dip:
2 tbsp (30ml) tomato sauce
salt and Sichuan pepper

Shell the shrimps (prawns); dry them well and marinate with salt for 5 minutes, then chop them into rice-grain-size pieces.

Fried prawn-balls garnished with cucumber slices and fresh coriander

Finely chop the water chestnuts; mix them with the shrimps (prawns), egg, glutinous rice powder, rice wine or sherry and monosodium glutamate; blend well.

Heat the oil in a deep-fryer, before it gets too hot, take a handful of the shrimp (prawn) mixture and squeeze it through your fist between the thumb and forefinger to form a ball about the size of a walnut. Scoop it off with a wet spoon and dip it into the oil (you should be able to make about 20 balls); fry for about 2 minutes. Stir to separate them and when they start to turn golden, scoop them out and drain.

Serve with the tomato sauce, and salt and pepper mixed as a dip.

Buddhist & Taoist dishes

We have already (page 66) looked at one religious school of cooking, the Moslem School. There is another, the Buddhist and Taoist School – their vegetarian foods are found throughout the country.

A good Buddhist abhors the killing of any living creature and would certainly never dream of eating meat in any form. This philosophy was grafted into the scientific and hygienic study of vegetables which was a part of Taoism. So a new school of cuisine was formed – at the same time varied, nutritious and delicious.

Chinese vegetarians are not allowed anything remotely connected with animals, including eggs or milk. They get their protein mainly from the soy bean and its by-products, such as bean – curd and imitation meat. Curiously these imitation meats (known as vegetarian-meat, -chicken, -fish and so on) bear an amazing resemblance to their fleshy counterparts in form, texture and flavor.

For some unknown reason, the best vegetarian restaurants are to be found in Shanghai – a thriving commercial center and seaport which had a very racy reputation in the past. Most dishes are too complicated for the untrained layman even to contemplate; others require such weird ingredients that they could put a person off food for life! I have selected two dishes: one very simple, the other a little more unusual.

THE TWO WINTERS
The 'Two Winters' are winter bamboo shoots and winter mushrooms.

1 oz (25g) Chinese dried mushrooms
⅔ cup (4 oz, 100g) winter bamboo
*   shoots*
2 tbsp (30ml) soy sauce
½ tbsp (10ml) sugar
1 tsp (5ml) monosodium glutamate
4 tbsp (60ml) mushroom stock
3 tbsp (45ml) vegetable oil
½ tbsp (10ml) cornstarch (cornflour)
½ tbsp (10ml) sesame seed oil

Try to select mushrooms of uniform small size. Soak them in warm water; squeeze dry and keep the water as mushroom stock.

Cut the shoots into thin slices not much bigger than the mushrooms.

Heat up the oil until it smokes; stir-fry the mushrooms and bamboo shoots for about 1 minute; add soy sauce and sugar, stir, add mushroom stock. Bring it to the boil and cook for about 2 minutes; add monosodium glutamate and cornstarch (cornflour). Blend well, then add sesame seed oil and serve.

The Two Winters. Bamboo shoots and Chinese mushrooms are two of the most common ingredients in Chinese cooking

BUDDHA'S FRY

The original recipe calls for eighteen different ingredients (mainly mixed vegetables to represent the eighteen Buddhas (*Luohan* in Chinese), but it is more common to use only eight to ten.

½ oz (15g) Chinese dried mushrooms
½ oz (15g) Golden Needles (dried Tiger Lily)
½ oz (15g) Wooden Ears
1 oz (25g) dried bean-curd skin
⅓ cup (2 oz, 50g) fresh straw mushrooms
⅓ cup (2 oz, 50g) bamboo shoots
⅓ cup (2 oz, 50g) Chinese cabbage or celery
⅓ cup (2 oz, 50g) snow peas (mange-tout), or French beans
⅓ cup (2 oz, 50g) broccoli or cauliflower
⅓ cup (2 oz, 50g) carrots
4 tbsp (60ml) vegetable oil
2 tbsp (30ml) soy sauce
½ tbsp (10ml) sugar
1 tsp (5ml) monosodium glutamate
1 tbsp (15ml) cornstarch (cornflour)
⅝ cup (¼ pt, 150ml) mushroom stock

Soak all the dried ingredients in separate bowls; cut the larger dried mushrooms into 4 pieces, smaller ones can be left uncut. Cut the Golden Needles in half; tear the bean-curd skin into pieces roughly the same size as the Wooden Ears. Cut all the fresh vegetables into a roughly uniform size.

Heat up about 2 tablespoons (30ml) oil; stir-fry the dried mushrooms, Golden Needles, bamboo shoots, snow peas (mange-tout) and carrots for about 1 minute, add about half the soy sauce and sugar; stir a few times more, then add about half of the monosodium glutamate and stock. Cover and cook for about 1 minute; mix in ½ tablespoon (10ml) cornstarch (cornflour) to thicken the gravy, then dish it out and keep warm.

Meanwhile heat up the remaining oil and stir-fry the other ingredients (i.e. Wooden Ears and bean-curd skin, fresh mushrooms, Chinese cabbage and broccoli), add the remaining soy sauce, sugar, monosodium glutamate and stock. Cover and cook for about 1 minute, then add ½ tablespoon (10ml) cornstarch (cornflour), blend

well and put it on top of the first group of vegetables. Garnish with sesame seed oil and serve.

Ideally these two groups of vegetables should be cooked simultaneously, for there will be a loss of quality if the gap between the finishing time of each is too long.

Left: *Buddha's fry ready to serve.*
Above: *Some of the ingredients used to make it.* **Top:** *Golden Needles;* **middle:** *Wooden Ears;* **bottom:** *dried bean-curd*

Hangzhou dishes

From Shanghai, we went on to Hangzhou (Hangchow), famous for its beautiful West Lake and many other delights. Our hotel was right by the lake and the view from our window was truly breathtaking. There is an old Chinese saying: 'In heaven, there is Paradise; on earth we have Suzhou and Hangzhou'; it refers not only to the scenic beauty of these two places, but also to the gastronomic delights and the general well-being of the local inhabitants. For instance, their silk and embroideries are world famous, and people from other parts of China always had the notion that everybody in Suzhou and Hangzhou wore only silk and satin and ate delicacies all the time. It all started during the Song dynasty (960–1279) when the capital was moved from Kaifeng to Hangzhou after 1127. This was one of the most culturally developed and economically prosperous periods in Chinese history. The history of Hangzhou, however, goes back more than 2,000 years, and its prosperity must have developed in the seventh century with the building of the Grand Canal, which linked it with the ancient capital Luoyang.

'More beautiful than Venice!' Marco Polo is supposed to have exclaimed on seeing Hangzhou in the thirteenth century. He stated that it was the greatest city to be found in the world, 'where so many pleasures may be found that one fancies oneself in Paradise'. Marco Polo is credited with introducing pasta dishes to Europe, not to mention ice-cream, which was invented in Hangzhou.

Like many other great cities all over the world, Hangzhou suffered many catastrophes in its history including total destruction in 1862. The city never recovered its past glory but, today, the West Lake, enclosed by wooded hills on three sides and as smooth and glistening as a mirror, reflects the surrounding landscape to form a panorama of great beauty, a testimony of the former splendor of Hangzhou.

Summer house in a park in Suzhou. The curved roof is typical of the old Chinese style of architecture which remained unchanged for centuries.

You can hire either an open-topped boat which gives you a panoramic view of the lake, or a covered boat which offers you a restricted view through the windows but the comfort of soft seats and a table, with services of hot tea and snacks.

To me this was sheer bliss, and after the hustle and bustle of a big city like Shanghai one truly feels as though in heaven on earth.

Legends and literary associations abound here, and for centuries Hangzhou with its West Lake seemed to have a special attraction for poets and artists. The name of each scenic spot has a romantic story behind it,

DRAGON WELL TEA

Right: *Very little of this superb tea is exported. If you are lucky you might get some in a specialist Chinese store.* **Below:** *Freshly-picked tea-leaves in the process of being dried.* **Bottom:** *This old postcard shows the site of the Dragon Well.*

中國綠茶
龍井

123

Center: *A panoramic view of the West Lake, Hangzhou– one of the souvenirs of my childhood visit. The Dragon Well is the small red building, top left of the picture. The Su causeway cuts across from left to right.* **Below:** *Summer house on an islet in the West Lake.* **Right:** *Jade fountain fish pond* (**front**)*; the Su causeway* (**behind**) *in the 1930s.* **Far right:** *The Su causeway, an aerial view.* **Lower right:** *Lotus flowers in bloom – their roots* (**below**) *can be eaten raw or cooked.*

places like 'Peak Flown from Afar', 'Pagoda of Six Harmonies', 'Listening to Orioles in the Willows', 'Autumn Moon on the Tranquil Lake' or 'Three Pools Mirroring the Moon'. Then there is Bai Causeway named after the great Tang poet Bai Chuyi (772–846), and Su Causeway named after Su Tung-po (1036–1101) whose recipe for lamb we have already sampled (p.67), and there will be more about him later (see p.135).

Tea from West Lake's 'Dragon

圖全湖西州杭

景風一第下天

Well' (*Longjing*) is considered by many connoisseurs to be the best green tea in China. The lotus seeds and roots from the lake are particularly delicious; normally lotus roots are eaten cooked as a vegetable but those from the West Lake are so delicate that they can be eaten raw as a fruit.

The most famous dish of all is the fish from the West Lake. There are several ways of cooking it; I have given two examples on pages 129-130.

A fish-farm in Zhejiang province. The inland lakes provide a great variety of fish for the many Chinese fish dishes.

STEAMED FISH

Carp, perch or bream are best, but bass or trout can be substituted.

1 fish weighing about 1½ lb (0.75kg)
⅙ cup (1 oz, 25g) cooked ham
⅙ cup (1 oz, 25g) bamboo shoots
2 large Chinese dried mushrooms, soaked
⅛ cup (1 oz, 25g) pork fat
1½ tsp (7ml) salt
1 tsp (5ml) sugar
½ tsp (2ml) monosodium glutamate
½ tbsp (10ml) Shaoxing wine or sherry
2 scallions (spring onions)
2 slices ginger root
2 tbsp (30ml) lard

Scale and gut the fish; clean and dry well. Trim off fins and tail, score the body three or four times half way down, then place it on an oblong dish. Cut the ham, bamboo shoots, mushrooms and pork fat into match-size shreds; arrange them in four different rows according to color in a star shape. Spread the salt, sugar, monosodium glutamate, wine, lard, onions and ginger root evenly on top of the fish. Steam vigorously for 20 minutes; discard the onions and ginger root before serving.

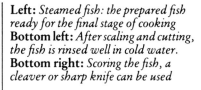

Left: *Steamed fish: the prepared fish ready for the final stage of cooking*
Bottom left: *After scaling and cutting, the fish is rinsed well in cold water.*
Bottom right: *Scoring the fish, a cleaver or sharp knife can be used*

As West Lake fish is hard to obtain outside China, you can adapt the recipe and use any ordinary freshwater fish, as in this picture. Our chef has modified the dressing too, adding bamboo shoots, peas and Wooden Ears

WEST LAKE FISH IN VINEGAR SAUCE

The West Lake fish is also known as grass carp, a species of mirror carp with very delicate flesh. It is the usual practice to keep the fish in a specially made cage in the lake without any food for one or two days in order to rid it of its muddy taste.

1 mirror carp weighing about 1½ lb (0.75kg)
2 slices ginger root, peeled and finely chopped
1 tbsp (15ml) Shaoxing wine or sherry
2 tbsp (30ml) soy sauce
2 tbsp (30ml) sugar
1 tbsp (15ml) vinegar
1 tbsp (15ml) cornstarch (cornflour)
2–2½ pt (about 1l) water

Scale and gut the fish; clean well. Split it in half lengthways with its back bone still attached to one half, known as the male side (the half without the bone is known as the female side).

Score the 'male' side through the skin five times not quite as deep as the bone, but cut all the way down at the third cut so it becomes two halves. Then score the 'female' side through the flesh not quite as deep as the skin.

Bring the water to the boil, put in the fish opened out with skin side up and the tail piece on top, but try to keep the head out of the water. Place the lid on and boil rapidly for 5 minutes; ladle out most of the water leaving about ⅝ cup (¼ pt, 150ml) in the pan. Add soy sauce, wine and half the ginger root, then immediately scoop the fish out; place it on a plate still with skin side up and the tail piece restored to its original position. Add sugar and the remaining ginger root together with the cornstarch (cornflour) mixed with the vinegar; stir to make a thickish smooth gravy. Pour it all over the fish and serve. This is the traditional way of cooking West Lake fish, which is supposed to resemble crab in its flavor.

HAM AND BROAD BEANS

Ham from Jinhua (Kin Hwa) further down south in Zhejiang has a wide reputation. It is unique to China. You may substitute Virginia or Parma ham.

4 oz (100g) best ham
2 cups (½ lb 225g) peeled, fresh
 broad beans
2 tbsp (30ml) lard
1 tsp (5ml) salt
¼ tsp (1ml) monosodium glutamate
1 tsp (5ml) sugar
½ tsp (2 ml) cornstarch (cornflour)
4 tbsp (60ml) stock

Use the young, tender broad beans when in season. Peel off the skin. Dice the ham into small cubes.

Warm up the lard and stir-fry the broad beans and ham at the same time. Add sugar, salt and stock, continue cooking for a while, then add monosodium glutamate and the cornstarch (cornflour) mixed with a little cold water; blend well and serve.

Ham and broad beans. The ham is evenly sliced into pieces roughly the same size as the beans

Rapidly-fried shrimps, served in their shells with a strong Chinese spirit

RAPIDLY-FRIED SHRIMPS (PRAWNS)

Shrimps (prawns) from the West Lake are succulent and tender; substitute freshwater shrimps (prawns) where available rather than sea varieties for a more authentic result.

½ lb (225g) uncooked, unshelled
    shrimps (prawns)
1½ tbsp (10ml) soy sauce
1 tbsp (15ml) Shaoxing wine or sherry
½ tbsp (10ml) sugar
½ tbsp (10ml) vinegar
1 stick ginger root, peeled and finely
    chopped
1 scallion (spring onion), finely
    chopped
2½ cups (1 pt, 600ml) lard for
    deep-frying

Trim the shrimps (prawns), but keep the shell on. Dry well.

Heat the lard in a *wok* and when it is bubbling deep-fry the shrimps (prawns) twice (3–4 seconds only each time); scoop out and drain.

Pour out all the lard, then return the shrimps (prawns) to the same *wok*. Add soy sauce, wine sugar, onions and ginger root; stir a few times; add vinegar and serve.

EIGHT TREASURE BEAN-CURD

This recipe used to be called 'Prince's Bean-Curd' and originally appeared in *Sui-yuan Shihtan* ('Recipes of Sui-yuan') by the eighteenth century man of letters and gourmet, Yuan Mei. It has been modified somewhat by the chefs of a leading restaurant by the West Lake. Readers might be intrigued by the use of butter among the ingredients, but only canned butter was suggested as fresh butter is very hard to come by in China.

2 cakes of bean-curd
⅓ cup (2 oz, 50g) cooked ham, finely
    chopped
1 tbsp (15ml) frozen lard
½ tbsp (10ml) cornstarch (cornflour)
1 tbsp (15ml) butter
⅙ cup (1 oz, 25g) cooked chicken
    meat, finely chopped
2 Chinese dried mushrooms, soaked,
    finely chopped
3 egg whites
1 tsp (5ml) salt
½ tsp (2 ml) monosodium glutamate
⅝ cup (¼ pt, 150ml) chicken stock
2 tbsp (30ml) lard
1 tsp (5ml) sesame seed oil

Chop up the bean-curd; add 1½ egg whites and salt; mix well. Add the remaining egg whites, frozen lard, butter, cornstarch (cornflour), monosodium glutamate and a little water; beat until stiff.

Heat the lard in a *wok*, put in about half the chicken stock followed by the bean-curd mixed with the remaining chicken stock. Stir for about 1 minute until smooth, add the chicken meat, about half of the ham and mushrooms, blend well and garnish with the remaining ham and sesame seed oil before serving.

Above: *Fresh bean-curd on a Chinese market stall*

Bamboo shoots with shrimp (prawn) roe. The roe gives a subtle taste, but shrimp sauce may be used instead

'DRAGON-WELL' SHRIMPS (PRAWNS)

The original recipe called for the shrimps to be cooked with tea-leaves. The exquisite flavor of 'Dragon-Well' tea has to be tasted to be believed, and the fresh shrimps (prawns) from the West Lake also have a truly superlative flavor; but to mix these two together is something I personally find difficult to approve, so I have omitted the tea-leaves from this recipe.

1 lb (0.5kg) freshwater shrimps (prawns)
1 egg white
1 tbsp (15ml) Shaoxing wine or sherry
1/4 tsp (1ml) monosodium glutamate
1 tsp (5ml) salt
1 tbsp (15ml) cornstarch (cornflour)
1 scallion (spring onion), cut into 1 in (2.5cm) lengths
lard for deep-frying

'Dragon-Well' shrimps (prawns). Be careful not to overcook the prawns during the last stage, otherwise they will toughen and lose their tender texture. There is a picture of the Dragon-Well on page 123.

Shell the shrimps (prawns), put them in cold water and stir with chopsticks for 2–3 minutes. Change the water two or three times, then drain. Mix them with the salt, monosodium glutamate, egg white and the cornstarch (cornflour); marinate for 3 hours.

Heat the lard and deep-fry the shrimps (prawns), separate them with chopsticks after 15 seconds or so, scoop them out and drain. Pour off the excess lard, return the shrimps (prawns) to the *wok*, add the wine, and stir a few times. It is then ready to serve.

BAMBOO SHOOTS WITH SHRIMP ROE

Another specialty of the region is bamboo shoots which are fat and round with a color like ivory, with tender and crunchy flesh.

2²/₃ cups (1 lb, 450g) winter bamboo shoots
1 tbsp (15ml) shrimp (prawn) roe
1/2 tbsp (10ml) sugar
1 1/2 tbsp (25ml) rice wine (or sherry)
2 tbsp (30ml) soy sauce
1/2 tsp (2ml) monosodium glutamate
1 tbsp (15ml) cornstarch (cornflour)
lard for deep-frying

Peel the bamboo shoots; discard the tough parts at the root, then cut into thin slices the size of a stamp.

Heat the lard; deep-fry the bamboo shoots for about 2 minutes; turn into a sieve to drain.

Put about 1 tablespoon (15ml) lard back into the *wok*, put in shrimp roe, bamboo shoots, soy sauce, rice wine or sherry and sugar, in that order. Add a little boiling water (about 2–3 tablespoons (30–45ml)). Place a lid on; reduce heat and cook for 3 minutes. Now add monosodium glutamate and the cornstarch (cornflour) mixed with a little cold water; increase heat to high; stir a few times to blend it well, serve.

133

FU-YANG PORK

This recipe, dating back over a thousand years, was only recently discovered in Hangzhou.

6 oz (150kg) pork fillet
¼ cup (2 oz, 50g) pork fat
20 shrimps (prawns), peeled, uncooked
1 tsp (5ml) Sichuan peppercorns
2 tbsp (30ml) soy sauce
¼ tsp (1ml) monosodium glutamate
1 tbsp (15ml) rice wine (or sherry)
¾ cup (6 fl. oz, 175ml) sesame seed oil
for deep-frying

Cut the pork into twenty thin pieces of roughly the same size. Cut the pork fat into twenty pieces too; place a piece of pork fat on each piece of pork. Use the flat side of a cleaver to tap the pork and fat together gently, then place a peeled shrimp (prawn) on top of that and give it a tap.

Bring the sesame seed oil to boiling point; toss in the Sichuan peppercorns and scoop them out after 2–3 seconds when they turn dark. Using a wire basket or a large Chinese perforated spoon, lower the pork into hot oil to deep-fry for 1–2 seconds; take out to let the oil get hot again, then lower

once more. Repeat this once or twice more, then pour off the oil and put the pork pieces flat in the pan. Add wine or sherry, soy sauce and monosodium glutamate, cook for 3–4 seconds then arrange them carefully on a plate.

BACON AND BAMBOO SHOOT SOUP

4 oz (100g) unsmoked fatty (streaky) bacon in one piece
1 cup (6 oz, 175g) bamboo shoot tips
½ cup (2 oz, 50g) seasonal greens
1 tbsp (15ml) rice wine (or sherry)
½ tsp (2ml) monosodium glutamate
1 tsp (5ml) salt
1 tbsp (15ml) lard
2½ cups (1 pt, 600ml) water

Dice the bacon into small cubes and the bamboo shoot tips into small triangles.

Bring water to the boil; put in both the bacon and bamboo shoots at the same time; add wine or sherry, then reduce heat and simmer for 10 minutes. Add greens, monosodium glutamate and salt; increase heat to high again and when the soup starts to boil put in the lard and serve.

The 'Three Whites' Assembly, garnished with peas to give a touch of color.

THE 'THREE WHITES' ASSEMBLY

4 oz (100g) abalone
4 oz (100g) white asparagus (canned)
⅔ cup (4 oz, 100g) winter bamboo shoot tips
¼ cup (2 oz, 50g) green peas
2 tbsp (30ml) lard
1 tsp (5ml) salt
1 tbsp (15ml) rice wine or sherry
1 tsp (5ml) sugar
1 tsp (5ml) cornstarch (cornflour)
½ cup (4 fl oz, 100ml) stock

Drain the abalone and asparagus. Cut the bamboo shoot tips half-way through so that they open up like a flower petal.

Warm the lard in a *wok* or pan and stir-fry the bamboo shoot 'flowers' for a short while. Add the abalone and asparagus together with salt, rice wine or sherry, sugar and stock; when it starts to bubble, add cornstarch (cornflour) mixed in a little water. Garnish with the green peas, and serve when the gravy thickens.

TUNG-PO PORK

There are several different recipes for this famous dish. Since Mr. Su Tung-po actually lived in Hangzhou for a number of years, this may well be the authentic one. At any rate, my grandmother used to cook it this way, and that is good enough for me.

10 oz (275g) fresh belly of pork
1 tbsp (15ml) crystal sugar
2 tbsp (30ml) soy sauce
2 tbsp (30ml) rice wine (or sherry)
2 scallions (spring onions)
2 slices ginger root, peeled

Cut the pork into four equal squares. Put enough cold water in a sand-pot (or casserole) to cover the meat; bring it to the boil, then blanch the meat for 5 minutes. Take it out and rinse in cold water.

Discard the water in which the meat has been blanched; place a bamboo rack at the bottom of the pot, then place the meat skin side down in it; add crystal sugar, soy sauce and rice wine or sherry. Place the onions and ginger root on top; seal the lid tightly with flour and water paste and cook gently for at least 2 hours or until tender. Discard the ginger root and onions and transfer the meat into a bowl, skin side up this time, with three pieces on the bottom layer and one piece on top. Pour the juice over them, cover and steam vigorously for at least 2 hours before serving.

The partly-cooked Tung-po pork is prepared for steaming

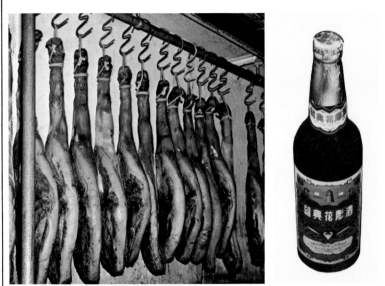

Before leaving Zhejiang, mention must be made of two other famous regional products: the yellow wine of Shaoxing (Shao Hsing) and ham from Jinhua (Kin Hwa). Both names are so illustrious that they are synonymous with superlative quality and are often 'borrowed' by imitators throughout China.

Yellow wine is the term commonly used for rice wine because of its color. It is very like a dry sherry both in appearance and flavor, though they taste quite different. Dry sherry is best served chilled while rice wine should be warmed up. Rice wine does not give you a hangover the morning after!

To return to Shaoxing, the best-known yellow wine there is called *Hua Tiao*, which means 'carved flower'. It is the name given to the pretty pattern carved on the urns in which wines are stored in underground cellars for maturing. The best ones are supposed to be over a hundred years old, but those offered for sale on the market nowadays are probably about 10 years old and deep amber in color. Once I tasted one that was over 40 years old; when the seal of the urn was broken the bouquet was so tremendously powerful that it filled the entire room and lingered in the air for hours afterwards.

All yellow wines are made from a blend of glutinous rice, millet and ordinary rice, but what gives Shaoxing wine its unique flavor is the special type of yeast used, the mineral water taken from the local lake and the spring water from a nearby stream.

Another name for Shaoxing wine is 'Daughter's Wine' because it used to be the local custom to store a few urns of *Hua Tiao* on the birth of a daughter in order to drink them at her wedding feast (normally 18 to 20 years later). It is interesting to compare this charming tradition with the more male-oriented English custom of the past of laying down port for a son.

The ham from Jinhua owes its well-deserved reputation to the special species of pigs reared in its surrounding towns, and to the elaborate method of curing employed. If kept properly, the ham can last up to three years without any deterioration in flavor. The meat has a bright red color like the flame of a fire, which is why the Chinese name for ham is 'fire leg'. It is succulent and fragrant with a natural sweet flavor, not sugary sweet but with an indefinable and delectable quality as in 'sweet air'.

Fujian dishes

Zhejiang is linked in the south with the province of Fujian (Fukien), and the two provinces are collectively known as the South East Coastal Uplands. The inclusion of Fujian in the Eastern School is purely geographical, for here we leave the sophistication of Shanghai and Zhejiang behind, and the accent is on locally produced delicacies, particularly seafood and agricultural products. As southern Fujian borders Guangdong (Kwangtung), its culinary art is strongly influenced by its great neighbor, so much so that cookery writers would very often group Fujian and Guangdong together as China's Southern School of cuisine – I can see their point. There are others who would place Fujian on its own as an individual school, and I will not quarrel with that either.

Fujian's culinary centers are all situated on the coast. They are, from north to south, Fuzhou (Foochow), Quanzhou (Chuanchow), Xiamen (Amoy) and Zhangzhou (Changchow).

Fuzhou, the provincial capital, is famous for its lacquerware, which became identified with the traditional Chinese export trade in the past. Here are three very simple recipes from the specialties of the region.

SALT AND PEPPER SPARERIBS

10 oz (275g) pork spareribs
1 egg
1 tsp (5ml) salt
2 tsp (10ml) cornstarch (cornflour)
½ tbsp (10ml) Kao Liang spirit (or
    1½ tbsp (25ml) rice wine or sherry)
½ tsp (2ml) five-spice powder
1 tsp (5ml) Sichuan pepper, freshly
    ground
oil for deep-frying

Chop the spareribs into small pieces; marinate with salt, pepper, Kao Liang spirit and five-spice powder for 15 minutes. Add egg and cornstarch (cornflour); mix well.

Heat the oil until hot; deep fry the spareribs for 3 minutes, then soak them in cold oil for 1 minute. Just before serving, crisp them in hot oil once more.

Above: *Drunken spareribs, succulent and juicy, are an ideal accompaniment for wine*

DRUNKEN SPARERIBS

10 oz (275g) pork spareribs
1 tbsp (15ml) cornstarch (cornflour)
2 tbsp (30ml) rice wine (or sherry)
1 tbsp (15ml) curry powder
1 tsp (5ml) sugar
1 tbsp (15ml) soy sauce
1 scallion (spring onion), finely
    chopped
1 clove garlic, finely chopped
1 small green pepper, shredded
1 small red pepper, shredded
1 tbsp (15ml) sesame seed oil
1 tbsp (15ml) tomato paste (purée)
oil for deep-frying

Chop the spareribs into small pieces; mix in cornstarch (cornflour), wine or sherry and curry powder. Deep fry in hot oil for 3 minutes; scoop them out and drain. Pour the excess oil out, put in the finely chopped onion and garlic, followed by shredded red and green peppers; add sugar, soy sauce, tomato paste (purée) and sesame seed oil. Stir to make a smooth sauce, then put in the spareribs; blend together well; serve.

Left: *Salt and pepper spareribs. The leftover marinade can be made into a coating sauce*

SNOW-FLOWER CHICKEN

This dish comes from Xiamen (Amoy), Fujian's second largest city. It used to be an island but now a causeway links it with the mainland. Both Xiamen and Fuzhou are among the original treaty ports opened to foreign trade in 1842.

3 cups (8 oz, 225g) glutinous rice
1 young chicken about 2 lb (1kg)
⅓ tbsp (10ml) salt
1 tbsp (15ml) rice wine (or sherry)
1 egg white
1½ tbsp (25ml) cornstarch (cornflour)
1 tsp (5ml) lard or oil

Wash and rinse the glutinous rice, soak in cold water for 2 hours.

Chop the chicken into four large pieces, then remove all skin and bones. Cut a criss-cross pattern on the surface of each piece, then cut into 1 in (2.5cm) squares; marinate with salt and wine or sherry for 5 minutes.

Make a paste with egg white and cornstarch (cornflour).

Spread out the glutinous rice on a plate, dip each piece of chicken in the paste then roll it in the glutinous rice to make sure that the entire piece is covered by rice. Place it on a large plate greased with lard or oil, leaving a small space between each piece of chicken. Steam vigorously for 40 minutes; remove and pile the pieces on a dish. Pour the juice over.

OIL-SOAKED DUCK

1 duckling weighing over 3 lb (1.5kg)
3 tbsp (45ml) rice wine (or sherry)
6 tbsp (90ml) stock
3½ tbsp (55ml) sugar
3 tbsp (45ml) soy sauce
a few fennel seeds
1 slice ginger root
5 tbsp (75ml) orange juice
oil for deep frying

Serving:
2 tomatoes
6 scallions (spring onions), white parts only
8 oz (225g) Chinese pickled turnip (or radish)

Clean the duck; discard the pinions (wing tips); blanch in a large pot of boiling water; place it on a long dish with its stomach side up. Mix 2 tablespoons (30ml) rice wine or sherry with 2 tablespoons (30ml) sugar, stock, soy sauce, fennel seeds and ginger root; pour it all over the duck; steam it vigorously for 15 minutes. Pierce the stomach with a sharp-pointed chopstick or knitting needle a dozen times or so; turn the bird over, steam for another 15 minutes, then turn it over once more and steam for a further 15 minutes. Now deep-fry it in hot oil until dark brown. Remove.

Pour off the excess oil, put in the remaining rice wine or sherry, sugar, orange juice and about one-third of the juice from the duck. Add the duck; turn it round a few times to make sure that the bird is well coated, then remove and chop it into small pieces. On a serving plate, rearrange it in the shape of the original duck; pour the juice over it.

Serve it with sliced tomato, shredded onion and pickled turnip or radish. You can make your own pickle as follows. Cut some turnip or radish into thin slices; marinate with a little salt for a while, squeeze out the liquid, then in a jar mix it with sugar and vinegar and leave for several hours.

'THREE FAIRIES' IN THEIR OWN JUICE

This dish originated from Zhangzhou, a former commercial centre which has been supplanted by Xiamen in importance. The city is known for its satin and sugar products.

1 young chicken (poussin) weighing about 1½ lb (0.75kg)
1 duckling weighing about 2½ lb (1.25kg)
½ leg of pork weighing about 2 lb (1kg)
1 oz (25g) Chinese dried mushrooms, soaked
1⅓ cups (8 oz, 225g) bamboo shoots, sliced
1½ tbsp (25ml) salt
5 cups (2 pt, 1.2l) duck, chicken and pork stock

Clean the chicken, duck and pork well; parboil them together in the stock (which is made from duck, chicken and pork in the first place, thus the term 'in their own juice' in the name of this dish).

Place the chicken, duck and pork in a large bowl or deep dish; add soaked mushrooms, bamboo shoot slices and salt; steam vigorously for at least 2½ hours.

Obviously you will need a very large steamer for this dish. Those who would like to try it out at home can reduce the quantity of the ingredients by three-quarters.

'CASSIA' CRAB

The recipe is from Quanzhou, formerly known as Tsinkiang, one of China's leading ports during the Song (960–1279) and Yuan (Mongol; 1279–1368) dynasties. Like Xiamen, Quanzhou is the place of origin of many Chinese emigrants overseas.

½ lb (225g) crab meat
½ cup (2 oz, 50g) water chestnuts
⅓ cup (2 oz, 50g) bamboo shoots
3–4 Chinese dried mushrooms, soaked
3–4 scallions (spring onions)
¼ cup (2 oz, 50g) pork fat
4 eggs
3 tbsp (45ml) lard
½ tbsp (10ml) salt
1½ tbsp (25ml) rice wine (or sherry)

Garnish:
freshly ground Sichuan pepper
Chinese parsley (fresh coriander)

Finely shred the crab meat, water chestnuts, bamboo shoots, mushrooms, onions and pork fat; add them to the beaten eggs with salt; mix well.

Warm up the lard; put in the egg mixture; scramble for 4–5 minutes; add rice wine or sherry, dish it out. Garnish with freshly ground pepper; place a little parsley on each side of the plate and serve.

'LYCHEE' PORK

Although lychee is one of the local products it is not used in this dish – the pork is cut in such a way that, when cooked, it resembles the fruit.

10 oz (275g) lean pork
1 tbsp (15ml) cornstarch (cornflour)
1 tbsp (15ml) sugar
1½ tsp (7ml) vinegar
1 tbsp (15ml) soy sauce
2 scallions (spring onions), white parts only
1 tsp (5ml) sesame seed oil
2 tbsp (30ml) stock
oil for deep-frying

First cut the pork into large slices of ¼ in (1cm) thickness; score a crisscross pattern on each slice, then cut them into diamond-shape pieces; coat each piece with cornstarch (cornflour). Cut the onion whites into short lengths.

Heat up the oil, pùt in the pork piece by piece and deep fry 3 minutes. The pieces should curl up slightly to look like lychee. Scoop them out and drain.

Pour off the excess oil; put in onions, sugar, vinegar, soy sauce, and stock. When it starts to bubble, add the pork and sesame seed oil; blend well; serve.

'LET A HUNDRED FLOWERS BLOOM' CHICKEN

Do not think I am trying to cash in on this topical quotation – this is the original name. The 'flowers' are the scallions, leeks and green peppers cut into the shapes of flowers. If you find the decoration is too much bother, just ignore it.

1 young chicken (poussin) weighing about 1½ lb (0.75kg)
½ lb (225g) shrimps (prawns), uncooked
¼ cup (2 oz, 50g) pork fat
¼ cup (1 oz, 25g) water chestnuts
¼ cup (1 oz, 25g) celery
1 egg white
2½ tsp (12ml) salt
½ tsp (2ml) oil
2 tsp (10ml) cornstarch (cornflour)
1 tsp (5ml) sesame seed oil
5 scallions (spring onions)
1 leek
1 green pepper

Clean the chicken and boil in water for about 30–40 minutes; take out and discard the skin and bones.

Shell the shrimps (prawns), finely grind (mince) them together with chicken and pork fat. Add egg white, mix well, next add water chestnuts, and then the celery finely chopped with 2 teaspoons (10ml) salt.

Grease a dish with oil; spread out the chicken and shrimp (prawn) mixture flat on it, about ½ in (1cm) thick; smooth the surface. Steam for 15 minutes; take out and cut into small pieces not much bigger than a stamp; arrange them on a serving dish in neat rows overlapping each other rather like a fish's scales.

Heat in a pan about ½ cup (100ml) stock in which chicken has been cooked. Add ½ teaspoon (2ml) salt, sesame seed oil and cornstarch (cornflour), stir to make a smooth gravy, pour it all over the chicken.

Decorate the edge of the plate with the onions, leek and green pepper cut into shapes of various flowers.

'Cassia' Crab. The small picture in the left corner shows a spray of cassia in bloom. Chinese egg dishes are often given the name 'cassia' because of the yellow color

FUJIAN WINE AND TEA

In the area around Xiamen, where the climate is sub-tropical and the land particularly fertile, the people seem to devote all their leisure time to the art of cooking and eating. The soy sauce produced locally is generally regarded as the best in China.

Excellent yellow wine, almost as famous as Shaoxing wine, is produced at a place called Longyan (*Dragon Cliffs*) in southern Fujian; it is called *Chen Gang* (Sunken urn). Here the word 'sunken' means 'stored' because during the maturing process the wine urns are stored deep underground. Like Shaoxing wine, *Chen Gang* has a fragrant bouquet but tastes a little sweeter, a taste which lingers in the mouth long after swallowing. It is often used as a tonic, particularly by women during pregnancy and after confinement.

Fujian also produces a variety of teas of high quality. The best red tea in China is undoubtedly Wuyi Cliff tea, which is known as the bohea leaf in the West, from the Bohea Hills, a Western corruption of the name of the Wuyi Mountains, which lie on the borders of Fujian and Jiangxi (Kiangsi). It is said that, because the cliffs are so steep, monkeys were trained to climb them to pluck the tea leaves. One of the best-known varieties is called 'Iron Goddess of Mercy'; it has an exquisite fragrance with a very full flavor and is almost black in color, hence the name *iron*.

Top right and left: *The soaring cliffs of the Wuyi Mountains.* **Right:** *In this early nineteenth century print monkeys are trained to pick tea*

Jiangxi dishes

Strictly speaking, we have now covered all the major schools of Eastern Chinese food, but I simply must take you into Jiangxi (Kiangsi), the province where my parents come from and where I spent more than 10 years of my childhood.

Compared with Fujian, the landscape in Jiangxi is less rocky and assumes a more lustrous appearance. We are now in the heart of the 'Lands of Fish and Rice'. In the countryside, wherever you look you will see people either busily working the land or fishing in the shallow ponds and small

rivers. Here the style of cooking is 'national' rather than regional, yet retaining a style of its own.

In Jiangxi, we first lived in Nanchang, the provincial capital. After my parents left for Europe my sister and I were in the care of our maternal grandparents and, since my grandfather was a classical scholar, he was well versed in the art of gastronomy. Likewise, my grandmother was an excellent cook and she used to make delicious rice wine; I soon learned to like it. Here are a few recipes passed down by my grandmother.

STIR-FRIED CHICKEN CUBES
This is one of my favorites and very easy to prepare. It is my children's favorite, too.

½ lb (225g) chicken breast meat
1½ tsp (7ml) salt
1 egg white
1½ tbsp (25ml) cornstarch (cornflour)
2 scallions (spring onions)
1 small green pepper
1 small red pepper
1 tbsp (15ml) rice wine (or sherry)
3 tbsp (45ml) stock

Cut the chicken meat into cubes the size of playing dice, mix them with a little salt, the egg white and 1 tablespoon (15ml) cornstarch (cornflour), in that order which is very important.

Cut the onions, green and red peppers to the same size as the chicken cubes.

Deep-fry the chicken cubes in oil on a medium heat for a few seconds only; scoop out and drain.

Pour off the excess oil leaving about 1 tablespoon (15ml) in the *wok*; put in the onions, green and red peppers; stir and add the stock, wine or sherry, the remaining salt and cornstarch (cornflour); mix well then add the chicken cubes; blend together and serve. A few drops of sesame seed oil can be added as garnish.

'THREE CUP' CHICKEN
It is so called because you use one cup each of rice wine, soy sauce and lard. No other liquid whatever is added to this dish.

1 young chicken weighing about 2 lb (1kg)
1 cup (8 fl. oz, 225ml) rice wine (or sherry)
1 cup (8 fl. oz, 225ml) light soy sauce
1 cup (8 fl. oz, 225ml) lard
2 scallions (spring onions), white parts only
2 slices ginger root, peeled
1 tsp (5ml) sesame seed oil

Clean the chicken, cut it into small pieces about 3–4 in (7.5–10cm) square; cut the giblets (liver and gizzard) to

Left: *Stir-frying the chicken cubes in a wok*

the same size and put them together with the chicken, into a sand-pot (casserole).

Cut the onions and ginger root into small pieces; add to the pot; pour in the wine or sherry, soy sauce and lard. Cook gently for 30 minutes; by then there should be little juice left; add the sesame seed oil and serve it from the sand-pot.

BRAISED TEA-EGGS

This is actually a national dish with regional variations. Tea is one of Jiangxi's foremost products and my grandmother used to cook eggs in tea to be eaten as part of a snack.

12 eggs
2 tsp (10ml) salt
5 tbsp (75ml) soy sauce
2–3 star anise
1½ tbsp (25ml) red tea leaves (the better the quality tea, the better the result)

Boil the eggs in warm water for 5–10 minutes. Remove and gently tap the shell of each egg with a spoon until it is cracked finely all over. Put the eggs back into the pot and cover with fresh water. Add salt, soy sauce, star anise and tea leaves. Bring to the boil and simmer for 30–45 minutes. Let the eggs cool for a while in the liquid.

When you peel the shells off, the eggs will have a beautiful marbled pattern.

Braised tea-eggs: a very popular snack, usually eaten between meals

JIANXI TEA AND CERAMICS

Before leaving Jiangxi, a quick word about two world-famous products. The first is 'Cloud Mist', tea from the Lu Mountains, 5,000 ft (1520m) above sea level; the beautiful scenery and cool climate make Lu Shan a popular resort in the summer. The second product is the porcelain and ceramics of Jingdezhen (Kingtehchen or Ching-te-Chen).

Ceramics in the form of crudely baked pottery dates back to about 2700 B.C. in China. During the Han dynasty (206 B.C.–A.D. 220) the art of pottery-making underwent a big improvement, but porcelain as we know it today probably was not invented until the third century A.D. True porcelain is made from *kaolin* (China clay) and a fusible rock known as *petuntse* (*pai-tun-tzu*, white stone), and only certain localities yield this clay and rock. They vary in quality according to the different districts. Jingdezhen is the undisputed leader amongst the kilns in the whole of China.

The word kaolin came from Kao Ling (High Mound), a hill to the east of the city which supplied the white clay for the kilns. The original deposit has been largely exhausted through centuries of porcelain-making, but today Jingdezhen is still a flourishing concern, obtaining most of its clay, glazes, coloring agents and other resources from the

Eighteenth-century porcelain bowl (**above**)*; hand-painting porcelain* (**below**)

vicinity as well as from Qimen in adjoining Anhui.

A history of Jingdezhen would be too long and too technical for this book. Suffice it to say that the Song dynasty in the tenth century marked a distinct and important advance in refined porcelain-making. An Imperial kiln was established at Jingdezhen which attracted potters and artists from all over the land; an experimental spirit prevailed and competition was keen. It was then that Jingdezhen became the empire's center for porcelain and ceramics.

FRIED RICE-NOODLES

Rice-noodles, also known as rice-sticks, are another specialty of the region. They are very popular with children, particularly the way my nanny used to cook them.

1 lb (0.5kg) rice-noodles
1 oz (25g) dried shrimps
2 oz (50g) pork
⅓ cup (2 oz, 50g) bamboo shoots
3–4 small dried Chinese
    mushrooms
⅓ cup (2 oz, 50g) celery
⅙ cup (1 oz, 25g) leeks
1 tsp (5ml) salt
2 tbsp (30ml) soy sauce
4 tbsp (60ml) stock
4 tbsp (60ml) oil

Soak the rice-noodles in warm water until soft; soak the dried shrimps and mushrooms. Cut the pork, bamboo shoots and leeks into match-size shreds.

Stir-fry the pork, bamboo shoots, shrimps, celery and leeks in a little hot oil; add salt and stock; cook for about 2 minutes, remove.

Heat up the remaining oil; stir-fry the rice-noodles for 2–3 minutes; add the other cooked ingredients and soy sauce; stir for a further 2 minutes until there is no juice at all left; serve hot.

TEN VARIETY FRIED RICE

The ingredients can be varied as you wish or according to availability. Another recipe will be found on p 195.

1⅓ cup (½ lb, 225g) rice
4 oz (100g) shrimps (prawns)
4 oz (100g) cooked ham or pork
2 scallions (spring onions)
3 eggs
salt
1 cup (4 oz, 100g) green peas
2 tbsp (30ml) soy sauce

Wash the rice in cold water just once, then cover it with more cold water so that there is about 1 in (2.5cm) of water above the surface of the rice in the saucepan. Bring it to the boil; stir to prevent it sticking to the bottom of the pan when cooked. Replace the lid tightly and reduce the heat so that it is as low as possible. Cook for about 15–20 minutes.

Peel the shrimps (prawns), dice the ham or pork into small cubes the size of the peas. Finely chop the onions. Beat up the eggs with a little salt; heat up about 1 tablespoon (15ml) oil and make an omelette; set aside to cool. Heat up the remaining oil, stir-fry the finely chopped onions, followed by the shrimps (prawns), ham or pork, and peas; stir, adding a little salt, then add the cooked rice and soy sauce. When all the ingredients are mixed well, add the omelette, breaking it into little bits. When everything is well blended it is ready to serve.

The dishes in the picture below are:
Fried rice noodles (**left**)*; raw noodles*
(**above**)*; Ten variety fried rice* (**right**)

*Noodle-making is a highly skilled craft. Years of apprenticeship are required to perfect the skill. The chef (**left**) is throwing and pulling the dough to achieve an elastic consistency. The dough is doubled repeatedly (**top**) until it falls naturally into fine, thin shreds – the noodles. The whole process takes less than ten minutes*
Below: *The finished product – a dish of fresh fried noodles from the batch made by our chef in the pictures above*

FRIED NOODLES (CHOW MEIN)

Chow mein ('fried noodles') is always a popular dish in overseas Chinese restaurants. Try to obtain freshly-made noodles from oriental stores if you can – they taste much better than the dried ones.

½ lb (225g) egg noodles
4 oz (100g) pork or chicken meat
1 bamboo shoot
1 cup (4 oz, 100g) Chinese cabbage
1½ tbsp (25ml) soy sauce
1 tbsp (15ml) rice wine (or sherry)
1 tsp (5ml) cornstarch (cornflour)
1 tsp (5ml) sugar
1 tsp (5ml) salt
3 tbsp (45ml) oil

Shred the pork or chicken into small, thin strips; mix with a little soy sauce, rice wine or sherry, sugar and cornstarch (cornflour). Shred the bamboo shoot and cabbage into thin strips.

Heat up the oil and stir-fry the meat and vegetables together with a little salt for about 1½ minutes; add the noodles and the remaining soy sauce; mix well and cook gently until the noodles soften (fresh ones cook very quickly). Serve hot.

Bean-curd à la maison – I have given the dish this name because it is such a typical everyday Chinese dish

BEAN-CURD A LA MAISON

4 cakes bean-curd
¼ lb (100g) pork
⅓ cup (2 oz, 50g) leeks
5–6 red chilis
1 tbsp (15ml) rice wine (or sherry)
1 tbsp (15ml) soy sauce
2 tbsp (30ml) crushed yellow bean
    sauce
½ tsp (2ml) salt
½ tsp (2ml) sesame seed oil
oil for deep-frying

Split each cake of bean-curd into three or four thin slices crossways, then cut each slice diagonally into two triangles.

Cut the pork into small, thin slices; diagonally cut the leek into chunks; cut the dried red chilis into small pieces.

Heat up the oil; deep-fry the bean-curd pieces for about 2 minutes;

remove and drain.

Pour out the excess oil, leaving about 1 tablespoon (15ml) in the *wok*. Put in the pork and red chilis, stir; add rice wine or sherry, soy sauce, bean-curd, leek and crushed bean sauce; cook for about 3 minutes. Add sesame seed oil and serve.

STEWED PORK WITH BAMBOO SHOOTS

Bamboo shoots are the specialty of the region, particularly winter bamboo shoots, which are collected by digging underground when the shoots first begin to grow. They are relatively small and taste extra tender. This is very much a seasonal dish. Either carrots or white turnips may be substituted for the bamboo shoots.

1½ lb (0.75kg) pork, not too lean
6 cups (1½ lb, 0.75kg) bamboo
    shoots (carrots, turnips)

2 tablespoons (30ml) lard or oil
4 tbsp (60ml), soy sauce
2 tbsp (30ml) rice wine (or sherry)
1 tbsp (15ml) sugar
½ cup (4 oz, 100ml) stock
5 cups (2 pt, 1.2l) water

Cut the pork into 1 in (2.5cm) squares. Cut the bamboo shoots into triangular-shaped chunks of the same size.

Blanch the pork in boiling water, remove as soon as the water starts to boil again. Rinse the pork in cold water and drain.

Warm up the lard or oil, put in the parboiled pork, stir for 30 seconds, add soy sauce, wine or sherry and sugar. When the color starts to darken, add stock, reduce heat, cover with a lid, and cook gently for 1½ hours. Now add the bamboo shoots; blend well and cook for another 30 minutes. This dish can be re-heated and served again.

'LION'S HEAD' (PORK MEATBALLS WITH CABBAGE)

Let me reassure you that the rather alarming name of this dish refers to the pork meatballs which are supposed to resemble the shape of a lion's head and the cabbage which is supposed to look like its mane.

1 lb (0.5kg) ground (minced) pork, not too lean
½ cup (2 oz, 50g) water chestnuts, peeled
1 oz (25g) dried shrimps, soaked
2 scallions (spring onions)
1 slice ginger root
2 tbsp (30ml) rice wine (or sherry)
2 tbsp (30ml) soy sauce
½ tbsp (10ml) sugar
1 tsp (5ml) salt
4 cups (1 lb, 0.5kg) Chinese cabbage
3 tbsp (45ml) oil
1 cup (8 fl. oz, 225ml) stock

Finely chop the pork, water chestnuts, shrimps, onions and ginger root. Mix them together well; add salt, wine or sherry, sugar and soy sauce. Shape the meat mixture into four round balls.

Wash and cut the cabbage into quarters lengthwise. Heat oil until smoking; stir-fry the cabbage until soft, then place the meatballs on top; add stock, bring to a boil and simmer with a lid on for 20–30 minutes.

When serving make sure the meatballs are on top of the cabbage, otherwise it will not look anything like a lion's head.

STEAMED PORK WITH GROUND RICE

As a child, this was one of my favorite recipes, perhaps because it was only eaten on special occasions such as the Beginning of Summer festival (usually early in May).

1 lb (0.5kg) belly of pork, boned but with skin on
⅔ cup (4 oz, 100g) rice, uncooked
1 star anise
2 tbsp (30ml) soy sauce
½ tbsp (10ml) sugar
1 tbsp (15ml) rice wine (or sherry)
2 tbsp (30ml) stock

Cut the pork into 2×4 in (5×10cm) thin slices; marinate with soy sauce, sugar, rice wine or sherry and stock for 20 minutes.

Put the rice and star anise in a *wok* or frying-pan; stir over a high heat for a while, then reduce heat and continue stirring until golden; remove the rice and crush it with a rolling pin until fine. Coat each piece of pork with the ground rice, pressing it in well.

Place the pork piece by piece into a bowl, skin side down; steam vigorously for at least 2 hours or until the meat is very soft. To serve, turn the meat onto a dish so that the skin side is up.

My mother in wartime England used breadcrumbs instead of ground rice; the result was entirely satisfactory.

Above: *Steamed pork with ground rice. This dish is so delicious that children in China eat mounds of it. As a joke, they are weighed before and after the meal to see how much weight they have put on*

Below: *'Lion's head' – this dish is traditionally served with rice*

STIR-FRIED PORK SLICES WITH FRESH VEGETABLES

½ lb (225g) pork fillet
1⅓ cups (½ lb, 225g) fresh mushrooms
1 small Chinese cabbage
1 tbsp (15ml) soy sauce
1 tbsp (15ml) rice wine (or sherry)
1 tsp (5ml) sugar
½ tbsp (10ml) cornstarch (cornflour)
1 scallion (spring onion)
1 tsp (5ml) salt
3 tbsp (45ml) oil

Cut the pork into small slices about the size of an oblong stamp; mix with soy sauce, rice wine or sherry, sugar and cornstarch (cornflour). Wash the mushrooms and cut them into thin slices. Cut the cabbage into pieces about the same size as the pork. Finely chop the onion.

Heat up about 1 tablespoon (15ml) oil; before it gets too hot, stir-fry the pork about 1 minute or until the color of the meat changes; then dish out and keep it aside.

Wash and dry the *wok*; heat up the remaining oil. When it smokes, toss in the finely chopped onion followed by the mushrooms and cabbage; add salt and stir constantly for about ½ minute, then return the pork to the *wok* and mix it well with the vegetables; add a little stock or water if necessary. As soon as the gravy starts to bubble it is ready to serve.

Stir-fried pork slices with fresh vegetables
1. *The raw ingredients and seasonings are assembled*
2. *The pork is cut into small slices*
3. *The pork is mixed with the marinade*
4. *The pork is cooked first, then removed*
5. *The vegetables are stir-fried in very hot oil*
6. *Finally the pork is added to the vegetables in the* wok *for the last stage in cooking*
7. *The finished dish*
This is the basic method for cooking meat and vegetables in China

China tea

Controversy and mystery surround the origin of tea. Indeed, it is very difficult to establish an exact date when tea was first known in China as a drink. The Chinese character for tea, *Cha*, made its first appearance during the early Han dynasty (206 B.C.–A.D. 24), therefore one can assume tea was known as a drink in China for more than 2,000 years. Some scholars argue that the ancient Chinese character for a bitter-tasting plant, *tu*, was also used to signify tea; in that case, the origin of tea drinking must go further back by at least 600 years.

It was not until the eighth century, however, when the first treatise on tea, *Cha Jing* ('Classics of Tea') was written by Lu Yu, that tea became a common beverage drunk by all classes of people.

From Lu Yu's book we learn all about the tea plant (*Camellia* or *Thea sinensis*) and its cultivation. The seed is planted in October in sandy or rocky soil. It grows on ground that would not support any edible crops, and its

Left: *Picking tea at dawn, Hangzhou.* **Below:** *Shelves of high-quality tea in a Chinese teashop – among them are Puer* (**top left**) *with jasmine next to it, and Iron Goddess* (**bottom right**) **Bottom:** *Teas picked later in the season are coarser and therefore cheaper. They are usually sold loose and used for everyday drinking*

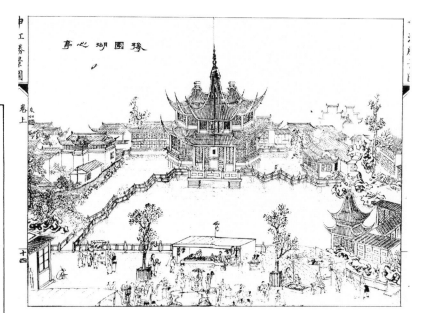

THE ART OF
TEA DRINKING

Since the best China teas are seldom exported, people in the West cannot truly appreciate the fine art of tea drinking as practised in China. However, the least we can do is to observe a few basic rules in our tea making.

Choose your tea carefully; buy only good quality varieties.

Use only freshly boiled water; always let the cold tap run for a while before filling the kettle.

Do not use silver or metal teapots. Similarly, the tea cups should be of porcelain or glass.

Always rinse the teapot thoroughly and warm with boiling water before putting in the tea.

Allow the tea to draw for about 3 minutes before pouring out.

Drink it while still hot, even in summer.

Never add milk or sugar to Chinese tea; it will spoil the fragrant aroma.

Everything used in the preparation of tea must be absolutely clean and free from oil.

Good teas can be infused three times – in fact the second time is generally regarded as the best, because by then the tea will release its full fragrance and aroma.

quality is improved by clouds, snow, and the misty atmosphere of high altitudes; therefore most of the best teas come from the mountain tops.

A tea planter has to wait three years for his first harvest. Left alone, the plant would grow to a tree more than 50 feet high, but like olive trees in the Mediterranean countries, it is diligently pruned to a height of 5 feet or less to make it easy to harvest and to ensure an explosion of leaves or 'flush' rather than growth in height.

The tea leaves are picked in April, May and September. The April picking, when the leaves are covered with down, is regarded as the best crop and is known as *pekoe* tea. The picking, usually done by girls and women, has to be completed in a few days, otherwise the leaves will grow too tough. The higher the leaves are on the shrub, the better their quality. Sometimes these leaves are called *sproutings*, like the best 'Dragon-Well' tea from the West Lake in Hangzhou. They are further classified as *Before the Rains* – denoting that they were picked before the rainy season which gives leaf growth an extra boost.

Although there are hundreds of varieties of tea, they all fall into two basic categories: green and red (or black) tea. Green teas are unfermented and are dried in the sun or in drying rooms where they may also be steamed, while the red or black teas are fermented before drying. Processes vary considerably from district to district.

Most tea leaves are curled. This is usually done by hand or, nowadays, by machine. After sorting and blending, the tea leaves are packed in chests lined with lead or pewter foil, ready for the market. In China, teas are

seldom sold in small packages. I used to accompany my grandfather, who was a tea connoisseur, to the tea shops to select his favorite teas, which were always sold loose. The shops were rather like the old-fashioned wine merchants in England where the customer used to be treated with respect and courtesy.

Lu Yu laid down the law that tea leaves should not be picked on a rainy or cloudy day: 'Pick tea only on a clear day at dawn, when the morning air is clear on mountain tops and the fragrance of dew is still on the leaves.' Tea drinking became so popular that the Taoists, with their conception of Yin and Yang, claimed that the dew actually stands for the 'juice of heaven and earth' when the two principles unite at night. The dew is an important ingredient in the elixir of immortality.

With the Taoists' insistence on the return to nature and purity, a Chinese tea connoisseur has to be most fastidious in the preparation and making of tea. Cleanliness is of utmost importance; everything used in the preparation and making of tea must be absolutely clean and free from oil, and therefore tea must not be made in the kitchen. The setting is important, too; ideally one should find a quiet spot away from earthly activity, and drink tea using only water from a mountain spring, with a good book to read or in the company of a few close friends – the smaller the number the better, for one cannot appreciate the fine quality of really good tea in a large and therefore noisy gathering. Tea houses in a city are not meant for a true tea connoisseur; they are more like an institution for all sorts of people to have refreshments, to gossip or to transact business.

Far left: Nineteenth-century tea-house in Shanghai (top); present-day workers' tea-house in Suzhou (lower left); tea-shop in Shanghai (lower right) Above: 'Accomplishments of a gentleman', one of which is the appreciation of good tea

Of course, we are here talking about tea as drunk by connoisseurs. But how about the millions of others who treat tea as an everyday beverage? As you know, tea-drinking is universal amongst the Chinese; they drink it all day long. A visitor is always offered tea on arrival. A pot of strong tea is kept warm all day long; one need only pour out a small amount into a cup and dilute it with hot water from a vacuum flask. But when a special guest or somebody important arrives, then freshly made good quality tea would be offered.

SICHUAN/THE WESTERN SCHOOL

Sichuan

The province of Sichuan (Szechuan) is the most populous in China, with an estimated 75 million inhabitants, or about 10 per cent of the nation's total population.

The Sichuan basin is encircled by high mountains. About 135 million years ago the basin was a lake; later the surrounding land gradually rose to become mountains and then, through an opening on its eastern edge which was to become the famous Yangtse Gorges, the water flowed out and the lake became dry land. Today, wells sunk into the basin floor will yield salt water formed by saline compounds from an ancient lake that seeped underground.

With high mountains to the north fending off the cold air, the basin has hot summers and mild winters. It is virtually frost free with abundant rainfall in winter and spring. Plant growth continues the whole year round. One of China's important 'rice bowls', the Sichuan basin also yields a wealth of sub-tropical products including fruits, silk, tea and herb medicines, all of which have earned Sichuan the name 'Land of Abundance'.

Geographically and historically, Sichuan was a small kingdom which developed in isolation. Up to the middle of this century, it was virtually inaccessible from the rest of China; the famous Tang poet Li Po (699–762) wrote, 'It is harder to enter Sichuan than to go to heaven!'

The cuisine of Sichuan has the reputation of being richly flavored and peppery hot, but that is not the whole truth. At least one third of Sichuan's dishes are not hot at all; in fact only everyday dishes prepared in the home are highly seasoned and have a piquant taste. When it comes to formal dinners or banquets no peppery hot dishes are served at all.

Hot red chili is used, not to paralyze the tongue, but to stimulate the palate. One of the characteristics of Sichuan cuisine is that each dish usually contains a number of different flavors such as sweet, sour, bitter, hot, salty, aromatic and fragrant. When the palate is stimulated by hot chili, it becomes more sensitive and is capable of taking in several different flavors simultaneously.

Chengdu, the provincial capital, is also Sichuan's culinary center. It is an old walled town with a history going as far back as the third century B.C., when it became the capital of the King of Sichuan in the later Chou dynasty.

Chengdu is a picturesque city with many beautiful sights. Bamboos grow plentifully there, and one of the local specialties is bamboo shoots. A very good family friend, who is a native of Chengdu, told me that when she was 16 she had the symptoms of tuber-

Left: *Rice and vegetable fields: typical farming country in Sichuan.* **Below:** *The famous Sichuan gorge. These dangerous rapids and high mountains for centuries isolated Sichuan from the rest of the world*

culosis. That was in the days before there were any drugs to treat the condition. But her mother was told of a traditional remedy which she followed. She used to get up at dawn before the sun rose and go into their garden and pick the bamboo leaves which were still full of the morning dew. My friend had to drink the water in which the tips of the bamboo leaves had been boiled. She was completely cured from her illness, thanks to her kind mother *and* the bamboo leaves. I have never discovered any scientific basis for this!

Far left: *Palm trees provide shade in the hot climate of south-western China (top); bamboo groves surround a house in Chengdu (below).* **Center:** *Rice fields and fishing boats on a lake in Yunnan.* **Below:** *Vegetables in a Sichuan market, and (bottom) fresh bamboo shoots*

Chengdu dishes

Food from the Sichuan School – a complete, well-balanced meal, enough for six people. **Top:** *Jadeite shrimps (prawns);* **left:** *Hot and sour kidney;* **right:** *Tea-smoked duck, with salt and Sichuan pepper dip*

JADEITE SHRIMPS (PRAWNS)

The white and green of jadeite are provided by the shrimps (prawns) and the peas. The red of the tomato and ham is used to give a contrast in color. Here we garnished the dish with a few cocktail cherries.

1 lb (0.5kg) uncooked shrimps
    (prawns), peeled
1 egg white
½ tsp (2ml) salt
½ tbsp (10ml) cornstarch (cornflour)
½ cup (2 oz, 50g) green peas
⅙ cup (1 oz, 25g) cooked ham or
    1 small red tomato
1 scallion (spring onion)
oil for deep-frying

Sauce mixture:
½ tsp (2ml) salt
½ tsp (2ml) pepper
1 tbsp (15ml) rice wine (or sherry)
½ tbsp (10ml) cornstarch (cornflour)
3 tbsp (45ml) stock or water

Marinate the peeled shrimps (prawns) with the egg white, salt and cornstarch (cornflour). Dice the ham or tomato into small cubes; cut the onion into short lengths. Mix the sauce in a bowl or jug.

Heat up the oil; deep-fry the shrimps (prawns) for about 15 seconds; stir to separate them; scoop them out and drain. Pour off the excess oil; return the shrimps (prawns) to the *wok* together with the green peas, ham or tomato. Stir for a little while; add the sauce mixture. When the sauce thickens, the dish is ready to serve.

and pepper. Stir a few times, then add the sauce mixture; blend well. As soon as the sauce starts to bubble, dish out and serve.

This is a typical Sichuan dish in that you are served several flavors (sweet, salt, sour and hot) all at once.

TEA-SMOKED DUCK

*1 duckling weighing about 3½–4 lb
(1.5–1.75kg)*

Marinade:
½ tbsp (10ml) salt
2 Sichuan peppercorns
½ tsp (2ml) ground pepper
3 tbsp (45ml) rice wine (or sherry)
2 tbsp (30ml) Hoi Sin sauce

Smoking material:
2 oz (50g) tea leaves
2 oz (50g) camphor leaves
¼ lb (100g) saw dust
¼ lb (100g) cypress tree branch
oil for deep-frying

Garnish:
Chinese parsley (fresh coriander)
salt and pepper

Make the marinade; rub it all over the duck both inside and out; leave to marinate for 12 hours, then let it dry in an airy place.

Mix the smoking materials together, then divide into three portions and put one portion in an earthenware bowl; place the bowl inside a large container such as a wine barrel sawn in half. Light a piece of charcoal until red; put it inside the bowl and place a sheet of wire netting on top. Lay the duck on the wire netting and place the other half of the wine barrel on top so that it keeps the smoke in. After 10 minutes, add the second portion of the smoking material to the bowl together with a new piece of burning charcoal, then turn the duck over and replace the lid. After 7 minutes add the last portion of the smoking material with another piece of burning charcoal, turn the duck over again and smoke for another 5 minutes. The duck should be nice and brown all over.

HOT AND SOUR KIDNEY

½ lb (225g) pig's kidney
1 tsp (5ml) salt
1 tbsp (15ml) rice wine (or sherry)
½ tbsp (10ml) cornstarch (cornflour)
1 tbsp (15ml) dried red chili
1 slice ginger root, peeled
2 scallions (spring onions)
1 clove garlic
oil for deep-frying
1 tsp (5ml) Sichuan pepper, ground

Sauce mixture:
1 tbsp (15ml) sugar
1½ tbsp (25ml) vinegar
1½ tbsp (25ml) soy sauce
2 tsp (10ml) cornstarch (cornflour)
water or stock

Split the kidneys in half lengthwise and discard the fat and white parts in the middle. Score the surface of the kidneys diagonally in a criss-cross pattern and cut them into oblong stamp-size pieces. Marinate in salt, rice wine or sherry and cornstarch (cornflour).

Cut the dried red chili into small bits, discard the seeds; finely chop the ginger root, garlic and onions. Mix the sauce in a bowl or jug.

Heat up the oil and deep-fry the kidney pieces for about 1 minute; scoop them out and drain. Pour off the excess oil leaving about 1 tablespoon (15ml) in the *wok*; put in the red chili and cook until it turns dark. Add kidney pieces, onions, garlic, ginger

CARVING THE DUCK

Using a sharp cleaver, chop the duck into four pieces

Chop each piece into several small slices

Arrange the slices neatly on a plate in the shape of the bird

Take it out and steam it for about 3 hours; remove to cool.

Heat up the oil and deep-fry the duck for 5 minutes, turning it over once or twice to ensure the skin is crispy.

Chop the duck into small pieces; arrange on a dish and garnish with Chinese parsley. Mix a little salt and freshly ground pepper as a dip.

This duck has gone through four processes: marinating, smoking, steaming and frying. It should be aromatic, crisp, tender and delicious; – an ideal accompaniment for wine.

CHICKEN SLICES WITH BAMBOO SHOOTS

½ lb (225g) chicken breast meat
½ tsp (2ml) salt
1 egg white
2 tsp (10ml) cornstarch (cornflour)
1 carrot
⅔ cup (4 oz, 100g) bamboo shoots
3 dried Chinese mushrooms, soaked
2 scallions (spring onions)

Opposite: Tea-smoked duck. The smoked duck is deep-fried in a wok and turned over frequently. This last stage of the cooking ensures that the skin becomes crispy.

Sauce:
1 tbsp (15ml) soy sauce
1 tbsp (15ml) sugar
1 tbsp (15ml) vinegar
1½ tbsp (25ml) cornstarch (cornflour)
2 tbsp (30ml) water

Cut the chicken into small slices not much bigger than the size of a postage stamp; mix with salt, egg white and cornstarch (cornflour).

Slice the bamboo shoots, mushrooms and carrots; cut the onions into short lengths; mix the sauce in a bowl.

Heat up the oil, stir-fry the chicken until its color changes; scoop out with a perforated spoon; toss the bamboo shoots, mushrooms and carrots into the *wok*, stir a few times, put the chicken back, stir a few more times, add the sauce with the crushed peanuts, blend well. As soon as the sauce thickens, dish out and serve.

TANGERINE PEEL CHICKEN

The tangerine peel is peel that has been dried in the sun. You can easily dry it yourself if you have difficulty finding it in the shops.

1 lb (0.5kg) chicken meat, boned
2 slices ginger root, peeled
1 scallion (spring onion)
1½ tbsp (25ml) rice wine (or sherry)

1 tsp (5ml) salt
2 tsp (30ml) soy sauce
1 tbsp (15ml) sugar
1 tbsp (15ml) vinegar
3–4 dried chilis
½ tsp (2ml) Sichuan pepper
1 tsp (5ml) dried tangerine peel
oil for deep-frying
½ tsp (2ml) sesame seed oil

Cut the chicken meat into small pieces and crush the ginger root and onion; add them to the chicken meat together with salt, rice wine or sherry and 1 tablespoon (15ml) soy sauce. Let it marinate for a while.

Mix the remaining soy sauce with the sugar and vinegar in a bowl to make sweet and sour sauce.

Heat up the oil; discard the ginger root and onion; deep-fry the chicken until golden; remove and drain.

Pour off the excess oil leaving about 2 tablespoons (30ml) in the *wok*; put in the dried red chilis, Sichuan pepper and tangerine peel. Add chicken, stir a few times, then add the sweet and sour sauce; blend well and serve hot.

When eating, savor each mouthful slowly. After the initial hot taste is passed, you will be able to distinguish all the other different flavors, with the subtle fragrance of tangerine peel.

WINE-MARINATED SHRIMPS

½ lb (225g) fresh shrimps (prawns)
3 tbsp (45ml) rice wine (or sherry)
2 scallions (spring onions), white parts only
⅓ cup (2 oz, 50g) celery
⅓ cup (2 oz, 50g) carrots
1 tbsp (15ml) peas

Sauce:
2 tbsp (30ml) soy sauce
1 tsp (5ml) sesame seed oil

Wash the shrimps well, and place in a dish. Pour the wine or sherry over them, add the onion whites cut to 1 in (2.5cm) lengths; cover and marinate for 5 minutes.

Slice the celery and carrot; parboil with the peas for 5 minutes. Drain and add to the shrimps. Pour the sauce over and serve. Mix the sauce; pour it over the shrimps (prawns), serve.

Wine-marinated shrimps (prawns): the fresher the shellfish the better

CRYSTAL SUGAR 'SILVER' EARS

'Silver' Ears are a specialty of Sichuan. They are similar to Wooden Ears but are much more expensive, as they are considered to be a tonic which will help in maintaining good health.

½ oz (15g) 'Silver' Ears
2 cups (½ lb, 225g) crystal sugar
1 egg white
3¾ cups (1½ pt, 900ml) water

Soak the 'Silver' Ears in warm water for 1 hour; discard the hard 'roots'; rinse well.

Use a *wok* or saucepan that is free from oil, dissolve the crystal sugar in water over a moderate heat, add the egg white beaten with a little water. Bring to the boil, and skim off any bubbles or impurities; pour the liquid into a large bowl (again make sure it is clean and free from oil); add the 'Silver' Ears and steam for 1½ hours. This dish deserves to be served in the best porcelain you have.

CHRYSANTHEMUM FISH POT

This is a seasonal dish. Chrysanthemums start to bloom in September, marking the end of summer. If you compare this dish with 'Rinsed lamb in fire-pot' (p.68) you will notice the differences. To start with, the northerners use charcoal, while in the south it is more common to use a spirit burner which does not smell so pleasant, but it is less of a bother as you do not have to add more fuel in the middle of eating.

The fish maw is the same as that used in 'Happy Family' p.103.

4 oz (100g) fish maw
4 oz (100g) chicken breast meat, boned and skinned
2 chicken gizzards
½ lb (225g) pig's tripe
4 oz (100g) Beche-de-mer
⅔ cup (4 oz, 100g) snow peas (mange-tout)
2 cups (½ lb, 225g) spinach leaves
⅓ cup (2 oz, 50g) Chinese parsley (fresh coriander)
2 slices ginger root, peeled
2–3 scallions (spring onions)
2 tsp (10ml) salt
1 tsp (5ml) freshly ground Sichuan pepper
9 cups (3½ pts, 2l) stock
1 large chrysanthemum (white or yellow)

Cut the fish maw, chicken gizzards, Beche-de-Mer and tripe into slices.

Wash the cabbage, snow peas (mange-tout), spinach and Chinese parsley; cut them into small pieces.

Finely chop the ginger root and onions; place them with salt and pepper in a small bowl. These are the 'four seasonings'.

Bring the stock to a rolling boil in the fire-pot; arrange the meat and vegetables in the moat. They will only need to be cooked for about five minutes. Everybody just helps themselves from the pot with chopsticks, and dips their helping in the 'four seasonings' before eating it.

What happens to the chrysanthemum? I will tell you on the next page.

Crystal sugar 'Silver Ears : the finished dish, with (inset) 'Silver' Ears as you would see them in a store

Chrysanthemum fish pot, seen from the top. Clockwise from 12 o'clock: *bêche-de-mer, with Chinese cabbage heart dividing it from chicken breast meat; egg omelette, sliced chicken gizzards and cabbage; tripe; another omelette, fish maws, and a third omelette. Fish-balls are placed all the way round the 'chimney'. Traditionally the chrysanthemum petals were scattered over the finished dish, but personally I find them rather tasteless and would prefer to use the flower as a decoration.*

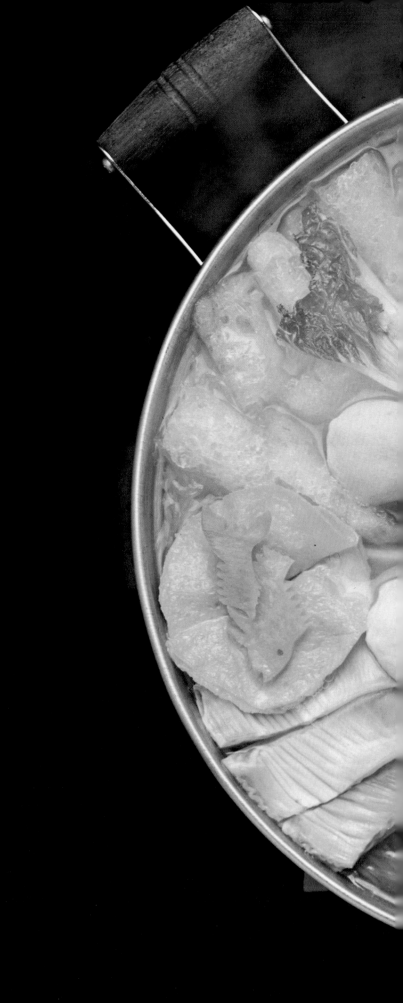

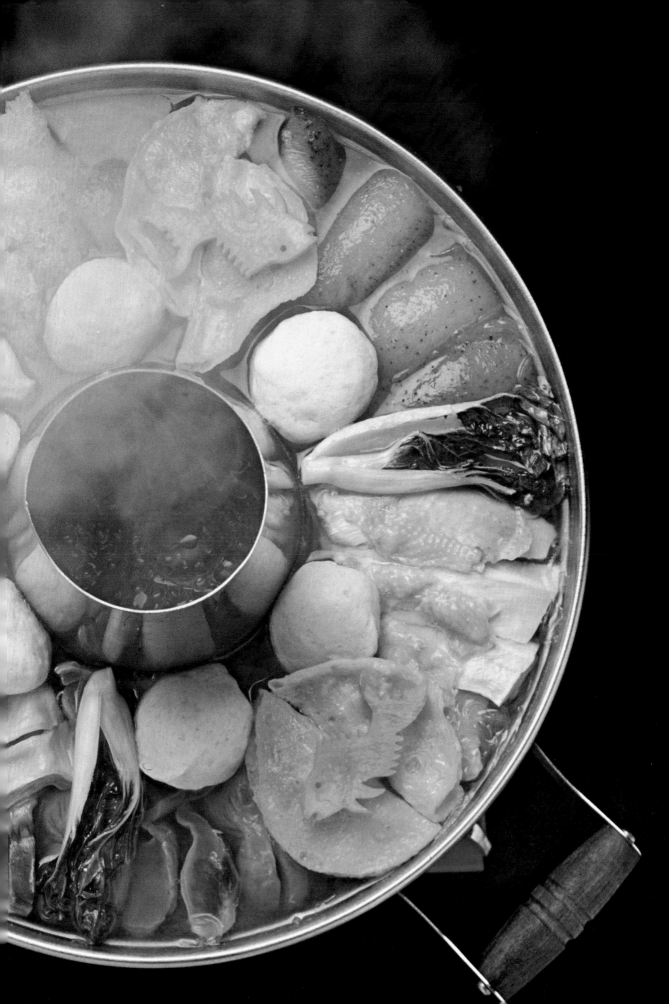

BEAN-CURD FISH IN CHILI SAUCE

The original recipe recommends a carp for this dish but there is no reason why you should not use a sea fish if preferred.

1 lb (0.5kg) mullet or mackerel
2 scallions (spring onions), white parts only
1 clove garlic
2 slices ginger root, peeled
2 cakes bean-curd
1 tsp (5ml) salt
4 tbsp (60ml) oil
2 tbsp (30ml) chili paste (purée)
1 tbsp (15ml) soy sauce
2 tbsp (30ml) rice wine (or sherry)
1 tbsp (15ml) cornstarch (cornflour)
1½ cups (12 fl. oz, 350ml) stock

Cut the heads off the fish and remove the backbone; crush the garlic, cut it and the ginger root into small pieces; cut the onion whites into short lengths.

Cut each bean-curd into about 10 pieces. Blanch them in boiling water; remove and soak them in stock with salt.

Heat up the oil until hot; fry the fish until both sides are golden; put them to one side; tilt the *wok*, and put in the chili paste (purée). When it starts to bubble, return the *wok* to its original position, push the fish back, add soy sauce, rice wine or sherry, onion, ginger root, garlic and a little stock – about ½ cup (4 fl. oz, 100ml). At the same time add the bean-curd taken from the stock and cook with the fish for about 10 minutes.

Now pick out the fish with chopsticks and place them on a serving dish, then quickly mix the cornstarch (cornflour) with a little cold water. Add to the *wok* to make a smooth sauce with the bean-curd; pour it all over the fish and serve.

Below: *Bean-curd fish in chili sauce, garnished with shredded scallions (spring onions) to give a touch of color*

SWEET-SOUR CRISP FISH

1 carp (or freshwater fish) weighing 1½ lb (0.75kg)
2 tbsp (30ml) rice wine (or sherry)
4 tbsp (60ml) soy sauce
½ cup (2 oz, 50g) cornstarch (cornflour)
1 clove garlic
2 scallions (spring onions)
2 slices ginger root, peeled
2 dried red chilis, soaked
⅙ cup (1 oz, 25g) bamboo shoots
2–3 Chinese dried mushrooms, soaked
oil for deep-frying
1½ tbsp (25ml) sugar
1½ tbsp (25ml) vinegar
½ cup (4 fl. oz, 100ml) stock

Above: *Sweet-sour crisp fish, surrounded by its rich sauce*

Clean the fish; make six or seven diagonal cuts as deep as the bone on each side of the fish. Marinate in rice wine or sherry and 2 tbsp (30ml) soy sauce for 5 minutes; remove and wipe dry. Make a paste with ⅜ cup (1½ oz, 40g) cornstarch (cornflour) and water and coat the entire fish evenly.

Finely chop the garlic, 1 onion and 1 slice ginger root. Cut the other onion and ginger root into thin shreds. Cut the soaked red chilis (discarding the seeds), bamboo shoots and mushrooms all into thin shreds.

Heat up the oil to boiling point, pick up the fish by the tail, lower it

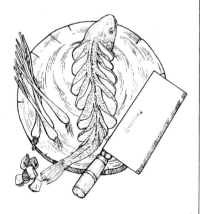

How to cut the fish for Sweet-sour crisp fish

head first into the oil, turn it around and deep fry for about 7 minutes or until golden; remove and drain.

Pour off the excess oil leaving about 2 tablespoons (30ml) in the *wok*; add finely chopped onion, ginger root, garlic and red chili, bamboo shoots and mushrooms followed by the remaining soy sauce, sugar, vinegar and stock. Stir a few times, then add the remaining cornstarch (cornflour) mixed with a little water; blend well to make a slightly thick smooth sauce.

Place a cloth over the fish, press gently with your hand to soften the body, then put it on a serving dish and pour the sauce over it; garnish with onion and ginger root shreds.

165

Chongqing dishes

Chongqing (Chungking), Sichuan's largest city and the wartime capital of the Kuomintang government, is situated at the confluence of the Yangtse and one of its tributaries, Jialing River. (By the way, the name Sichuan means 'four rivers' in Chinese. There seem to be different opinions as to the identity of these four rivers since there are more than twice that number in the province and all are tributaries to the great Yangtse; it is generally accepted, however, that the 'four rivers' are the Yangtse plus three of its left bank tributaries, the Jialing, Tuo and Min rivers.)

The city center is situated on a rocky promontory between the two rivers, but the city limits extend south of the Yangtse River as far as the Guizhou (Kweichow) border. Chongqing now has a population of nearly 5 million and is a focal point of the province's transport network, as well as the main industrial center.

Because of its strategic position and the recent influx of 'foreigners' (i.e., people from other provinces), the cuisine of Chongqing is regarded as not quite as orthodox Eastern School as that of Chengdu. There is no doubt however, that it is still unmistakably 'Sichuan' in character.

FRAGRANT AND CRISPY DUCK

*1 duckling weighing about 3 lb
    (1.5kg)
1 tbsp (15ml) salt
2 slices ginger root, crushed
2 cloves garlic, crushed
2 scallions (spring onions), cut into
    short lengths
3 tbsp (45ml) rice wine (or sherry)
2 tsp (10ml) five-spice powder
1 tsp (5ml) Sichuan peppercorns
oil for deep-frying*

Serving:
*4 scallions (spring onions), cut into thin
    strips
6 tbsp (90ml) Hoi Sin sauce*

Clean the duck well; rub with salt inside and out; place it in a deep dish; add ginger root, garlic, onions, rice wine or sherry, five-spice powder and Sichuan peppercorns. Steam vigorously for at least 2½ hours; remove and discard the ginger root, garlic, onions and Sichuan peppercorns. Turn the duck over and let it marinate in the juice. After about 2–3 hours take it out to cool until the skin is dry.

Heat up the oil and deep-fry the duck until golden and crispy.

To serve, either leave it whole or split it in half lengthwise. It is eaten like a Peking duck, wrapped in pancakes or steamed buns with strips of onion and Hoi Sin sauce.

Fragrant and crispy duck surrounded by steamed buns. The buns can be made from the same dough as Cha Shao dumplings (recipe page 190)

about 1 tablespoon (15ml) in the *wok*; toss in the finely chopped garlic, ginger root and onions, followed by pork. Stir for a while then add soy sauce, wine or sherry and chili paste (purée); blend well then add the aubergine. Cook together for another 1–2 minutes; add the cornstarch (cornflour) mixed with a little water, stir a few more times; serve when the juice is reduced to almost nothing.

CHICKEN IN VINEGAR SAUCE

½ lb (225g) chicken breast meat, boned
⅔ cup (4 oz, 100g) bamboo shoots
1 egg white
1 tbsp (15ml) rice wine (or sherry)
1 tsp (5ml) salt
1 tbsp (15ml) cornstarch (cornflour)
3–4 dried red chilis, soaked
3 tbsp (45ml) oil

Vinegar sauce:
1 tbsp (15ml) vinegar
1 tbsp (15ml) soy sauce
1 tbsp (15ml) sugar
1 slice ginger root, peeled and finely chopped
1 clove garlic, finely chopped
1 scallion (spring onion), finely chopped
3 tbsp (45ml) stock
1 tbsp (15ml) cornstarch (cornflour)

Score the skinless surface of the chicken in a criss-cross pattern; cut it into oblong pieces about the size of a stamp. Marinate it with the egg white, wine or sherry, salt and cornstarch (cornflour).

Cut the bamboo shoots to roughly the same size as the chicken; finely chop the soaked red chilis.

Finely chop the ginger root, garlic and onion; mix the sauce in a bowl.

Chicken in vinegar sauce: the fiery sauce is typical of Sichuan cooking

Warm up the oil and stir-fry the chicken pieces for about 2 minutes; add chilis and bamboo shoots, stir a few times more then add the sauce. Blend well; serve as soon as the sauce thickens.

AUBERGINE IN 'FISH SAUCE'
No fish is used in this recipe – the sauce is normally used for a fish dish, hence the name 'fish sauce'.

2 cups (½ lb, 225g) aubergine
¼ lb (100g) lean pork
1 slice ginger root, peeled and finely chopped
1 clove garlic, finely chopped
2 scallions (spring onions), finely chopped
1 tbsp (15ml) soy sauce
1 tbsp (15ml) rice wine (or sherry)
1 tbsp (15ml) chili paste (purée)
½ tbsp (10ml) cornstarch (cornflour)
oil for deep-frying

Skin the aubergine; cut it into strips rather like potato chips. Cut the pork into thin shreds the size of matches.

Heat up the oil; deep-fry the aubergine for about 1–2 minutes, then scoop out and drain.

Pour off the excess oil leaving

*The aubergines are peeled (**top**), cut into thick chunks, and (**bottom**) deep-fried in oil like potato chips*

LIVER PATE SOUP

½ lb (225g) pig's liver
2 egg whites
1 tbsp (15ml) rice wine (or sherry)
1 tsp (5ml) salt
3 cups (1¼ pts, 1l) stock
salt and pepper to taste

Chop the liver into a pulp; squeeze it through a muslin cloth; mix it with ¼ cup (1 tablespoon, 60ml) stock and the egg whites; add wine or sherry and salt. Place in a bowl, and steam for 15 minutes; by then it will have become a solid liver pâté; let it cool.

Place the liver pâté on the bottom of a large soup bowl; cut it into small squares (but keep the whole pieces together). Bring the stock to the boil and gently pour it over the liver. Season with salt and pepper and serve.

STEAMED BEEF WITH GROUND RICE

1 lb (0.5kg) beef steak
1 tbsp (15ml) salted black beans, crushed
2 tbsp (30ml) soy sauce
1 tbsp (15ml) chili paste (purée)
1 tbsp (15ml) oil
2 tbsp (30ml) rice wine (or sherry)
2 slices ginger root, peeled and finely chopped
½ tsp (2ml) Sichuan pepper, freshly ground
⅔ cup (4 oz, 100g) coarsely-ground rice (use 20 per cent glutinous rice with 80 per cent ordinary rice)

Cut the beef into 2 in (5cm)×1 in (2.5cm)×¼ in (5mm) slices; mix with crushed salted black beans, soy sauce, chili paste (purée), oil, rice wine or sherry, ginger root and ground pepper. Marinate for 30 minutes, then coat each piece of beef carefully with ground rice.

Ideally, use small *dim sum* bamboo steamers as seen in Cantonese restaurants, otherwise any other type of steamer will do. Steam the beef vigorously for 30 minutes (if using the tenderest rump steak, then 15 minutes will do).

Serve hot, garnished with finely chopped onions or Chinese parsley (fresh coriander) if desired.

Twice-cooked pork: bright contrasting colors, a most attractive dish

TWICE-COOKED PORK

This is a traditional Sichuan dish that has become a national favorite.

½ lb (225g) pork
1 leek
1 small green pepper
1 small red pepper
1 tbsp (15ml) chili paste (purée)
1 tbsp (15ml) soy sauce
3 tbsp (45ml) oil
1 tsp (5ml) salt

Choose a piece of pork that is not too lean. Boil in water for 20 minutes; remove and cool a little then cut it into thin slices the size of a matchbox. Cut the leek, green and red peppers into chunks of roughly the same size.

Heat up the oil, stir-fry the leek, green and red peppers till soft. Add salt, chili paste (purée) and soy sauce followed by the pork slices. Blend well and cook together for 1–2 minutes; serve hot.

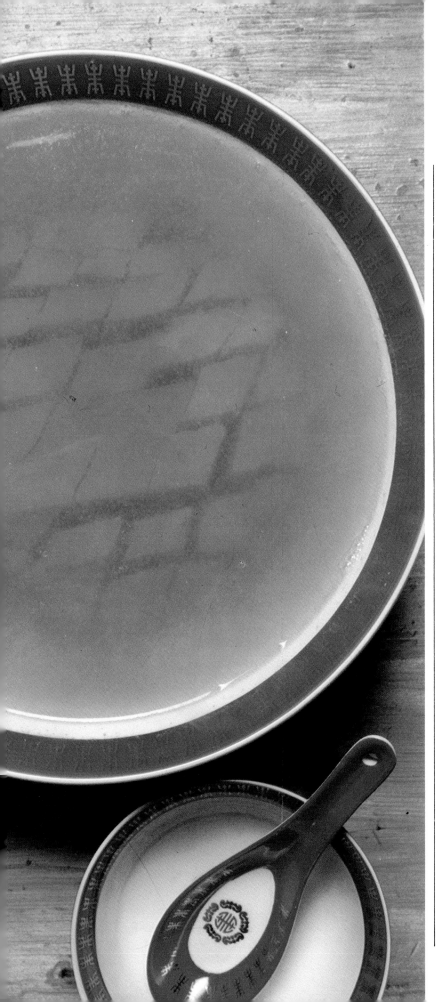

Liver pâté soup. **Above:** *The liver pâté is cut into small squares or diamonds, before the stock is poured over.* **Left:** *The finished dish, ready to be served*

*Chili chicken cubes, **left**, with Shredded pork in 'fish sauce' on the **right**. In the **center** you can see a pile of dried Wooden Ears.*

CHILI CHICKEN CUBES

This is another Sichuan dish that has gained nationwide popularity. It is reputed to have been one of the late Chairman Mao's favorites.

½ lb (225g) chicken breast meat, boned
1 egg white
½ tsp (2ml) salt
1½ tbsp (25ml) cornstarch (cornflour)
1 slice ginger root, peeled
1 clove garlic
2 scallions (spring onions), white parts only
1 small green pepper
1 small red pepper
1 tbsp (15ml) rice wine (or sherry)
1 tbsp (15ml) soy sauce
3 tbsp (45ml) stock
oil for deep-frying
1 tbsp (15ml) chili paste (purée)
½ tsp (2ml) sesame seed oil

Dice the chicken into ½ in (1cm) cubes, mix with the egg white, salt and ½ tbsp (10ml) cornstarch (cornflour).

Cut the ginger root and garlic into thin slices; cut the onion diagonally into short lengths. Cut the green and red peppers into small squares roughly the same size as the chicken cubes.

SHREDDED PORK IN 'FISH SAUCE'

Like 'Aubergine in "fish sauce"', there is no fish involved in this dish.

½ lb (225g) pork fillet
1 cup (225ml) soaked Wooden Ears
2–3 stalks celery
1 tsp (2ml) salt
1½ tbsp (25ml) cornstarch (cornflour)
1 slice ginger root, peeled and finely chopped
1 clove garlic, finely chopped
2 scallions (spring onions), finely chopped
1½ tbsp (25ml) soy sauce
1 tbsp (15ml) chili paste (purée)
1 tsp (5ml) sugar
2 tsp (10ml) vinegar
3 tbsp (45ml) oil

Cut the pork into thin shreds the size of matches; mix with salt and ½ teaspoon (2 ml) cornstarch (cornflour). Shred the soaked Wooden Ears and celery.

Heat 1 tablespoon (15ml) oil and stir-fry the pork until the color changes; remove and add the remaining oil to the *wok*; put in Wooden Ears and celery together with ginger root, garlic and onions; add pork, soy sauce, chili paste (purée), sugar and vinegar. Cook together for 1–2 minutes, then add the remaining cornstarch (cornflour) mixed in a little water; blend well; serve.

Shredded pork in 'fish sauce'. The sauce ingredients are added to the meat, ready for final serving

Mix together the rice wine or sherry, soy sauce, stock and the remaining cornstarch (cornflour) in a bowl.

Heat up the oil and deep-fry the chicken cubes until pale golden; scoop out and drain.

Pour off the excess oil leaving about 1 tablespoon (15ml) in the *wok*; toss in the ginger root, garlic, onions, green and red peppers, the chicken and chili paste (purée). Stir a few times.

Now add the sauce mixture to the *wok*; blend well; add the sesame seed oil just before serving.

FISH IN HOT SAUCE

*1 freshwater fish weighing about
1½ lb (0.75kg)
2 tbsp (30ml) chili paste (purée)
1 tbsp (15ml) tomato paste (purée)
1 tbsp (15ml) soy sauce
2 tbsp (30ml) rice wine (or sherry)
½ tbsp (10ml) sugar
1 cup (8 fl. oz, 250ml) stock
2 slices ginger root, peeled and finely
chopped
1 clove garlic, finely chopped
1 tbsp (15ml) vinegar
2 scallions (spring onions), finely
chopped
1 tbsp (15ml) cornstarch (cornflour)
oil for deep-frying*

Scale and gut the fish, clean well. Slash
each side diagonally four or five times
as deep as the bone.

Heat up the oil, deep-fry the fish
until golden, turning it over once or
twice; remove and drain.

Pour off the excess oil leaving
about 1 tablespoon (15ml) in the *wok*;
put in the chili paste (purée), tomato
paste (purée), soy sauce, rice wine or
sherry, sugar, stock, finely chopped
ginger root and garlic. Bring it to the
boil, put the fish back; reduce heat and
cook gently for a few minutes turning
it over two or three times. Place the
fish on a serving dish. Increase the heat,
add vinegar and onions to the sauce,
thicken it with the cornstarch (cornflour) then pour it over the fish and
serve.

At the top of the picture, *Fish in hot
sauce*; **below it**, *Pock marked woman
bean-curd*.

'POCK MARKED WOMAN' BEAN-CURD

This is another nationally popular dish that originated from Sichuan. The 'pock marked woman' was the wife of a well-known chef who worked in Chengdu about a hundred years ago; it was she who created this dish.

3 cakes of bean-curd
¼ lb (100g) ground (minced) beef (or pork)
¼ tsp (1ml) salt
1 tsp (5ml) salted black beans
1 tbsp (15ml) chili paste (purée)
3 tbsp (45ml) stock
1 leek or 3 scallions (spring onions)
½ tbsp (10ml) soy sauce
1 tbsp (15ml) cornstarch (cornflour)
Sichuan pepper, freshly ground

Cut the bean-curd into ½ in (1cm)

The bean-curd and other ingredients are blended in the wok

square cubes; blanch for 2–3 minutes to get rid of its plaster odor; remove and drain. Cut the leek or onions into short lengths.

Heat up the oil until smoking; stir-fry the ground (minced) beef or pork until it turns dark in color; add salt, stir a few times, then add salted black beans. Crush them with the cooking ladle to blend well with the meat, then add chili paste (purée); continue stirring. When you can smell the chili, add stock followed by the bean curd and leek or scallion. Reduce heat; cook gently for 3–4 minutes; add soy sauce and the cornstarch (cornflour) mixed in a little water; stir gently to blend well and serve with freshly ground Sichuan pepper as a garnish.

Aromatic and colorful 'four seasonal beans', an everyday dish in Sichuan

STRING (FRENCH) BEANS A LA SICHUAN

String beans (*haricots verts* or *Phaseolus vulgaris*) are known in this part of the world as 'four seasonal beans' since they are grown in Sichuan all year round.

1 lb (0.5kg) string beans (French green beans)
½ oz (15g) dried shrimps, soaked
2 tbsp (30ml) Sichuan preserved vegetables
1 scallion (spring onion), chopped
1 slice ginger root, peeled and finely chopped
½ tbsp (10ml) salt
½ tbsp (10ml) sugar
1 tsp (5ml) sesame seed oil
1 tbsp (15ml) vinegar
oil for deep-frying

Wash and cut the ends off the beans; snap them in half if they are too long. Finely chop the soaked shrimps and Sichuan preserved vegetables.

Heat up the oil, deep-fry the beans for 1–2 minutes or until soft, scoop out and drain. Pour off the excess oil leaving about 1 tablespoon (15ml) in the *wok*; stir-fry the finely chopped ginger root, dried shrimps and Sichuan preserved vegetables; add the beans with salt, sugar and 2 table-spoons (30ml) water or stock. After 1–2 minutes add onions, vinegar and sesame seed oil; blend well; serve either hot or cold.

HOT AND SOUR SOUP

This is another Sichuan dish that has nationwide appeal – indeed, one could almost say worldwide since it was introduced to the West.

¼ lb (100g) pork
3–4 Chinese dried mushrooms, soaked
2 tbsp (30ml) bamboo shoots
1 cake bean-curd
1 scallion (spring onion)
1 slice ginger root, peeled
2 tbsp (30ml) Sichuan preserved vegetables
2 tbsp (30ml) Wooden Ears, soaked
2 eggs
2 tsp (10ml) salt
2½ tbsp (40ml) cornstarch (cornflour)
1 tbsp (15ml) soy sauce
2 tbsp (30ml) vinegar
5 cups (2 pt, 1.2l) stock

Garnish:
Sichuan pepper, freshly ground
sesame seed oil
Chinese parsley (fresh coriander)

Cut the pork into thin shreds the size of matches, mix with ½ teaspoon (2ml) salt and ½ tablespoon (10ml) cornstarch (cornflour).

Cut the mushrooms, bamboo shoots, bean-curd, onions, ginger root, Sichuan preserved vegetables and Wooden Ears all into strips of uniform size (i.e., same as the pork).

Bring the stock to the boil, put in the pork followed by all the other prepared ingredients. Cook for 2 minutes, then add soy sauce, vinegar, salt and the remaining cornstarch (cornflour) mixed with a little water, stir. Meanwhile beat the eggs and pour into the bubbling soup very slowly, ideally through a very small opening so that it falls like a thin thread. Pour the soup into a large serving bowl, add 1 teaspoon (5ml) sesame seed oil, freshly ground pepper (the more the better), and finely chopped Chinese parsley to garnish; serve hot.

Hot and sour soup: a typical Sichuan dish which has become popular all over China, and abroad

Braised shrimps (prawns) cooked in their shells with a piquant sauce

BRAISED SHRIMPS

½ lb (225g) shrimps, unshelled
1 tbsp (15ml) rice wine (or sherry)
4 tbsp (60ml) stock
4 dried red chilis, soaked and finely
*   chopped*
1 tbsp (15ml) chili paste (purée)
½ tbsp (10ml) Kao Liang spirit
1 slice ginger root, peeled and finely
*   chopped*
1 scallion (spring onion) finely
*   chopped*
1 tsp (5ml) salt
½ tsp (2ml) Sichuan pepper
2 tbsp (30ml) tomato paste (purée)
1 tbsp (15ml) cornstarch (cornflour)
oil for deep-frying
½ tsp (2ml) sesame seed oil

Clean the shrimps, cut them into two or three pieces but keep the shells on.

Heat up the oil and deep-fry the shrimps until they turn bright pink. Scoop them out and pour off the excess oil. Put the shrimps back in the pan, together with the rice wine or sherry and a little stock; cook for about 1 minute; remove.

Heat about 1 tbsp (15ml) oil in the *wok*; add the red chilis, chili paste (purée), Kao Liang spirit, ginger root, onions, salt and pepper, the remaining stock and the shrimps. Reduce heat and braise for 2 minutes, then add the tomato paste (purée) and the cornstarch (cornflour) mixed with a little water. Blend well; add sesame seed oil and serve.

OX TAIL SOUP

What makes this soup so special is that you make more use of the chicken than the ox tail, so it is really chicken soup with ox tail as the decorative piece. Its flavor also makes it special.

1 ox tail
1 chicken (boiler)
2 cups (½ lb, 225g) carrots
1 oz (25g) ginger root, crushed
1 tbsp (15ml) Sichuan peppercorns
4 tbsp (60ml) rice wine (or sherry)
salt to taste
15 cups(6 pt, 3l) water

Trim off the excess fat on the ox tail

Two bowls of ox tail soup ready to be served. This is such a rich soup that it is almost a meal in itself

and cut into pieces. Cut the carrots into thick chunks.

Place the ox tail in a large pot with water, bring to the boil, skim off the scum; add ginger root, Sichuan peppercorns, wine or sherry and chicken. Reduce heat when it starts to boil, simmer for 4 hours or more turning the chicken and ox tail over every hour or so. Add the carrots in the last 20 minutes of cooking time. Discard chicken before serving; add salt to taste.

ANTS CLIMBING TREES GROUND (MINCED) PORK WITH TRANSPARENT NOODLES

½ lb (225g) pork
2 tbsp (30ml) soy sauce
1 tbsp (15ml) sugar
1 tsp (5ml) cornstarch (cornflour)
½ tsp (2ml) chili paste (purée)
1 small red chili
2 scallions (spring onions), chopped
4 oz (100g) transparent noodles
3 tbsp (45ml) oil
About ¼pt (100ml) stock or water

Grind (mince) the pork; mix it with the soy sauce, sugar, cornstarch (cornflour) and chili paste (purée). Soak the noodles in warm water for 10 minutes.

Heat up the oil; first fry the chili and onions, then the pork. When the color of the meat starts to change, drain the noodles and add them to the pan. Blend well, then add the stock or water; continue cooking. When all the liquid is absorbed, it is done.

BEEF AND CELERY SALAD

1 lb (0.5kg) beef or ox tongue
2 cups (½ lb, 225g) celery or other seasonal vegetables
2 tbsp (30ml) soy sauce
1 tbsp (15ml) chili sauce
1 clove garlic, finely chopped
1 tsp (5ml) Sichuan pepper, finely ground
2 tsp (10ml) sugar
1 tbsp (15ml) vinegar
1 tbsp (15ml) sesame seed oil

Sirloin or fillet steak are the best cuts for this dish, but you can use any tender cut of beef in one piece. Parboil for 15–20 minutes (30 minutes if you like your beef done well); take out to cool.

Shred the celery or any other seasonal greens, place it on the bottom of a large bowl; thinly slice the beef (or ox tongue skinned first) and place it on top of the celery. Mix the soy sauce, chili sauce, garlic, Sichuan pepper, sugar, vinegar and sesame seed oil, pour it all over the beef and serve.

Ants climbing trees. Beside the dish is a bundle of transparent noodles. The ground (minced) pork forms the 'ants'; the transparent noodles the 'trees'

Hunan dishes

Of the eight provinces that border on Sichuan, only Hunan to the south—east is closely affiliated with the cuisine of its distinguished neighbor. What they have in common is a passion for hot chilis, and the Hunanese eat even hotter food than do the people of Sichuan. The spiciest variety, which is abundant in Hunan, is a fingertip-size bomb called 'To the Sky', because it grows facing upwards (*Capsicum frutescens* or *C. conoides*).

One of China's 'rice bowls', Hunan produces 15 per cent of China's total rice crop. Tea is the province's other main crop, accounting for 17 per cent of the nation's total.

Traditionally, people from Hunan and Jiangxi call each other 'cousins'. I have happy memories of an idyllic summer up in the hills south of Changsha, the provincial capital.

FRIED CRAB

Since Hunan is a land-locked province, only freshwater crab is available there, however, you can use sea crab for this recipe.

1 crab weighing about 1 lb (0.5kg)
2 tbsp (30ml) cornstarch (cornflour)
2 tbsp (30ml) soy sauce
1 tbsp (15ml) vinegar
1 tbsp (15ml) sugar
1 tbsp (15ml) rice wine (or sherry)
2 slices ginger root, peeled and finely chopped
2 scallions (spring onions), finely chopped
1 tsp (5ml) sesame seed oil
3 tbsp (45ml) oil

Trim off the tips of the crab's legs, remove the body from the shell, crack the claws and remove their meat; chop the meat from the body into four pieces; sprinkle some cornstarch (cornflour) on the meat's surface.

Mix in a bowl the soy sauce, vinegar, sugar, rice wine or sherry, finely chopped ginger root, onions and remaining cornstarch (cornflour).

Heat up the oil, fry all the crab meat until brown; add the sauce mixture; blend well, garnish with sesame seed oil and serve.

Pork in hot and sour sauce – a spicy and colorful dish

PORK IN HOT AND SOUR SAUCE

½ lb (225g) pork fillet
3–4 Chinese dried mushrooms, soaked
1 tbsp (15ml) Chinese pickled cabbage
2 tbsp (30ml) bamboo shoots
⅓ cup (2 oz, 50g) green hot chilis
1 leek
1 egg
2 tbsp (30ml) cornstarch (cornflour)
1 tsp (5ml) salt
2 tbsp (30ml) chili paste (purée)
1 tbsp (15ml) soy sauce
1 tsp (5ml) sesame seed oil
oil for deep-frying

First cut the pork into thick slices, score the surface with a criss-cross pattern, then cut them into small squares; marinate with salt, egg and 1 tablespoon (15ml) cornstarch (cornflour).

Finely chop the mushrooms, pickled cabbage, bamboo shoots, green chilis and leek.

Warm up the oil, deep-fry the pork until each piece opens up like a flower, scoop out and drain.

Pour off the excess oil leaving about 2 tablespoons (30ml) in the *wok*; stir-fry all the chopped ingredients, add chili paste (purée) and pork; blend well. Now add soy sauce and the remaining cornstarch (corn-

flour) mixed with a little cold water. When the sauce thickens, add the sesame seed oil and serve.

STEAMED CARP AND PORK

In addition to hot chili dishes, Hunan is also known for its preserved food. This recipe is a typical example of the wide range of specialties.

1 lb (0.5kg) pork leg
1 lb (0.5kg) carp
10 Sichuan peppercorns
2 tbsp (30ml) salt
½ tbsp (10ml) sugar
a pinch of saltpeter
sawdust and fruit peel for smoking

Clean the pork and gut the carp, but keep the scales on. Mix the peppercorns, salt, sugar and saltpeter and rub both the pork and carp with this mixture. Marinate in a closed earthenware vessel for about 4 days, longer in cold weather (5–6 days) and shorter (2–3 days) when hot.

Take them out, wipe off the salt and hang them up to dry in the air. Smoke them over some smoldering sawdust and fruit peels (lemon, orange, etc) until they turn dark brown.

Scale the carp, wash both the fish and pork in warm water; cut them into thick slices and steam for 30 minutes.

'GOLD-COIN' EGGS

6 eggs
1½ tbsp (25ml) cornstarch (cornflour)
oil for shallow-frying

Sauce:
1 slice ginger root, peeled and finely
    chopped
1 scallion (spring onion), finely
    chopped
2 green hot chilis, finely chopped
2 tbsp (30ml) soy sauce
1 tbsp (15ml) vinegar
1 tsp (5ml) sugar
1 tbsp (15ml) rice wine (or sherry)
½ tsp (2ml) monosodium glutamate
½ tsp (2ml) sesame seed oil
1 tbsp (15ml) cornstarch (cornflour)

Hard boil the eggs for 5–6 minutes,
shell and cut each egg into five coin-
shaped slices. Coat each slice with a
little cornstarch (cornflour); shallow-
fry both sides in a little hot oil until
golden. Mix the sauce and pour it over
the egg slices; stir gently to blend then
very carefully; arrange the 'gold coins'
on a serving dish.

DONG'AN CHICKEN

1 young chicken weighing about 2 lb
    (1kg)
3–4 dried red chilis
2–3 Chinese dried mushrooms, soaked
2 slices ginger root, peeled
2 scallions (spring onions)
½ tsp (2ml) Sichuan peppercorns
3 tbsp (45ml) oil
2 tsp (10ml) salt
1½ tbsp (25ml) vinegar
1 tbsp (15ml) soy sauce
1 tbsp (15ml) Kao Liang spirit
1 tbsp (15ml) cornstarch (cornflour)
1 tsp (5ml) sesame seed oil

*Dong'An chicken. Dong'An is the
small town in Hunan from which the
dish originally came*

Plunge the chicken into a pot of boiling water for 10 minutes, then rinse it
in cold water and leave it to cool. Take
the meat off the bone, and cut it into
1 in × ½ in (2.5cm × 1cm) strips.

Cut the mushrooms, dried red
chilis, ginger root and onions into
shreds, crush the peppercorns.

Warm up the oil, first put in the
chilis, ginger root, onions and pepper,
then add the chicken and mushrooms,
stir for a few seconds. Now add salt,
soy sauce, vinegar and spirit; when the
juice starts to bubble, add the cornstarch (cornflour) mixed with a little
water; blend well; add the sesame seed
oil just before serving.

You may think this a Sichuan dish,
but there is a subtle difference.

Yunnan & Guizhou dishes

Picking Puer tea in Menghai, Yunnan, near the Burmese border. About twenty groups of China's minority nationalities live in Yunnan. The workers in the picture are from one of these groups

The Yunnan-Guizhou (Kweichow) Plateau, south of Sichuan, has a high, rugged terrain dissected by deep valleys and crossed by mountains. Its elevation gradually decreases from about 6,000 ft (2,000 m) in Yunnan to 4,000 ft (1,250 m) in Guizhou. The climate is humid with abundant rainfall.

Kunming, the capital of Yunnan, is situated north of Dian Chi or Kunming Lake. The climate is so mild here that it is called the 'City of Spring', with flowers of many colors in full bloom the year round.

Two local products of world renown distinguish Yunnan on the map of gastronomy. A strong black tea is produced in the area of Puer (Puerh) which is so powerful that it is often used as a medicine. If drunk after a meal, it has the same effect as strong coffee, and is particularly good for hangovers!

The other product is the famous Yunnan ham from Xuanwei (Hsuanwei). It rivals the ham from Jinhua in Zhejiang.

Steamed chicken. When the steam-pot is placed in boiling water, the heat can reach the chicken through the central funnel

STEAMED CHICKEN

This is a traditional method of cooking unique to Yunnan. The special 'steam-pot' can be obtained in some Chinese stores.

1 young chicken weighing about 3 lb (1.5kg)
⅓ cup (2 oz, 50g) cooked ham
2 tsp (10ml) salt
1 tsp (5ml) sugar
2 tbsp (30ml) rice wine (or sherry)
1 slice ginger root, peeled
½ tsp (2ml) Sichuan pepper

Chop the chicken into about 24 pieces. Dice the ham into small cubes.

Place the chicken pieces with the ginger root in the 'steam-pot', put the ham cubes on top, then add salt, sugar, pepper and wine or sherry; replace the lid.

Place the 'steam-pot' on a rack in a large pot of boiling water. Make sure the water does not reach beyond the handles of the 'steam-pot'. Cook for at least 2–3 hours over a high heat adding more boiling water if necessary. Serve out of the 'steam-pot'.

Braised tripe, here served with carrots and cucumber to give extra color

FISH SOUP

1 freshwater fish such as trout
⅓ cup (2 oz, 50g) cooked ham
3–4 Chinese-dried mushrooms, soaked
1 cake bean-curd
2 tbsp (30ml) bamboo shoots
5 cups (2 pt, 1.2l) good stock
1 slice ginger root, peeled
1 scallion (spring onion)
1 tbsp (15ml) lard
1 tbsp (15ml) salt
1½ tbsp (25ml) rice wine (or sherry)
½ tsp (2ml) Sichuan pepper, ground

Clean the fish. Cut the mushrooms and ham into thin strips, cut the bamboo shoots into thin slices and the bean-curd into small cubes. Finely chop the onions and ginger root.

Warm up the lard, pour in the stock, bring it to the boil. Add the fish, followed by the ham, mushrooms, bamboo shoots, wine or sherry, salt, ginger root and onion. Cook over a high heat for 15 minutes, then add the bean-curd. Reduce heat and cook a further 5 minutes; garnish with ground pepper and serve.

BRAISED TRIPE

2 lb (1kg) tripe (pig's stomach)
salt
2 slices ginger root, peeled
2 scallions (spring onions)
2 tbsp (30ml) rice wine (or sherry)
4 tbsp (60ml) soy sauce
1 tbsp (15ml) sugar
1 tsp (5ml) five-spice powder
2 tbsp (30ml) oil
1 tsp (5ml) sesame seed oil

Wash the tripe thoroughly, rub both sides with the salt several times and rinse well.

Blanch it in boiling water for 20 minutes. Drain and discard the water.

Heat oil, brown the tripe lightly, add ginger root, onions, rice wine or sherry, soy sauce, sugar and five-spice powder. Add 5 cups (2 pt, 1.2l) water and bring it to the boil, reduce heat and simmer under cover gently for 2 hours.

Remove the tripe and cut into small slices; garnish with sesame seed oil and serve hot or cold.

SOY BRAISED DUCK

1 duckling weighing about 3½ lb
(1.5kg)
3 tbsp (45ml) rice wine (or sherry)
2 tbsp (30ml) Wooden Ears, soaked
2 tbsp (30ml) bamboo shoots, sliced
½ cup (2 oz, 50g) carrots, sliced
2 slices ginger root, peeled and crushed
2 scallions (spring onions), cut into
*   short lengths*
2 tbsp (30ml) Hoi Sin sauce
1 tbsp (15ml) sugar
3 tbsp (45ml) soy sauce
1 tbsp (15ml) cornstarch (cornflour)
seasonal greens
oil for deep-frying

Clean and parboil the duck, then rub
it all over with rice wine or sherry.

Heat the oil and deep-fry the duck
until golden; remove, chop it into
halves lengthwise.

Pour off the excess oil, leaving
about 2 tablespoons (30ml) in the
wok; add the ginger root, onions, Hoi
Sin sauce, sugar, and soy sauce with
the duck. Turn it over once or twice to
cover it with the sauce. Take the duck
out; place it on a plate and steam
vigorously for 1–2 hours.

Meanwhile blanch the greens and
place them on a large serving dish; put
the duck on top of the greens.

Fry the Wooden Ears, bamboo
shoots and carrots in a little hot oil,
add the sauce in which the duck was
cooked, and the cornstarch (cornflour) mixed with a little water; when
it is smooth pour it over the duck and
serve.

Soy braised duck, served on a bed of
lettuce – one of my favorite dishes

KUNG-PO CHICKEN

This dish from Guizhou has obviously
been influenced by the cuisine of its
northern neighbor, Sichuan.

1 young chicken weighing about 2½ lb
(1.25kg)
1 tsp (5ml) salt
1½ tbsp (25ml) soy sauce
1 tbsp (15ml) cornstarch (cornflour)
4 tbsp (60ml) oil
4–5 dried red chilis, finely chopped
2 slices ginger root, peeled
2 tbsp (30ml) crushed yellow bean
*   sauce*
1 tbsp (15ml) sugar
2 scallions (spring onions), cut into
*   short lengths*

A GUIZHOU SPECIALTY: MAO TAI SPIRIT

Guizhou's most distinguished product is the famous *Mao Tai* ('Thatched Terrace') spirit. It is made from Kao Liang (sorghum) and other grains. Its alcoholic strength is 55 per cent (110° proof), stronger than pure Russian vodka.

Mao Tai comes from a village of the same name in Renhuai, just south of the Sichuan border in north Guizhou. The special feature of this spirit is the water used, taken from a stream flowing through a gorge nearby. The climate is moist and warm and a thin layer of mist hovers permanently over the fast-running stream. In 1704 a salt merchant from Shaanxi in north China visited Renhuai on business and was so enchanted by the beauty of the village that he decided to settle down there. Following the technique employed in his native province for making the famous *Xifeng* ('West Phoenix'), the ex-salt merchant started to distill Kao Liang using the water from the nearby stream. It soon attracted attention all over the country. *Mao Tai* was first introduced abroad at the 1915 Panama International Exposition and its reputation is now worldwide.

Left: *Farmers examine the Kao-Liang from which Mao Tai spirit is made.*
Top: *Bottles of spirit are packed for market.* **Right:** *Special labels are produced for exports*

Bone the chicken, but keep the skin on. Cut the chicken meat into small cubes the size of a cherry; marinate with salt, soy sauce and cornstarch (cornflour).

Heat 3 tablespoons (45ml) oil, stir-fry the chicken for about 2 minutes, remove. Heat the remaining oil, put in the red chilis and ginger root. When they turn dark, add crushed bean sauce; stir a few times then put the chicken back followed by sugar and onions. Continue stirring until well blended, serve hot.

Right: *Kung-po chicken. This dish is named after Kung-po, a court official from Sichuan*

CANTON/THE SOUTHERN SCHOOL

The colorful Southern school of Chinese cooking has its center in Guangzhou (Canton), a major industrial city and the capital of Guangdong (Kwantung) province.

Geographically and historically, the former Guangxi province (now an Autonomous Region) and Guangdong are known as the 'two Guangs' or as *Lingnan*. This is a reference to the mountains collectively known as *Nan Ling* (Southern Mountains) which run along the northern boundary of the region, and act as a major climatic divide, sheltering the south from cold northern air masses.

South of the divide are the Guangdong-Guangxi hills, which are dissected by the region's three main rivers and their tributaries, the Xi Jiang (West River), Bei Jiang (North River) and Dong Jiang (East River). The confluence of these three rivers forms Zhu Jiang (the Pearl River) Delta which runs into the South China Sea.

Fisheries play a major role in the coastal economy, and Guangdong contributes about one-quarter of China's total fish catch (over 20% of the fish caught in Guangdong are freshwater fish). Rice is the dominant food grain; the principal rice areas are the lowlands of the Canton delta, the Luichow coastal plain (including Hainan Island) and the major river valleys.

Other crops are tea, tobacco, peanuts and sugar cane, and subtropical fruits such as bananas, pineapples, oranges, tangerines and lychees. Hainan Island is the only truly tropical area of China and produces coconuts, coffee, natural rubber and figs.

North of the Pearl River Delta lies Canton (Guangzhou), the provincial capital. The delta, in many respects very similar to the Yangtse Delta around Shanghai, is the economic and industrial center of this region. Its climate is subtropical. The summer lasts for almost six months from May to October, with the rest of the year divided into autumn and spring; there is no winter season. Vegetation grows luxuriantly all year round, producing a rich green landscape contrasting with the numerous low hills of red sandstone.

Canton has a population of over 3 million. Its history dates back over 2,800 years. It was the first Chinese port opened for foreign trade, after early contacts with Hindu, Persian and Arab traders. Canton was first visited by the Portuguese in 1516, followed by the British, Dutch and French. Its foreign trade prospered after foreign concessions were granted in the mid-nineteenth century, but the phenomenal growth of the British colony of Hong Kong eclipsed Canton as a foreign trade center for the first half of this century. Today, with the help of the biannual trade fairs, Canton has once again regained

Some Cantonese specialties: **Top:** *Chinese salami or sausages, hung on racks to dry in wind and sun.* **Above:** *A multi-colored carp – one of the many varieties of freshwater fish which abound in the rivers and lakes.* **Left:** *A wide variety of fresh vegetables.*
Cantonese agriculture: **Top right:** *For centuries water buffaloes have been the daily companions of Chinese farmers, plodding in circles to work water and grain mills, and drawing the heavy ploughs through the rice fields.* **Below right:** *A heavy crop of rice ready for harvest.* **Below far right:** *Drying the rice after harvest*

Limestone mountains
above the Li River in Guangxi.

its former position as China's major foreign trade center.

The Southern School consists of three distinctive regional styles of cooking: Canton, Chaochow (Swatow), and Dong Jiang. Canton cuisine has a greater variety of dishes than any other School because the Cantonese are interested in creating new dishes. They eat a number of 'delicacies' which people of other provinces do not care for at all, such as frogs' legs, turtles, dogs, snakes and all kinds of game. Chaochow excels in seafood and in products from the surrounding countryside.

Dong Jiang's food, in contrast to that from both Canton and Chaochow, is richer – and has a strong regional character. This school is sometimes known as Hakka, meaning 'family of guests', which refers to the immigrants from north China who settled in the south during the Song dynasty after the invasion by invading Mongols in the thirteenth century.

There was a mass emigration overseas after the seventeenth century by both Cantonese and Hakkas. When Chaochow was opened to foreign trade in 1858 it became a major port for Chinese emigration to south-east Asia, America and Europe. Since most Chinese emigrants are Cantonese, the first Chinese restaurants to open abroad introduced Cantonese cooking to the West; it was not until the mid-1950s that other schools of Chinese cuisine started to make their appearance in restaurants overseas. This helped to improve the then generally poor standard of Cantonese cooking abroad and for the first time the West was introduced to China's true gastronomy.

Top left: *Hakka woman in traditional costume.* **Below left:** *Live turtles for sale in a market.* **Top right:** *Qingdao beer has a wide appeal.* **Below right:** *Roast ducks.* **Right:** *A general store in Canton*

Dim sum

The Cantonese are particularly famous for *dim sum* ('dot on heart'), snacks which consist of steamed dumplings with meat or seafood fillings, sweet paste and cakes, etc. These are usually eaten between meals or as a light luncheon, but never in the evening.

CHA SHAO DUMPLINGS

Pastry:
4 cups (1 lb, 0.5kg) plain flour
1½ tbsp (25ml) dried yeast
2½ tsp (12ml) sugar
3 tbsp (45ml) lukewarm water
1¼ cups (½ pt, 300ml) lukewarm milk

Filling:
1 lb (0.5kg) cha shao pork (see recipe on p.216)
2 cloves garlic
2 tbsp (30ml) soy sauce
2 tbsp (30ml) sugar
1 tbsp (15ml) lard
½ tbsp (10ml) cornstarch (cornflour)

Mix together the yeast, sugar and warm water; stir to dissolve the yeast completely. Leave it in a warm place until frothy.

Sift the flour into a mixing bowl; gradually pour in the yeast mixture and warm milk; stir until a firm dough is formed.

Put the dough onto a lightly floured urface and knead well for about 10 minutes. Leave it in a warm place for 1½ to 2 hours or until the dough doubles in bulk.

Meanwhile prepare the filling. Cut the *cha shao* pork into small, thin slices; crush the garlic.

Heat up the lard and fry the garlic until brown; discard before adding the *cha shao* pork, soy sauce and sugar. Cook for about 2–3 minutes; thicken with cornstarch (cornflour) mixed with a little water, then divide into 24 portions.

Now knead the dough for about 5 minutes, then form into a long sausage roll shape. Slice the roll into 24 rounds. Flatten each round with the palm of your hand, then with a rolling pin roll out each piece until it is about 4 in (10cm) in diameter.

Place a portion of the filling in the center of each round, gather the sides

A selection of dim sum. *You can find most of these in a good Cantonese restaurant. Clockwise from twelve o'clock: Cha Shao dumplings; Shrimp (prawn) dumplings; Chicken and glutinous rice*

wrapped in lotus leaves; Stuffed pancakes (sweet); Spring rolls; Stuffed pancakes (savory); Steamed Shao-mai (pork dumpling); in the center: paper-wrapped prawns

around the filling to meet at the top, then twist the top to close tightly. Let the dumplings rest for 20–30 minutes.

Place the dumplings on a wet cloth on the rack of a steamer, leaving 1 in (2.5cm) space between each. Steam vigorously for 15 minutes. Serve hot or cold.

STEAMED SHAO-MAI (PORK DUMPLINGS)

To make the dough, follow instructions for 'Lotus-leaf pancakes' (p.44) but omit the oil, and add a beaten egg to the flour-water mixture. Roll out into thin pancakes. Alternatively, buy ready-made *wonton* skins at a Chinese grocer's.

Filling:

½ lb (225g) pork fillet
½ lb (225g) uncooked, shelled shrimps (prawns)
3–4 Chinese dried mushrooms, soaked
½ cup (2 oz, 50g) Chinese cabbage leaves
½ tsp (2ml) salt
2 tsp (10ml) sugar
1 tbsp (15ml) soy sauce
1 tsp (5ml) sesame seed oil

Clean and dry the shrimps (prawns). Add salt; mix well for 2 minutes.

Coarsely chop the pork, mushrooms and cabbage leaves to the size of rice grains. (Do not use a mincer for this.) Add them to the shrimps (prawns) together with soy sauce, sugar and sesame seed oil, blend well.

Place a pancake or *wonton* skin in the palm of your hand and cup it loosely. Put 1 tablespoon (15ml) of the filling in the 'cup'. Use your other hand to gather the sides of the skin around the filling, letting it fall into natural pleats. Squeeze the middle gently to give it a waist. Tap the dumpling to flatten its base so that it can stand upright. Place the dumplings on a lightly greased steamer rack; steam vigorously for 10–15 minutes. Serve hot.

SHRIMP (PRAWN) DUMPLINGS

To make the dough, follow the instructions on p.44 for 'Lotus-leaf pancakes', but use half the amount of plain flour and water to make about 50 pancakes to use as wrappers. Alternatively, buy ready-made dumpling wrappers from oriental stores.

Filling:

½ lb (225g) uncooked but shelled
*   shrimps (prawns)*
½ cup (4 oz, 100g) pork fat
⅔ cup (4 oz, 100g) bamboo shoots
1 tsp (5ml) salt
2 tsp (10ml) sugar
1 tbsp (15ml) soy sauce
1 tsp (5ml) sesame seed oil

Clean and dry the shrimps (prawns); mix with salt. Add coarsely chopped pork fat and bamboo shoots, sugar, soy sauce and sesame seed oil; blend well and leave to marinate in a refrigerator for 30 minutes.

Place about 1 teaspoon (5ml) filling in the center of each wrapper; fold into a half moon shape. Damp the edge and seal firmly by pressing it down with your fingers.

Lightly grease the steamer rack; place the dumplings on it and steam vigorously for 5-10 minutes. Serve hot.

CHICKEN AND GLUTINOUS RICE WRAPPED IN LOTUS-LEAVES

2⅔ cups (1 lb, 0.5kg) glutinous rice
4 oz (100g) chicken meat, boned
4 oz (100g) pork
4 oz (100g) Chinese salami or ham
4 oz (100g) shelled and cooked
*   shrimps (prawns)*
3-4 Chinese dried mushrooms, soaked
½ tbsp (10ml) salt
1 tbsp (15ml) soy sauce
1 tbsp (15ml) sugar
2 tbsp (30ml) lard
1 tbsp (15ml) rice wine (or sherry)
1 slice ginger root, finely chopped
1 tbsp (15ml) cornstarch (cornflour)
5 dried lotus-leaves, soaked
vegetable oil

Wash and rinse the glutinous rice. Add about 5 cups (2 pt, 1.2l) cold water, a little salt and lard; steam vigorously for 20 minutes. Divide into 20 portions. Cut the chicken into 10 small pieces; cut the pork, salami and mushrooms into small pieces about the size of a thumbnail.

Heat the lard in a *wok*; stir-fry the

chicken, pork, salami or ham, mushrooms and shrimps (prawns). Add salt, rice wine or sherry, soy sauce and sugar. Cook for about 5 minutes; add finely chopped ginger root. Thicken with cornstarch (cornflour) mixed with a little water. Divide it into 10 portions.

Soak the lotus-leaves in water until soft; divide them into 10 pieces. Grease each leaf lightly with a little vegetable oil. Place one portion of glutinous rice on it, flatten the surface and add one portion of the meat filling with one piece of chicken, place another portion of glutinous rice on top, wrap up the four corners of the lotus leaf like wrapping a package. You should have 10 'packages'. Steam vigorously for 15 minutes and serve hot. The leaves are not eaten. They may be washed carefully and used again.

Water chestnut cake, rich and moist, with a jelly-like texture

WATER CHESTNUT CAKE (Ma tai ko)

4 cups (1 lb, 0.5kg) water chestnuts, skinned
1 cup (4 oz, 100g) water chestnut flour
1¼ cup (½ pt, 300ml) milk
¼ cup (2 oz, 50g) lard
1 cup (½ lb, 225g) sugar
2½ cups (1 pt, 600ml) water

Make a paste with the water-chestnut flour and milk.

Finely chop the water chestnuts into a pulp. Add lard, sugar and water; bring to a boil; add about two-fifths of water chestnut paste, mix well and bring to the boil again; then take it off the heat to cool for 2 minutes. Now

add the remaining paste gradually, blending all the time. When it is mixed well, pour it into a greased cake tin; steam vigorously for 30 minutes.

When it is cool, cut into small squares for serving either cold or reheated by frying or steaming.

Sa Chi Ma – loosely translated as 'a stone riding a horse'

SA CHI MA

3 cups (4 oz, 350g) flour
2 tsp (10ml) baking powder
3 eggs
1 cup (8 oz, 225g) sugar
¾ cup (6 oz, 175ml) maltose or honey
1 cup (225ml) water
oil for deep-frying

Sift flour and baking powder onto a pastry board. Spread to form a hollow in the center; add eggs, blend well. Then knead the dough thoroughly until it is smooth.

Roll the dough with a rolling pin until it is like a big pancake about ⅛ in (3mm) in thickness. Cut it into 2 in (5cm) long thin strips; dust strips with flour so that they won't stick together.

Heat up the oil and deep-fry the thin strips in batches for 45 seconds or until light golden. Remove and drain.

Place the sugar, maltose or honey and water in a saucepan; bring it to the boil over a high heat; simmer and stir until the mixture is like syrup. Add the thin strips and mix thoroughly until each strip is coated with syrup. Turn it out onto a pre-greased cake tin and press to form one big piece. When cool, cut it into squares with a sharp knife.

Cantonese dishes

WHITE CUT CHICKEN

This famous Cantonese dish is about the simplest way of cooking a chicken. It is always served cold.

1 young chicken weighing about
  3 lb (1.5kg)
2 slices ginger root
2 scallions (spring onions)

Sauce:

1 tsp (5ml) salt
2 tbsp (30ml) soy sauce
1 tsp (5ml) sugar
1 clove garlic, crushed
1 slice ginger root, peeled
1 scallion (spring onion)
½ tbsp (10ml) sesame seed oil

Clean the chicken, place it in a large pot with enough water to cover. Add the ginger root and onions; cover the pot with a tight-fitting lid and bring it to the boil. Simmer for 5 minutes, then turn off the heat and let the chicken cook gently in the hot water for 3–4 hours. Do *not* lift the lid while you wait for it to cool.

To serve, remove the chicken and drain. Chop it into 20–24 pieces, then reassemble on a long dish.

Finely chop the garlic, ginger root and onion; mix with salt, sugar, soy sauce, sesame seed oil and a little stock. Either pour it all over the chicken or use as a dip.

BRAISED CHICKEN BREAST

10 oz (275g) chicken breast meat,
  boned
1 egg
1 tbsp (15ml) cornstarch (cornflour)
1 tbsp (15ml) soy sauce
1 tbsp (15ml) rice wine (or sherry)
1 tbsp (15ml) tomato paste (purée)
1 tsp (5ml) monosodium glutamate
½ tsp (2ml) sesame seed oil
1 tsp (5ml) sugar
a few shrimp (prawn) crackers
lard for deep-frying

Cut the chicken into small thin slices; mix with egg, soy sauce and cornstarch (cornflour). Deep-fry the chicken pieces in lard for 2–3 minutes or until golden; remove and drain.

Pour off the excess lard; return the chicken pieces to the pan, followed by the rice wine or sherry, tomato paste (purée), sugar, monosodium glutamate and sesame seed oil; blend well and place on a serving dish. Decorate the edge of the plate with shrimp (prawn) crackers and serve.

White cut chicken – an ideal starter, or part of a buffet meal.

Steamed spareribs in black bean sauce. This dish goes well with Steamed chicken and Chinese mushrooms

STEAMED SPARE RIBS IN BLACK BEAN SAUCE

¾ lb (350g) pork spareribs
1 clove garlic, crushed
1 slice ginger root, peeled
1 tsp (5ml) oil
1 small red chili

Sauce:

2 tbsp (30ml) crushed black bean sauce
1 tbsp (15ml) soy sauce
1 tbsp (15ml) rice wine (or sherry)
1 tsp (5ml) cornstarch (cornflour)

Garnish:

2 scallions (spring onions) cut into
  short lengths

Chop the spareribs into small pieces, finely chop the garlic, ginger root and red chili. Mix them all together with the sauce marinate for 15 minutes.

Grease a heat-proof plate with oil; place the spareribs on it. Steam vigorously for 25–30 minutes. Garnish with onions cut into short lengths. Serve.

Fried spring rolls – fillings and sauces can be varied as you please

FRIED SPRING ROLLS

This is a Chaochow (Swatow) version of a Hakka dish. It is very different from the spring rolls one encounters in overseas Chinese restaurants.

½ lb (225g) pork
2 oz (50g) shelled shrimps (prawns)
⅓ cup (2 oz, 50g) bean sprouts
2 Chinese dried mushrooms, soaked
3 eggs, beaten
1 tsp (5ml) salt
1 tsp (5ml) sugar
1 tsp (5ml) cornstarch (cornflour)
2 tbsp (30ml) plum sauce
oil for deep-frying

Coarsely chop the pork, shrimps (prawns) and mushrooms, cut the ends off the bean sprouts. Mix with salt, sugar, cornstarch (cornflour) and about one-third of the beaten egg; blend well.

Lightly grease the *wok* or pan with oil; pour in the remaining beaten egg. Tip the *wok* from side to side until a thin, round omelette forms. Gently lift it out with a fish slice and lay it flat on a plate.

Cut the omelette into three, and in the center of each place one-third of the pork and shrimp (prawn) filling; fold up the sides to make three long rolls. Deep-fry them in oil over a moderate heat for 2 minutes. Turn off the heat for about 1 minute and keep the rolls in the oil, then heat up the oil again and re-fry them until golden. Remove and drain.

Cut the rolls into slices and serve with plum sauce as a dip.

BRAISED GREEN CABBAGE WITH RED HAM

1 Chinese green cabbage
4 oz (100g) Yunnan ham (or
    other cooked ham)
1 tsp (5ml) salt
1 tsp (5ml) sugar
½ tsp (2ml) monosodium glutamate
½ cup (4 fl. oz, 100ml) stock
3 tbsp (45ml) oil

Parboil the cabbage for 2 minutes, then rinse in cold water to preserve the bright green color.

Heat up the oil; fry the cabbage with salt, sugar and monosodium glutamate. Add stock and ham cut into thin slices; simmer for 4–5 minutes. Serve.

Braised green cabbage, a beautiful combination of colors, and tastes

Fish and bean-curd casserole, with some of the raw ingredients used

FISH AND BEAN-CURD CASSEROLE

The original recipe calls for a species of fish only to be found hidden under rocks in the waters off the two Guangs. Its nearest Mediterranean equivalent is called the grouper and belongs to the family *Serranidae*. The flesh is firm, delicately flavored and free of bone. Bass or sea perch can be substituted.

Yangzhou fried rice – another version of Ten variety fried rice

YANGZHOW FRIED RICE

This dish must have originated in Yangzhow on the Yangtse River Delta, but it is now on the menu of every Cantonese restaurant.

1⅓ cups (½ lb, 225g) rice
4 oz (100g) peeled shrimps (prawns)
4 oz (100g) cha shao pork (see p.216)
1 cup (4 oz, 100g) green peas
2–3 Chinese dried mushrooms, soaked
1 cup (4 oz, 100g) carrots
2 eggs
2 scallions (spring onions)
1 tsp (5ml) salt
1 tbsp (15ml) soy sauce
3 tbsp (45ml) oil
cucumber for garnish

Cook the rice according to the recipe for *Ten variety fried rice* (p.142).

Dice the *cha shao* pork, mushrooms and carrots into small cubes the size of peas. Finely chop the onions. Beat the eggs with a little salt and the onions.

Heat up 1 tablespoon (15ml) oil and scramble the eggs. Remove.

Heat up the remaining oil, stir-fry the peas, mushrooms, carrots, *cha shao* pork and shrimps (prawns); add salt; blend all ingredients well. Now add rice and soy sauce; stir to make sure each grain of rice is separated. Add the scrambled eggs, breaking them into little bits; serve with finely chopped onions as a garnish. Decorate the edge of the plate with thinly sliced cucumber.

4 oz (100g) fish steak
2 cakes bean-curd
2 oz (50g) cooked ham
2 egg whites
1 tsp (5ml) salt
½ tsp (2ml) monosodium glutamate
1 slice ginger root, peeled
1 scallion (spring onion)
1 tsp (5ml) sesame seed oil
1 tbsp (15ml) cornstarch (cornflour)
1 pt (600ml) stock
freshly ground Sichuan pepper
2 tbsp (30ml) oil
Chinese parsley as garnish

Cut the fish into thin strips. Coarsely chop the bean-curd and finely chop the ham. Shred the ginger root and onion.

Heat up the oil; toss in the ginger root followed by the fish; stir gently for a while; add stock, salt, and bean-curd; bring it to the boil. Thicken with cornstarch (cornflour) mixed with a little water, then add egg whites, sesame seed oil and the onion; blend well. Transfer to a dish or serve in a sand-pot garnished with chopped ham and Chinese parsley.

Steamed chicken with Chinese mushrooms, one of my favorite dishes, and always popular with my family and friends

STEAMED CHICKEN WITH CHINESE MUSHROOMS

1 lb (0.5kg) chicken meat
3–4 Chinese dried mushrooms, soaked
2 slices ginger root, peeled
1 tsp (5ml) salt
½ tsp (2ml) monosodium glutamate
1 tbsp (15ml) rice wine (or sherry)
1 tsp (5ml) sugar
1 tsp (5ml) cornstarch (cornflour)
1 tsp (5ml) sesame seed oil
freshly ground Sichuan pepper

Use the breasts and thighs of a very young chicken; cut into small pieces and mix with salt, monosodium glutamate, rice wine or sherry, sugar and cornstarch (cornflour).

Thinly shred the mushrooms and ginger root.

Grease a heat-proof plate with a little oil or lard, place the chicken pieces on it with the mushrooms and ginger root shreds on top, add ground pepper and sesame seed oil.

Steam vigorously for 20 minutes. Serve hot.

½ tbsp (10ml) cornstarch (cornflour)
2 tbsp (30ml) flour
1 clove garlic
1 scallion (spring onion), cut into
    short lengths
oil for deep-frying

Sauce:
3 tbsp (45ml) vinegar
2 tbsp (30ml) sugar
½ tsp (2ml) salt
1 tbsp (15ml) tomato paste (purée)
1 tbsp (15ml) soy sauce
½ tbsp (10ml) cornstarch (cornflour)
1 tsp (5ml) sesame seed oil

Cut the meat into about two dozen small pieces, cut the bamboo shoots and green pepper into pieces of the same size.

Mix the meat pieces with salt and Kao Liang spirit for 15 minutes; add a beaten egg with cornstarch (cornflour); blend well, then coat each piece of meat with flour.

Deep-fry the meat in slightly hot oil for 3 minutes, then turn off the heat but leave the meat in the oil for 2 minutes; scoop out and drain. Heat up the oil again and re-fry the meat with bamboo shoots for another 2 minutes or until they are golden. Remove and drain.

Pour off the excess oil, put in the garlic and green pepper followed by onion and the sweet and sour sauce mixture; stir to make it smooth, add the meat and bamboo shoots; blend well. Serve.

CANTONESE ROAST DUCK
This is another famous and popular dish from Canton. These are the shining red ducks one sees hanging in the windows of Chinese restaurants abroad and in Hong Kong, though I do not remember seeing them displayed this way when I was in Canton.

1 duckling weighing about 4½–5 lb
    (2–2.5kg)
1 tsp (5ml) salt

Stuffing:
2 slices ginger root, peeled
2 scallions (spring onions)
2 tbsp (30ml) sugar
2 tbsp (30ml) rice wine (or sherry)
1 tbsp (15ml) yellow bean sauce
1 tbsp (15ml) Hoi Sin sauce
½ tsp (2ml) five-spice powder
1 tbsp (15ml) oil

Coating:
4 tbsp (60ml) honey
1 tbsp (15ml) vinegar
1 tsp (5ml) 'red powder' (or cochineal)
¾ pt (12 fl oz, 350ml) water

Clean the duck well; pat it dry with a cloth or kitchen paper inside and out. Rub both inside and out with salt, then tie the neck tightly with string so that no liquid will drip out when it is hanging head downward.

Heat up the oil in a saucepan, mix in the sugar, rice wine or sherry, bean sauce and Hoi Sin sauce, five-spice powder and finely chopped ginger root and onions. Bring it to the boil, pour it into the cavity of the duck and

Cantonese roast duck, usually served cold as a starter or a main course

sew it up securely.

Plunge the whole duck into a large pot of boiling water for a few seconds only; take it out and baste it thoroughly with the 'coating' mixture then hang it up to dry for at least 4–5 hours, ideally overnight in a well ventilated place.

Roast in a moderately hot oven – 400°C (200°C, Gas Mark 6) hanging on a meat hook with its head down; place a tray of cold water in the bottom of the oven to catch the drippings. After 25 minutes or so, reduce the heat to 350°F (180°C, Gas Mark 4), roast for a further 30 minutes, basting once or twice during the cooking with the remaining coating mixture. When it is done let it cool for a while, then remove the strings and pour the liquid stuffing out. Use as the sauce when serving the duck.

SWEET AND SOUR PORK
This is one of the few dishes that people in the West have come to associate with overseas Chinese restaurants. Though it is not Cantonese in origin, it has become one of the most popular dishes in that region.

½ lb (225g) pork, not too lean
⅔ cup (4 oz, 100g) fresh bamboo
    shoots
1 green pepper
1 tsp (5ml) salt
1½ tbsp (25ml) Kao Liang spirit
1 egg

Sweet and sour pork – you will find this recipe quite different from the version in some Chinese takeaways

BRAISED SHRIMPS (PRAWNS) IN THEIR SHELLS

1 lb (0.5kg) large shrimps (prawns) in their shells
2 tbsp (30ml) soy sauce
2 tbsp (30ml) rice wine (or sherry)
1 tsp (5ml) salt
½ tbsp (10ml) sugar
4 tbsp (60ml) stock
⁵⁄₈ cup (5 oz, 150g) lard

Trim off the legs and heads of the shrimps (prawns) but keep the shells and tails on.

Heat up the lard, fry the shrimps (prawns) for about 5 minutes or until golden; remove and drain off the excess lard from the *wok*. Return the shrimps (prawns); add rice wine or sherry, soy sauce, stock, sugar and salt. Cook until all the juice is absorbed. Serve either hot or cold.

EIGHT TREASURE STUFFED BEAN-CURD

This is a well-known Hakka dish. It may appear to be rather complicated, but I can assure you it is worth the extra effort.

6 cakes bean-curd
4 oz (100g) pork
2 oz (50g) fish fillet
2 oz (50g) shrimps (prawns), shelled
2 Chinese dried mushrooms, soaked
½ tsp (2ml) salt
1 tbsp (15ml) rice wine (or sherry)
½ tbsp (10ml) cornstarch (cornflour)
1 tbsp (15ml) soy sauce
2 tbsp (30ml) oyster sauce
2 scallions (spring onions)
3 tbsp (45ml) oil

Parboil the bean-curd in salted water – 1 teaspoon (5ml) salt in 7½ cups (3 pt, 1.5l) water – for 2 minutes in order to harden them; remove and drain. Then cut each cake into four triangular pieces.

Coarsely chop the pork, fish, shrimps (prawns), mushrooms and 1 onion; mix with salt, rice wine or sherry, soy sauce and cornstarch (cornflour). Cut a slit on each bean-curd triangle and stuff with meat/fish mixture.

Fry the stuffed bean-curd, with the meat side down first, in hot oil for

Eight treasure stuffed bean-curd, surrounded by braised lettuce heart

about 2 minutes, turning it over until both sides are golden. Add oyster sauce and a little water or stock and simmer for 3–4 minutes.

Garnish with onion cut into short lengths; serve.

STIR-FRIED SQUID-FLOWERS AND BROCCOLI

1 lb (0.5kg) squid
2 cups (½ lb, 225g) broccoli
2 scallions (spring onions)
2 slices ginger root, peeled
1 tbsp (15ml) rice wine (or sherry)
1 tbsp (15ml) cornstarch (cornflour)
2.tsp (10ml) salt
1 tsp (5ml) sugar
4 tbsp (60ml) oil
1 tsp (5ml) sesame seed oil

Clean the squid; discard the head and transparent backbone as well as the ink bag; make a criss-cross pattern on the outside, then cut into pieces about the size of a matchbox. Mix with 1 slice finely chopped ginger root, 1 teaspoon (5ml) salt, rice wine or sherry and cornstarch (cornflour).

Cut the broccoli into small florets,

cut the onions into 1 in (2.5cm) lengths, shred the remaining slice of ginger root.

Heat up 2 tablespoons (30ml) oil, toss in the onions and ginger root, followed by the broccoli; add salt and sugar, stir for 2 minutes; remove and put aside.

Heat up the remaining oil, stir-fry the squid for about 1 minute; add the broccoli; blend well. Add the sesame seed oil and serve.

STEAMED LOBSTER

Lobster is called 'dragon prawn' in Chinese: there may be a link between the mythological beast and the shell-fish – according to traditional Chinese paintings the two are not all that dissimilar in appearance.

1 lobster weighing about 1½–2 lb (0.75kg–1kg)

Sauce:
2 scallions (spring onions), finely chopped
2 slices ginger root, peeled and finely chopped
1 tsp (5ml) salt
1 tsp (5ml) sugar
½ tbsp (10ml) cornstarch (cornflour)
1 tsp (5ml) sesame seed oil
4 tbsp (60ml) stock
freshly ground Sichuan pepper
1 tbsp (15ml) oil

Steam the lobster for 20 minutes. Leave to cool, then split in two lengthwise, and cut each half into four pieces.

Crack the shell of the claws so that the flesh can be taken out easily.

Make the sauce by heating up the oil in a *wok* or saucepan; toss in the finely chopped onions and ginger root; add salt, sugar, stock and ground pepper. Thicken with the cornstarch (cornflour) mixed with a little water. Finally add the sesame seed oil; pour it all over the lobster and serve.

Aboard a floating restaurant overlooking one of the bays off Hong Kong Island; **left:** *Stir-fried squid-flowers and broccoli;* **right:** *Braised shrimps (prawns) in their shells;* **in the foreground:** *Steamed lobster*

CRAB WITH SCALLIONS (SPRING ONIONS) AND GINGER

1 lb (0.5kg) crab
4–5 scallions (spring onions), finely
*   chopped*
4–6 slices ginger root, peeled and finely
*   chopped*
2 tbsp (30ml) rice wine (or sherry)
1 tbsp (15ml) cornstarch (cornflour)
2 tbsp (30ml) soy sauce
1 tbsp (15ml) sugar
1 tbsp (15ml) vinegar
4 tbsp (60ml) oil
greens to garnish

Separate the legs and claws of the crabs. If the crabs are large, break the body into two or three pieces. Heat up the oil and fry the crab pieces until golden. Remove and drain.

Toss in the finely chopped onions and ginger root in what is left of the oil in the *wok*; add soy sauce, sugar, rice wine or sherry and vinegar. Thicken with cornflour mixed with a little cold water, then return the crab pieces to be coated by this sauce. Blend well and serve.

Decorate the plate with greens or other garnishes.

Crab with scallions (spring onions) and
ginger – fragrant and aromatic

FRIED GROUPER WITH VEGETABLES

¾ lb (350g) grouper or other firm
*   white fish steak*
1 cup (4 oz, 100g) seasonal greens
1 carrot
2–3 Chinese dried mushrooms, soaked
1 slice ginger root, peeled and finely
*   chopped*
1 scallion (spring onion), cut into
*   short lengths*
1 tsp (5ml) salt
1 egg white
2 tbsp (30ml) soy sauce
2 tbsp (30ml) rice wine (or sherry)
1 tbsp (15ml) sugar
½ tbsp (10ml) cornstarch (cornflour)
1 tsp (5ml) sesame seed oil
oil for deep-frying

Mix the fish steak with a little salt, the egg white and cornstarch (cornflour).

Left: *Fried grouper with vegetables, and Lettuce with crabmeat.* **Above:** *The Chinese attach great importance to the use of fresh ingredients. These grouper* (**top**) *and crab* (**below**) *are on sale live at a Chinese market*

Wash and cut the greens, cut the carrot into thin slices and cut each mushroom into two or three pieces.

Deep-fry the fish pieces until lightly golden; scoop out and drain.

Pour off the excess oil leaving about 2 tablespoons (30ml) in the *wok*; stir-fry the ginger root, onion, greens, mushrooms and carrot; add salt; blend well. Now add the fish pieces with soy sauce, rice wine or sherry and sugar; stir gently for 3–4 minutes, then thicken the gravy with cornstarch (cornflour) mixed with a little water. Finally add sesame seed oil and serve.

LETTUCE WITH CRAB MEAT

½ lb (225g) crab meat
1 lettuce
⅔ cup (4 oz, 100g) Chinese straw mushrooms
1 carrot
½ tbsp (10ml) salt
½ tsp (2ml) monosodium glutamate
1 tbsp (15ml) rice wine (or sherry)
1 tbsp (15ml) cornstarch (cornflour)
4 tbsp (60ml) stock
3 tbsp (45ml) oil

Wash the lettuce and separate the leaves, shake dry. Cut the carrot into thin slices.

Heat up 2 tablespoons (30ml) oil; stir-fry the lettuce leaves with a little salt for about 30 seconds or until soft. Place them on a serving dish.

Heat the remaining oil; stir-fry the straw mushrooms and carrot for about 1 minute; add the crab meat with salt, monosodium glutamate, rice wine or sherry and stock. Thicken with the cornflour mixed with a little cold water, blend well; then pour it over the lettuce leaves and serve.

SHRIMPS (PRAWNS) AND SEASONAL GREENS

½ lb (225g) uncooked shrimps (prawns)
2 cups (½ lb, 225g) Chinese cabbage or broccoli
1 egg white
½ tbsp (10ml) salt
1 tsp (5ml) cornstarch (cornflour)
1 tsp (5ml) sugar
3 tbsp (45ml) oil

Shell the shrimps (prawns) and cut each one into 2–3 pieces; mix in salt, egg white and cornstarch (cornflour).

Wash and cut the vegetable. Heat up the oil; fry the shrimps (prawns) in oil for 1–2 minutes; scoop out with a perforated spoon; then stir-fry the greens in hot oil until soft. Add salt and sugar, return the shrimps (prawns) to the *wok*; blend well. Serve hot.

SQUID AND PEPPERS WITH SHRIMP (PRAWN) BALLS

1 lb (0.5kg) squid
2 cups (½ lb, 225g) green peppers
1 tsp (5ml) salt
1 tsp (5ml) sugar
1 tbsp (15ml) crushed black bean sauce
2 green chilis
1 slice ginger root, peeled
1 scallion (spring onion)
1 tbsp (15ml) rice wine (or sherry)
1 tbsp (15ml) soy sauce
oil for deep-frying
20 deep-fried shrimp (prawn) balls
    (see recipe p.118)

Discard the soft bone, head and ink bag of the squid; peel off the skin and

Above: *Squid and peppers with Shrimp (prawn) balls.* **Top right:** *Fried squid with peppers.* **Right:** *Fresh squid in a Chinese market; squid are a Cantonese specialty*

Right: *Fish-head casserole. This everyday family dish is a Hakka specialty. It is both economical and delicious*

make a criss-cross pattern on the outside, then cut into slices not much bigger than a matchbox.

Cut the green peppers into slices roughly the same size as the squid; finely chop the ginger root, onion and green chili.

Deep-fry the squid for 1 minute; remove and drain. Pour off the excess oil leaving about 2 tablespoons (30ml) in the *wok*. Toss in the ginger root, onion and chilis followed by green peppers; add salt and sugar; stir for a short while then add the squid together with the crushed black bean sauce, rice wine or sherry and soy sauce. Cook for about 1½ minutes and blend everything well. Serve with deep-fried shrimp (prawn) balls decorating the edge of the plate.

FRIED SQUID WITH PEPPERS

¾ lb (350g) squid
1 red pepper
2 slices ginger root, peeled
1 tsp (5ml) salt
1 tbsp (15ml) rice wine (or sherry)
1 tbsp (15ml) soy sauce
½ tsp (2ml) fresh ground black pepper
1 tsp (5ml) vinegar
1 tsp (5ml) sesame seed oil
oil for deep-frying
Chinese parsley (fresh coriander)
*   for garnish*

Discard the head, transparent backbone and ink bag of the squid. Peel off the thin skin and score a criss-cross pattern on the outside, then cut into small pieces the size of a matchbox.

Thinly shred the red pepper and ginger root.

Deep-fry the squid in oil over a moderate heat for 30 seconds; scoop out and drain. Pour off the excess oil, leaving about 1 tablespoon (15ml) in the *wok*; toss in the ginger root and red pepper followed by the squid; add salt, rice wine or sherry, soy sauce, black pepper and vinegar. Stir-fry for about 1 minute, add sesame seed oil and serve. Garnish with Chinese parsley.

FISH-HEAD CASSEROLE
Normally the head of a variegated carp (also known as Bighead) is used.

1 fish-head weighing about 1 lb (0.5kg)
2 oz (50g) lean pork
3–4 Chinese dried mushrooms, soaked
2 cakes bean-curd
2 slices ginger root, peeled
2 scallions (spring onions)
1 tsp (5ml) salt
2 tbsp (30ml) rice wine (or sherry)
1 tbsp (15ml) sugar
2 tbsp (30ml) soy sauce
2 tbsp (30ml) flour
1¼ cup (½ pt, 300ml) stock
oil for deep-frying

Garnish:
scallions (spring onions)
red chili
Chinese parsley (fresh coriander)

Discard the gills from the fish-head; rub some salt both inside and out; coat the head with flour.

Cut the pork, mushrooms, bean-curd and ginger root into small slices; cut the onions into short lengths.

Deep-fry the fish-head over a moderate heat for 10 minutes or until golden. Remove.

Heat a little oil in a sand-pot or casserole. Put in the ginger root and onions, followed by pork, mushrooms and bean-curd; stir for a while then add rice wine or sherry, sugar, soy sauce, stock and the fish-head; bring it to the boil; add a little salt, reduce heat and simmer for about 7 minutes.

Garnish with onions, red chili and Chinese parsley (fresh coriander). Serve in a sand-pot or casserole. It is absolutely delicious.

ROASTED GOOSE

This dish originally came from a Moslem restaurant in Canton. You will notice the similarity between this and the famous Peking duck.

1 goose weighing about 6 lb (2.5kg)
½ cup (4 oz, 100g) maltose
or honey
3 slices ginger root, peeled
3 scallions (spring onions)
1 tsp (5ml) five-spice powder
1 tsp (5ml) sugar
½ tbsp (7ml) salt

Clean and dry the goose both inside and out. Dilute the maltose or honey in a little water and coat the entire goose with it, then hang it up to dry in an airy place overnight.

Finely chop the ginger root and onions; mix with five-spice powder, sugar and salt. Put it inside the cavity of the goose; shake it about to make sure it covers the entire area.

Like the Peking duck, it should be roasted hanging in a specially constructed kiln. Or, again like Peking duck, it can be roasted on the rack of an ordinary oven. Allow 10 minutes to the pound in a high oven 450°F (230°C, Gas Mark 8). When correctly done the goose should have a beautifully golden brown skin which is carved at the table and eaten wrapped in thin pancakes (recipe p.44), with onions and *Hoi Sin* sauce. (The meat is normally used for another dish, see recipe p.206 and of course the carcass is used to make soup or stock.)

Far left: *Carving the Roasted goose. It is served in the same way as Peking duck (p 40).* **Below:** *Geese and duck flocks by a lakeside on a chinese farm*

CANTONESE FRIED CHICKEN

1 young chicken weighing about
    3 lb (1.5kg)
2 tbsp (30ml) soy sauce
1 tbsp (15ml) rice wine (or sherry)
oil for deep-frying

Sauce:
2 scallions (spring onions), finely
    chopped
2 slices ginger root, peeled and
    finely chopped
1 tbsp (15ml) sugar
1 tbsp (15ml) vinegar

Clean the chicken well; parboil in a large pot of boiling water for 2–3 minutes; remove and drain.

Marinate in soy sauce and rice wine or sherry for 20–30 minutes.

Heat up the oil in a deep-fryer; brown the chicken all over, basting constantly for 20–30 minutes. Leave it to cool before chopping into small pieces. Arrange neatly on a serving dish.

Heat up the remains of the marinade with the sauce mixture; either pour it over the chicken or use as a dip.

MINCED GOOSE MEAT AND VEGETABLES

1 lb (0.5kg) goose meat
⅔ cup (4 oz, 100g) bamboo shoots
3–4 Chinese dried mushrooms,
soaked
2 slices ginger root, peeled
2 scallions (spring onions)
1 egg
1 tsp (5ml) salt
2 tbsp (30ml) rice wine (or sherry)
2 tbsp (30ml) soy sauce
½ tbsp (10ml) cornstarch (cornflour)
1 tsp (5ml) sesame seed oil
2 tbsp (30ml) oil
1 Webbs lettuce (or other crisp
    variety)

Coarsely chop the goose meat; mix

Above: Minced goose meat and vegetables, a subtle combination of flavors and textures

with a little salt, egg and cornstarch (cornflour).

Coarsely chop the bamboo shoots and mushrooms, finely chop the ginger root and onions.

Heat up the oil; toss in the ginger root, onions, bamboo shoots and mushrooms. Stir a few times then add the goose meat with rice wine or sherry, soy sauce and a little stock or water; when everything is well blended, add sesame seed oil and serve.

Traditionally you help yourself to a lettuce leaf, put a few spoonfuls of meat on it and eat it with your hands.

Cantonese fried chicken. Cantonese chefs pride themselves on the fine presentation of their food; this photograph shows a particularly fine example

RED-COOKED LAMB

However conservative the Chinese may be in their outlook on some aspects of life, they are quite open-minded about food, even daringly experimental. The following recipe for cooking lamb appears to be rather elaborate but, if followed correctly, it will taste like nothing on earth! If you tasted it blind-fold, you would never be able to guess what you were eating, but nevertheless you would marvel at the delicious flavor of this dish.

1½ lb (0.75kg) lamb fillet in one piece
4–5 Chinese dried mushrooms, soaked
1½ tbsp (1 oz, 25g) Chinese dried dates, soaked
1 cup (4 oz, 100g) water chestnuts, peeled
½ tsp (2ml) five-spice powder
2 slices ginger root, peeled
2 scallions (spring onions), cut into short lengths
1 tsp (5ml) salt
½ tsp (2ml) Sichuan ground pepper
½ tsp (2ml) sesame seed oil
2 tbsp (30ml) soy sauce
2 tbsp (30ml) rice wine (or sherry)
1 tbsp (15ml) cornstarch (cornflour)
7½ cups (3 pt, 1.5l) stock
oil for deep-frying

Wash the meat thoroughly; make a cut two-thirds the way through the piece of meat at ½ in (1cm) intervals. Blanch in boiling water for about 3 minutes; drain and coat with soy sauce.

Place the meat in a strainer and lower it into oil to deep-fry over a moderate heat for about 1½ minutes or until it turns red; remove and drain.

Pour off the excess oil; put the meat back with rice wine or sherry, salt, dates, water chestnuts, ginger root, onions, soy sauce, five-spice powder and stock; bring to the boil, then transfer into a sand-pot or casserole. Simmer gently for 1½ hours or until the stock is reduced by half; add the mushrooms and cook for another 10 minutes or so. Now remove the meat and cut it into ½ in (1cm) thick pieces. Place the water chestnuts, dates and mushrooms on a serving dish with the lamb pieces on top.

Remove the onions and ginger root from the gravy and discard them; warm up about 1 cup of the gravy in a small saucepan. Add sesame seed oil and thicken it with a little cornstarch (cornflour); stir to make it smooth, then pour it over the lamb and serve.

You will find the strong odor of the lamb (which most Chinese dislike) has almost completely disappeared. Instead it has acquired a new aroma which is strange and difficult to describe, yet at once most attractive.

Red-cooked lamb, served with plum sauce as a dip

THE FOUR SEASONS

1 small can baby corns (spring)
    Bamboo shoots or young carrots can be used instead
1 celery heart (summer)
½ lb (225g) pork fillet (autumn)
1 oz (25g) Chinese dried mushrooms (winter)
3 tbsp (45ml) oil
1 tsp (5ml) salt
1 tsp (5ml) sugar
1 tbsp (15ml) soy sauce
2 tbsp (30ml) rice wine (or sherry)

Soak the mushrooms in warm water for 20 minutes and discard the hard stalks. Cut the celery into small pieces. Drain the baby corns. (If you are using carrots or bamboo shoots, cut into thin slices.)

Heat up 1 tablespoon (15ml) oil in a *wok* or frying pan. Stir-fry the pork until the color changes. Remove the pork from the *wok*, add the remaining oil, and allow it to get hot. Put in the whole mushrooms and the other vegetables, and add the salt, sugar and pork. Stir a few times and add the soy sauce and rice wine or sherry. As soon as the juice starts to bubble, it is ready.

There is an illustration on page 19.

FRIED BASS IN SWEET AND SOUR SAUCE

*1 sea bass weighing about 1½–2 lb
    (0.75–1kg)
1 tsp (5ml) salt
2 tbsp (30ml) flour
oil for deep-frying*

Sauce:
*2 tbsp (30ml) sugar
2 tbsp (30ml) vinegar
1 tbsp (15ml) soy sauce
½ tbsp (10ml) cornstarch (cornflour)
2 tbsp (30ml) stock or water*

Garnish:
*2 scallions (spring onions)
2 slices ginger root, peeled
1 small red pepper
Chinese parsley (fresh coriander)*

Clean and scale the fish, slash both sides diagonally at intervals. Rub salt both inside and out, then coat with flour.

Thinly shred the onions, ginger root and red pepper.

Deep-fry the fish in hot oil until golden; place it on a long dish.

Pour off the excess oil from the *wok*, put in the sauce mixture and stir until smooth, then pour it over the fish. Garnish with shredded onions, ginger root, red pepper and Chinese parsley.

Below left: *Steamed bass in salted black beans.* **Below:** *Steamed sea bass*

STEAMED BASS IN SALTED BLACK BEANS

1 bass weighing about 1½ lb (0.75kg)
⅛ cup (1 oz, 25g) pork fat
⅙ cup (1 oz, 25g) bamboo shoots
2–3 Chinese dried mushrooms, soaked
2 cloves garlic
2 slices ginger root, peeled
2 scallions (spring onions)
2 tbsp (30ml) salted black beans
1 tbsp (15ml) lard or oil
½ tbsp(10ml)cornstarch (cornflour)

Sauce:
1 tbsp (15ml) soy sauce
2 tsp (10ml) sugar
1 tbsp (15ml) rice wine (or sherry)
2 tbsp (30ml) stock

Garnish:
shredded scallion (spring onion)
Chinese parsley (fresh coriander)

Scale and gut the fish, clean well then plunge it into a pot of boiling water; take it out as soon as the water starts to boil again. Place it on a plate.

Dice the pork fat, bamboo shoots and mushrooms into small cubes.

Crush one clove garlic with the salted black beans. Finely chop the remaining garlic with ginger root and onions.

Mix the sauce in a jug or bowl.

Heat up the lard or oil; first fry the garlic, ginger root and onions. When they start to turn golden, add the crushed garlic and black beans fol-lowed by the pork, bamboo shoots, mushrooms and the sauce mixture. Bring it to the boil, then add the corn-starch (cornflour) mixed with a little cold water; stir to make into a smooth sauce; pour it all over the fish.

Place the fish in a steamer and steam vigorously for 20 minutes.

STEAMED SEA BASS

1 sea bass weighing about 2 lb (1kg)
⅙ cup (1 oz, 25g) bamboo shoots
2–3 Chinese dried mushrooms, soaked
2 slices ginger root, peeled
2 scallions (spring onions)
1 leek
3 tbsp (45ml) soy sauce
½ tbsp (10ml) sugar
1 tbsp (15ml) oil
1 tbsp (15ml) rice wine (or sherry)
2 tbsp (30ml) stock
1 tsp (5ml) salt

Scale and gut the fish, clean thoroughly, then plunge it into a pot of boiling water; take it out as soon as the water starts to boil again. Place it on a long dish.

Shred the bamboo shoots, mush-rooms, ginger root, onions and leek; place them on top of the fish, then pour the soy sauce, oil, sugar, rice wine or sherry, stock and salt over it. Steam vigorously for 20 minutes.

Left : *Freshly-caught fish in a Chinese market.* **Below:** *Fried bass in sweet and sour sauce*

OYSTER SAUCE: A PEARL RIVER SPECIALTY

Left: *An oyster bed in Tai Shui Hang, Kowloon.* **Above:** *You can buy oysters and other shellfish to eat by the seashore, but in China most oysters are made into sauce* **(right)**

DUCK WEBS IN OYSTER SAUCE

5–6 duck webs
2 cups (½ lb, 225g) broccoli or other greens
2–3 Chinese dried mushrooms, soaked
2 slices ginger root, peeled
2 scallions (spring onions)
2 tbsp (30ml) rice wine (or sherry)
1 tbsp (15ml) soy sauce
½ tbsp (10ml) sugar
1 tsp (5ml) salt
1 star anise
2 tbsp (30ml) oyster sauce
1 tsp (5ml) sesame seed oil
1 tbsp (15ml) cornstarch (cornflour)
4 tbsp (60ml) oil

Remove the outer skin of the duck webs; wash and clean well. Crush the ginger root and onions.

Heat up 2 tablespoons (30ml) oil; toss in the crushed ginger root and onions followed by the duck webs; stir a few times; add rice wine or sherry and soy sauce. After 5 minutes or so, transfer the entire contents to a sand-pot or casserole. Add sugar, a little salt, star anise and a little stock or water. Simmer gently for 3 hours.

Just before serving, stir-fry the broccoli or greens with the Chinese dried mushrooms, a little salt and sugar. Place them on a serving dish, then arrange the duck webs on top of that. Meanwhile heat a little oil in a saucepan, add oyster sauce and sesame seed oil. Thicken with cornstarch (cornflour) mixed with a little cold water; when it is smooth, pour it over the duck webs and serve.

The oyster sauce enriches the subtle taste of the duck webs

STIR-FRIED BEEF WITH VEGETABLES

¾ *lb (350g) beef steak*
1 cup (4 oz, 100g) broccoli
⅔ *cup (4 oz, 100g) bamboo shoots*
3–4 Chinese dried mushrooms, soaked
2 slices ginger root, peeled
1 carrot
1 tsp (5ml) salt
1 tbsp (15ml) rice wine (or sherry)
2 tbsp (30ml) oyster sauce
1 tbsp (15ml) soy sauce
1 tbsp (15ml) cornstarch (cornflour)
3 tbsp (45ml) stock
oil for deep-frying

Cut the beef across the grain into thickish slices the size of matchboxes; mix with rice wine or sherry, soy sauce, cornstarch (cornflour) and a little oil; leave to marinate for 10 minutes.

Cut the bamboo shoots and carrot into slices the same size as the beef, cut the broccoli into small florets.

Deep-fry the beef in warm oil for 1½ minutes; remove and drain.

Pour off the excess oil leaving about 2 tablespoons (30ml) oil in the *wok*. Wait until it smokes, toss in the ginger root, broccoli, bamboo shoots, carrot and mushrooms; add salt, stir a few times then add the beef with oyster sauce and stock; cook together for 1 minute. Serve hot.

BEEF IN OYSTER SAUCE

Oyster sauce is a speciality of Canton. Beef cooked in oyster sauce is very popular throughout China but nobody can do it quite as well as the Cantonese.

1 lb (0.5kg) fillet of beef
1 green pepper
2 tbsp (30ml) rice wine (or sherry)
2 tbsp (30ml) oyster sauce
1 tbsp (15ml) soy sauce
1 tbsp (15ml) cornstarch (cornflour)
1 slice ginger root, peeled
2 scallions (spring onions)
1 tsp (5ml) salt
4 tbsp (60ml) oil

Cut the beef across the grain into thin slices, mix with rice wine or sherry, soy sauce, oyster sauce and 1 tablespoon (15ml) oil and cornstarch (cornflour). Marinate for at least 1 hour.

Cut the green pepper into roughly the same size as the beef pieces. Cut the ginger root into small pieces and the onions into short lengths.

Heat up the oil in a *wok* until really hot, stir-fry the beef for less than 1 minute; remove with a perforated spoon. Now toss in the ginger root and onions followed by the green pepper; add salt, stir a few times, then return the beef to the *wok*. Cook together for a further minute or less. Serve hot.

STUFFED GREEN PEPPERS

½ *lb (225g) pork*
4 oz (100g) fish fillet
4 cups (1 lb, 0.5kg) small round green peppers
1 tsp (5ml) salt
1 tbsp (15ml) rice wine (or sherry)
1 tbsp (15ml) soy sauce
1 tbsp (15ml) cornstarch (cornflour)
2 tsp (10ml) sugar
1 clove garlic, crushed
½ *tbsp (10ml) crushed black bean sauce*
2 tbsp (30ml) oil

Finely chop the pork and fish; mix with a little salt and cornstarch (cornflour).

Wash the green peppers; cut them in half and remove the seeds and stalks. Stuff them with the meat and fish mixture; sprinkle with a little cornstarch (cornflour).

Heat up 1 tbsp (15ml) oil in a flat frying pan; put in the stuffed peppers, meat side down; fry gently for 4 minutes adding a little more oil from time to time. When the meat side turns golden, add the crushed garlic, bean sauce, rice wine or sherry, sugar and a little stock or water. Simmer for 2–3 minutes, then add soy sauce and a little cornstarch (cornflour) mixed with cold water. Serve as soon as the gravy thickens.

Above: *Stuffed green peppers, garnished with shredded ham*

Previous page: *A representative selection of Cantonese dishes is here laid out against an attractive restaurant interior.* **Left:** *Salted chicken;* **at the back:** *Beef in oyster sauce;* **foreground:** *Mixed hors d'oeuvres;* **right:** *Chicken in bird's nest*

CHICKEN IN 'BIRD'S NEST'

2 cups (½ lb, 225g) potatoes
1 lettuce heart
½ lb (225g) chicken breast meat, boned
2 cups (½ lb, 225g) celery
2 scallions (spring onions)
1 slice ginger root, peeled
½ tbsp (10ml) salt
1 egg white
½ tbsp (10ml) rice wine (or sherry)
2½ tbsp (40ml) cornstarch (cornflour)
oil for deep-frying

Cut the potatoes into thin shreds; wash and rinse in cold water, drain and dry. Mix with a little salt and 2 tablespoons (30ml) cornstarch (cornflour). Arrange the shreds in a criss-cross pattern against the side of a strainer, then place another strainer on top of it. Submerge both in hot oil and deep-fry for about 4 minutes until golden. This is the 'bird's nest'.

Drain and take the 'bird's nest' out of the strainer, place it in a serving dish on a bed of lettuce heart.

Shred the chicken breast meat. Marinate in a little salt, egg white and cornstarch (cornflour). Shred the celery to the same size as the chicken. Finely chop the onions and ginger root.

Warm up about 2 tablespoons (30ml) oil; stir-fry the chicken meat for about 1 minute, remove; heat up a little more oil, toss in the onions and ginger root followed by celery. Add salt and rice wine or sherry, stir a few times then add chicken meat; cook together for about another minute, place it in the 'bird's nest' and serve.

Another method of making the 'bird's nest' is to use flour and water paste instead of potatoes. This may be the origin of the 'crispy noodles' one used to encounter in certain overseas Chinese restaurants.

MIXED HORS D'OEUVRES

This is an 'imported' dish from northern and eastern China in which a selection of thinly sliced cold cooked meats are neatly arranged on a large dish with some colorful garnishes. The center is usually topped with a roast, in this case a few slices of roast suckling pig which adds a bit of local color.

2 oz (50g) cooked ham
2 oz (50g) stewed beef (recipe p.73)
2 oz (50g) red-cooked lamb (recipe p.207)
1 pig's tongue or lamb's tongue
4 oz (100g) roast suckling pig (recipe p.217)

Blanch the tongue, remove the outer layer of skin and wash in cold water, then cook in stock for about 1 hour. Remove and marinate it for another hour in the sauce left over from either *Braised duck* (p.113) or *Braised tripe* (p.187). Now slice it as thinly as possible and lay it out on one side of a serving dish. Arrange the ham, beef and lamb, all thinly sliced, in uniform sizes and shapes on the other three sides and place the roast suckling pig pieces in the middle. Decorate the plate with fruit or vegetables.

SALTED CHICKEN

1 young chicken weighing about 2 lb (1kg)
2 tbsp (30ml) soy sauce
4 slices ginger root, peeled
4 scallions (spring onions)
2 star anise
4 tbsp (60ml) mei kuei lu chiew (rose petal wine) or fruit-based brandy
½ tbsp (10ml) salt
18 cups (4½ lb, 2kg) rock salt

Mei kuei lu chiew is fragrant liqueur used extensively in cooking. It is made from Kao Laing and specially grown rose petals, and it is very strong (96% proof!).

Clean the chicken; blanch for a short while. Remove and coat the whole chicken with soy sauce, then hang it up to dry.

Finely chop two slices ginger root and two onions, crush the star anise; mix them with ½ tablespoon (10ml) salt and *mei kuei lu chiew*, and place this 'marinade' inside the carcass of the chicken. Wrap it in a large sheet of aluminium foil.

In a large sand-pot or casserole, heat the rock salt over a high heat for a few minutes or until the salt is hot to

the touch, then make a hole in the middle and place the foil-wrapped chicken in it. Cover with salt so that it is completely buried. Place the lid on and turn off the heat for 15 minutes, after that turn the heat on again for 15 minutes. Remove the chicken (the salt can be kept for further use) and take it out of the foil. Chop it into small pieces and arrange on a serving dish.

Finely chop the remaining ginger root and onions; mix with a little salt and stock as a dip.

SCRAMBLED EGGS WITH SHRIMPS (PRAWNS)

Another name for this dish is *Fu Yung*, in which you are supposed to use the whites of eggs only.

4 oz (100g) shelled shrimps (prawns)
⅓ cup (2 oz, 50g) bamboo shoots
1 slice ginger root, peeled
1 scallion (spring onion)
5 eggs including 1 separated
1 tsp (5ml) salt
1 tbsp (15ml) rice wine (or sherry)
1 tsp (5ml) cornstarch (cornflour)
3 tbsp (45ml) oil
Chinese parsley (fresh coriander)
for garnish

Marinate the shrimps (prawns) in a

Top left: *Scrambled eggs with shrimps;* **below:** *Fried shrimp balls with baby corns*

---

little salt, half the egg white, rice wine or sherry and cornstarch (cornflour).

Cut the bamboo shoots into small slices, the onion into short lengths.

Heat 1 tablespoon (15ml) oil in a *wok*; stir-fry the shrimps (prawns) and bamboo shoots for 1 minute; remove and mix with beaten eggs.

Heat the remaining oil, toss in the onion followed by the beaten eggs. Stir for a few seconds until the eggs are set; do not over-cook. Serve with Chinese parsley as a garnish.

FRIED PRAWN BALLS WITH BABY CORNS

½ lb (225g) Pacific shrimps (prawns)
1 small can of baby corns
3–4 Chinese dried mushrooms, soaked
1 slice ginger root, peeled
2 scallions (spring onions)
½ tbsp (10ml) salt
1 egg white
1 tbsp (15ml) cornstarch (cornflour)
1 tbsp (15ml) rice wine (or sherry)
1 tsp (5ml) sugar
1 tsp (5ml) sesame seed oil
oil for deep-frying
Chinese parsley (fresh coriander)
for garnish

Shell the shrimps (prawns); use a sharp knife to make a deep incision down the back of each one, and pull out the black intestinal 'vein'. Cut each shrimp (prawn) into two or three pieces. Mix with a little salt, egg white and cornstarch (cornflour).

Finely chop the ginger root and onions, cut large mushrooms into two or three pieces; smaller ones can be left whole. Drain the baby corns. Deep-fry the shrimps (prawns) in warm oil for 30 seconds; remove and drain.

Pour off the excess oil, leaving about 2 tablespoons (30ml) oil in the *wok*; wait until it smokes, toss in the finely chopped ginger root and onions followed by mushrooms, baby corns and shrimps (prawns); add salt, rice wine or sherry and sugar. Stir until well blended; add sesame seed oil just before serving. Garnish with Chinese parsley (fresh coriander).

CHICKEN A LA KIN HWA

This colorful dish is also very simple to make. *Kin Hwa* refers to the delicious ham from Jinhua (see p.135)

1 young chicken weighing about
2½ lb (1.25kg)
½ lb (225g) cooked ham
4 cups (1 lb, 0.5kg) green cabbage or broccoli
½ tbsp (10ml) salt
1 tsp (5ml) sugar
½ tsp (2ml) monosodium glutamate
1 tbsp (15ml) cornstarch (cornflour)
1 tsp (5ml) sesame seed oil

Clean the chicken, plunge it into a pot of boiling water, immediately turn off the heat and put on a tight lid. Leave the chicken in the hot water for an hour, then take it out and leave it to cool.

Carefully remove the meat from the bone but keep the skin on; cut the chicken into 24 pieces. Cut the ham into 24 thin slices.

Arrange the chicken and ham slices in alternating overlapping layers on a plate, and steam for 10 minutes. Meanwhile parboil the greens in chicken stock until soft, then arrange them around the chicken and ham.

In a little saucepan, warm about half a cup of chicken stock with salt, sugar, monosodium glutamate and cornstarch (cornflour); stir to make it smooth; add sesame seed oil and pour it over the chicken and ham. Serve either as a starter for a banquet or as a main course for an informal meal.

Chicken à la Kin Hwa, traditionally served with the head as a centerpiece

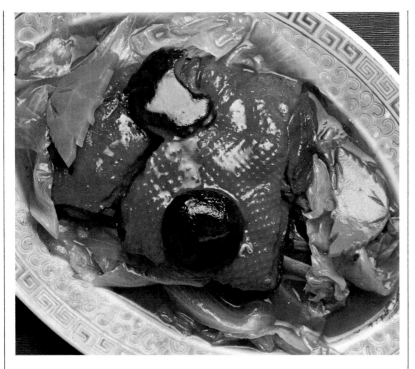

CHA SHAO (Roast pork)

This famous Cantonese dish is very popular throughout the world, apart from those countries where religion prohibits the eating of pork.

2 lb (1kg) pork fillet
2 tbsp (30ml) Kao Liang spirit
3 tbsp (45ml) sugar
2 tbsp (30ml) light-colored soy sauce
1 tbsp (15ml) dark soy sauce
1 tbsp (15ml) crushed yellow bean
  sauce
3 tbsp (45ml) honey

Cut the pork into thin strips lengthwise; marinate for about 45 minutes with Kao Liang spirit, sugar, soy sauce and bean sauce.

Roast it either suspended or on a rack in a moderately hot oven – 400°F (200°C, Gas Mark 6) – for 30 minutes (place a pan of water at the bottom of the oven to catch the dripping). Take it out to cool for about 3 minutes, then coat each piece with honey and put it back in the oven to roast for a further 2 minutes or so.

Traditionally *cha shao* is served cold or it can be used for a number of dishes such as Cha Shao dumplings (p.190)or Yangzhou fried rice (p.195).

Braised five-spice duck, a colorful and fragrant dish

BRAISED FIVE-SPICE DUCK

1 duckling weighing about 4½ lb (2kg)
2 slices ginger root, peeled
2 scallions (spring onions)
6–8 Chinese dried mushrooms, soaked
1 carrot
6 cups (1½ lb, 0.75kg) Chinese cabbage
4 tbsp (60ml) soy sauce
4 tbsp (60ml) rice wine (or sherry)
¼ cup (2 oz, 50g) candy sugar
1 tsp (5ml) five-spice powder

Cut the duck into four pieces (two breasts, two legs and thighs). Place them in a large pot or casserole of boiling water; boil rapidly for 4–5 minutes, then discard two-thirds of the water and add ginger root, onions, soy sauce, rice wine or sherry, candy sugar and five-spice powder. Bring it to the boil again, then put on the lid tightly and simmer gently for 1 hour.

Meanwhile cut the carrot into small slices, the cabbage into large chunks; add these and the mushrooms to the pot; continue cooking for 30 minutes. Serve with rice.

Ask a Cantonese in exile what food back home he misses most, and the answer invariably will be 'Roasted suckling pig'. It is a dish normally served only at festivals and on other special occasions. It is not an ordinary suckling pig but a particular species reared specially for the table, only one month old and weighing not much more than 10 lb (5kg).

Before cooking, the pig is coated with a mixture of red bean-curd sauce, bean sauce, five-spice powder, salt and sugar. It can either be spit-roasted over a charcoal fire in a specially built kiln for about 50–60 minutes, or barbecued over an open fire (as often is the case in the countryside). During a wedding feast I once attended on Hainan Island, the live pig arrived with the bride as part of her dowry, and a few hours later we were all eagerly savoring that delicious meat, barbecued over an open fire in the courtyard in full view of all the guests.

ROASTED SUCKLING PIG WITH ASSORTED MEAT
Like the Mixed hors d'oeuvres (p.214), this is a dish of assorted cold meats neatly arranged with the roasted suckling pig as the centerpiece. When you have finished eating the suckling pig you will discover a layer of roast duck.

4 oz (100g) cha shao *pork* (p.216)
4 oz (100g) *crystal sugar pork leg*
   (p.112)
1 pig's tongue
½ roast duck (p.197)
1 lb roasted suckling pig
3 preserved eggs
plum sauce, bean sauce, mustard,
   salt and pepper

Slice the *cha shao*, pork leg and tongue as thinly and as neatly as you can. Arrange them evenly on the edge of the serving dish. Cut up half of the duck for the center, then place the suckling pig pieces on top of the duck. Cut the preserved eggs in half; either use them as a garnish for the big dish, or serve on a separate dish.

Roasted suckling pig, served here with various sauces and with preserved eggs, shelled and halved, in the foreground

DRINKING – CANTONESE STYLE

It is generally acknowledged that the Chinese are more preoccupied with what they eat and the way their food is prepared than any other people in the world. It is also generally agreed that the Cantonese in particular are even more preoccupied with eating and cooking than the average Chinese. Therefore it is not an exaggeration to say that most Cantonese, rich or poor, can be regarded as natural gourmets in that they possess a good knowledge and skill regarding gastronomic matters.

I mentioned earlier the cultural division between northern and southern Chinese and their eating habits. In a wider sense both the Eastern (Shanghai) and Western (Sichuan) Schools are regarded as 'southern' because they are in the 'rice' region. But to the Cantonese, southern Chinese food means only Cantonese food, and anything north of Guangdong is northern Chinese. The wide variety of local natural ingredients certainly helps to develop the distinct character of this regional cuisine; the true flavors of these ingredients remain unchanged, all the culinary art being concentrated on the texture.

In China the Cantonese are the only people I know of who drink tea with their meals. They favor a semi-fermented tea called Oolong (*Wu Lung* 'Black Dragon'), the strongest of which is Iron Goddess of Mercy from the Wuyi Mountains.

As far as alcoholic beverages are concerned, the Cantonese appear to be rather casual in their choice; they seem to like anything that is strong, be it distilled rice spirit or Kao Liang liqueur. One of the best-known local products is called *Ng Ga Pei* ('Five-layer-skin'), a strong spirit flavored with herbs. It is bottled in an attractive dark brown, wide-lipped porcelain jar and makes an ideal gift for special occasions.

The Cantonese have an obsession with medicinal wines. The most common ones are snake wine and tiger bones wine; ginseng wine, although made in the north, is also very popular.

North or south, the main concerns of the Chinese in their daily diet are color, aroma, flavor and texture. For example, a roast duck must look golden brown, it must be cooked with onions, ginger root and other spices to bring out the delicate flavor, and its meat must be tender and the skin crispy. Wherever the Chinese live they will never give up their distinct food culture, the art of its preparation and the way it is enjoyed.

Below left: *Iron Goddess of Mercy tea from the Wuyi Mountains.*
Center: *An advertisement for the popular brands of Cantonese wines – rice wine (top) and twice-distilled spirit (below).*
Right: *A selection of medicinal wines, including snake-bite wine.*

Glossary of main ingredients

Bamboo shoots: There are several kinds of bamboo shoots available in the West – all in cans only, which is a pity since they lose much of their crispy texture and flavor. Try to obtain *Winter bamboo shoots*; they are dug up from the cracked earth before the shoots grow to any great length or size, therefore they are extra tender and tasty. Spring bamboo shoots are much larger; they sometimes may reach several feet in length and 3–4 in (7.5–10cm) in diameter. Once the can is opened, the shoots may be kept in a covered jar of water in the refrigerator for several days. *Braised bamboo shoots* in cans should be eaten cold without any further cooking.

Bean-curd (toufu): Made from soaked yellow soy beans ground with water. A coagulant is added after some of the water is strained through muslin cloth, causing the ground beans to curdle and become firm bean-curd. Usually sold in squares about $2\frac{1}{2} \times 2\frac{1}{2}$ in (6×6cm), $\frac{3}{4}$ in (2cm) thick. Will keep a few days if submerged in water in a container and placed in the coldest part of a refrigerator. *Dried bean-curd skin* is usually sold either in thick sticks or thin sheets. It should be soaked in cold water overnight or in warm water for at least an hour before use.

Bean sauce: Sometimes called 'Crushed bean sauce', this thick sauce is made from black or yellow beans, flour and salt. It is sold in tins and, once opened, must be transferred into a screw-top jar and then it will keep in a refrigerator for months. (N.B. Black bean sauce is very salty, while yellow bean sauce is sweeter with sugar added.)

Bean sprouts: Two kinds are available: *yellow soy bean sprouts*, only to be found in Chinese provision stores, and *green mung bean sprouts*, which can be bought from almost every large city supermarket. (Never use canned bean sprouts, they do not have the crunchy texture which is the main characteristic of bean sprouts.) They can be kept in the refrigerator for two or three days if bought fresh.

1 *Hoi Sin sauce;*
2 *Salted Black beans;*
3 *Light soy sauce;*
4 *Dark soy sauce;*
5 *Red bean-curd sauce;*
6 *Crushed yellow bean sauce;*
7 *Yellowl bean sauce*

Cellophane or transparent noodles: Made from mung beans. They are sold in dried form, tied into bundles weighing from 2 oz (50g) to 1 lb (0.5kg). Soak in warm water for five minutes before use.

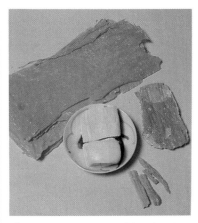

Above: *Various types of dried and fresh bean-curd.*

Chili paste: Also called 'Chili purée'. Is made of chili, soy bean, salt, sugar and flour. Sold in jars and will keep almost indefinitely.

Chili sauce: Hot, red sauce made from chilis, vinegar, plums, salt and sesame.

Chinese cabbage: There are innumerable varieties of cabbage grown in China, of which only two or three types are available in the West. The one most commonly seen is known as celery cabbage or Chinese leaves (*Brassica pekinensis*), it has a pale green color and tightly wrapped elongated head, two-thirds of the vegetable is stem which has a crunchy texture; another variety has a shorter and fatter head with curlier, pale yellow leaves. Then there is the dark green-leaved variety, also with white stems (*Brassica chinensis*); and the bright green-leaved variety with pale green stems, sometimes with a sprig of yellow flower in the center (*Brassica parachinensis*) which is very much prized by the Chinese. These last two varieties are sold only in Chinese stores.

Chinese dried mushrooms: There are two main types of Chinese mushrooms: those that grow on trees, known as Fragrant or Winter Mushrooms (*Lentinus edodes*); and those cultivated on a bed of straw, known as Straw Mushrooms (*Volvariella volvacea*). Fragrant or Winter Mushrooms are sold dried; they are used in many dishes as a complementary vegetable for their flavor and aroma. Soak in warm water for 20–30 minutes, squeeze dry and discard the hard stalks before use. Straw Mushrooms

1 Shaoxing wine;
2 Peanut oil;
3 Vinegar;
4 Monosodium glutamate;
5 Sesame seed oil;
6 Oyster sauce

are available in cans, they are completely different in texture and flavor. The Western varieties of common or field mushrooms (*Agaricus bisporus* or *Psalliota campestris*) can be used as substitutes.

Five-spice powder: A mixture of anise seed, fennel, cloves, cinnamon and pepper. It is very strongly piquant, so use a very small amount each time. It will keep for years if stored in a tightly covered container.

Fresh coriander: Sometimes known as Chinese parsley, this plant is available in oriental stores, or in Italian grocers where it is called *cilantro*.

Ginger root: Sold by weight. Should be peeled and sliced or finely chopped before use. Will keep for weeks in a dry, cool place. Dried and powdered ginger is not a satisfactory substitute for fresh ginger.

Green hot chili: Will keep fresh for a week or two in the vegetable compartment of the refrigerator in a plastic bag.

Green seaweed: This mosslike seaweed is dark green in color. It is sold dried, in wads or in matted chips. When deep-fried in oil, it is crisp and has a toasted fragrance. Dried green cabbage leaves can be used as a substitute.

Hoi Sin sauce: Also known as barbecue sauce. Made from soy beans, sugar, flour, vinegar, salt, garlic, chili and sesame.

Kao Liang liqueur: A spirit made from sorghum and millet. Brandy or vodka can be substituted.

You will have noticed that I have not listed **monosodium glutamate** (MSG). This chemical compound, sometimes known as 'taste essence' (*veh t'sin*), is often used to heighten the flavor of food. It is rather frowned upon by true gourmets as it can wipe out the subtle distinction of a dish when used to excess, so use with discretion.

Oyster sauce: A thick sauce made from oysters and soy sauce. Sold in bottles, will keep in the refrigerator indefinitely.

Red bean curd sauce: A thick sauce made from fermented bean curd and salt. Sold in cans or jars, will keep indefinitely.

Rice wine: Also known as Shaoxing wine, made from glutinous rice. Saké or pale (medium or dry) sherry can be substituted.

Salted black beans: Whole bean sauce, very salty.

Scallions: Also known as spring onions.

Sesame seed oil: Sold in bottles. Widely used in China as a garnish rather than for cooking. The refined yellow sesame oil sold in Middle Eastern stores has less flavor and therefore is not a very satisfactory substitute.

A few words must be said here regarding the types of oil used in Chinese cooking. The most commonly used in China are vegetable oils such as soy bean, peanut or rape seed oils. The Chinese never use butter or meat dripping, although lard and chicken fat are used in some regional cooking, notably in the Eastern School.

Sichuan preserved vegetable: This is a speciality of Sichuan province. It is the root of a special variety of the mustard green pickled in salt and hot chili. Sold in cans. Once opened it can be stored in a tightly sealed jar in the refrigerator for months.

Sichuan peppercorns: Reddish-brown peppercorns, much stronger than either black or white peppercorns of the West. Usually sold in plastic bags. Will keep indefinitely in a tightly sealed container.

Soy sauce: Sold in bottles or cans, this liquid sauce ranges from light to dark brown in color. The darker colored sauces are strongest, and more often used in cooking, whereas the lighter are used at the table.

Tiger lily or **golden needles:** The buds of a special type of lily (*Hemerocallis fulva*). Sold in dried form, should be soaked in warm water for 10–20 minutes and the hard stems removed. They are often used in combination with *Wooden Ears.*

Tomato sauce: Quite different from Western tomato ketchup. Italian tomato paste (purée) may be substituted when fresh tomatoes are not available.

Water chestnuts: Strictly speaking, water chestnuts do not belong to the chestnut family, they are the roots of a vegetable (*Heleocharis tuberosa*). Also known as *horse's hooves* in China on account of their appearance before the skin is peeled off. They are available fresh or in cans. Canned water chestnuts retain only part of the texture, and even less of the flavor, of fresh ones. Will keep for about a month in a refrigerator in a covered jar.

Water chestnut powder: A flour made from water chestnuts. Cornstarch (cornflour) is a good substitute.

Wooden Ears: Also known as *Cloud Ears*, they are dried tree fungus (*Auricularia auricula*). Sold in dried form, should be soaked in warm water for 20 minutes; discard any hard stems and rinse in fresh water before use. They have a crunchy texture and a mild but subtle flavor. According to the Chinese, Wooden Ears contain protein, calcium, Phosphorus, iron and carbohydrates, and one particular brand from Hubei province claims on the packet (in English) that it 'possesses such effect as cleaning gastroenteric (sic!) organs in human body'.

Dried and soaked Wooden Ears

Index of recipes

Index

Noted below are some everyday ingredients common to many of the recipes in this book. They are not listed separately in the index:

bamboo shoots
Chinese dried mushrooms
cornstarch (cornflour)
garlic
ginger root
scallions (spring onions)
sesame seed oil
shrimps (prawns)
Sichuan pepper
soy sauce
stock (chicken, duck)

PICTURE CREDITS:
All the pictures in this book, except those mentioned below, were taken specially in London and Hong Kong by Michael Freeman, Ian Howes and Jon Wyand.

2/3 Tim Megarry; 6/7 Tim Megarry; inset, Anglo-Chinese Educational Institute; 8/9 Anglo-Chinese Educational Institute; 10/11 Left, Nigel Cameron, Robert Harding Associates; right, Richard and Sally Greenhill; 12/13 Xinhua News Agency; 16 Left, British Museum; 25 Richard and Sally Greenhill; 31 Deh-Ta Hsiung; 32 Anglo-Chinese Educational Institute; 33 Xinhua News Agency; 34/35 Xinhua News Agency; 36/37 Centre and top right, Jane Taylor, Sonia Halliday Agency; left, Anglo-Chinese Educational Institute; 38 Anglo-Chinese Educational Institute; 39 Francis Wood; insets, Gina Corrigan; 46 Richard and Sally Greenhill; 53 Richard and Sally Greenhill; 66 Anglo-Chinese Educational Institute; 68 Gina Corrigan; 90 Jane Taylor, Sonia Halliday Agency; 94/95 Center, Richard and Sally Greenhill; bottom left, Francis Wood; inset, Anglo-Chinese Educational Institute; 96 Bottom right, Xinhua News Agency; 97 Top and bottom, Anglo-Chinese Educational Institute; 98 Top, Richard and Sally Greenhill; ·

bottom left, Francis Wood; bottom right, Xinhua News Agency; 99 Robert Harding Associates; 100/101 Gina Corigan; 110 Gina Corrigan; 112 Francis Wood; 123 Top, Francis Wood; bottom, Deh-Ta Hsiung; 124/125 Center and top left, Deh-Ta Hsiung; left and top right, Xinhua News Agency; 126/127 Anglo-Chinese Educational Institute; 139 Sonia Halliday Agency; 141 Center right, Sonia Halliday Agency; 148/149 Francis Wood; 150 Top, Deh-Ta Hsiung; lower left and right, Francis Wood; 151 British Museum; 152 Douglas Dickens; 153 Anglo-Chinese Educational Institute; 154 Top and centre, Xinhua News Agency; bottom right, Douglas Dickens; 181 Anglo-Chinese Educational Institute; 182/183 Center, Anglo-Chinese Educational Institute; top right, Xinhua News Agency; 184 Top right, Xinhua News Agency; 185 Bottom left, Anglo-Chinese Educational Institute; bottom right, Gina Corrigan; 186/187 Jane Taylor, Sonia Halliday Agency; 189 Richard and Sally Greenhill; 205 Xinhua News Agency; 218 Richard and Sally Greenhill. Endpapers Deh-Ta Hsiung

The quotation from Peking Cooking by Kenneth Lo on page 36 is reproduced with kind permission of Faber & Faber Ltd., London, and Pantheon Books, a division of Random House, Inc., New York.